The Educational Leader in a World of Covert Threats

Also Available from Bloomsbury

A New Theory of Organizational Ecology, and its Implications for Educational Leadership, *Christopher M. Branson and Maureen Marra*
Pluralist Publics in Market Driven Education, *Ruth Boyask*
Hannah Arendt on Educational Thinking and Practice in Dark Times, *edited by Wayne Veck and Helen M. Gunter*
Preparation and Development of School Leaders in Africa, *edited by Pontso Moorosi and Tony Bush*
Race, Education and Educational Leadership in England, *edited by Paul Miller and Christine Callender*
System Leadership, *Susan Cousin*
Sustainable School Leadership, *Mike Bottery, Wong Ping-Man and George Ngai*
Writing a Watertight Thesis, *Mike Bottery and Nigel Wright*
Educational Leadership for a More Sustainable World, *Mike Bottery*

The Educational Leader in a World of Covert Threats

Creating Multi-Level Sustainability

Mike Bottery

BLOOMSBURY ACADEMIC
LONDON • NEW YORK • OXFORD • NEW DELHI • SYDNEY

BLOOMSBURY ACADEMIC
Bloomsbury Publishing Plc
50 Bedford Square, London, WC1B 3DP, UK
1385 Broadway, New York, NY 10018, USA
29 Earlsfort Terrace, Dublin 2, Ireland

BLOOMSBURY, BLOOMSBURY ACADEMIC and the Diana logo are trademarks of
Bloomsbury Publishing Plc

First published in Great Britain 2022
This paperback edition published 2024

Copyright © Mike Bottery, 2022

Mike Bottery has asserted his right under the Copyright, Designs and
Patents Act, 1988, to be identified as Author of this work.

For legal purposes the Acknowledgements on p. xii constitute an extension
of this copyright page.

All rights reserved. No part of this publication may be reproduced or transmitted
in any form or by any means, electronic or mechanical, including photocopying,
recording, or any information storage or retrieval system, without prior
permission in writing from the publishers.

Bloomsbury Publishing Plc does not have any control over, or responsibility for, any
third-party websites referred to or in this book. All internet addresses given in this
book were correct at the time of going to press. The author and publisher regret any
inconvenience caused if addresses have changed or sites have ceased to exist,
but can accept no responsibility for any such changes.

A catalogue record for this book is available from the British Library.

Library of Congress Cataloging-in-Publication Data
Names: Bottery, Mike, author.
Title: The educational leader in a world of covert threats: creating
multi-level sustainability / Mike Bottery.
Description: First Edition. | New York: Bloomsbury Academic, 2022. |
Includes bibliographical references and index.
Identifiers: LCCN 2022004159 (print) | LCCN 2022004160 (ebook) |
ISBN 9781350160521 (Hardback) | ISBN 9781350226791 (Paperback) |
ISBN 9781350160538 (PDF) | ISBN 9781350160545 (ePub)
Subjects: LCSH: Educational leadership. | School management and
organization. | Education–Environmentaql aspects. | Sustainability.
Classification: LCC LB2806.B5994 2022 (print) |
LCC LB2806 (ebook) | DDC 371.2/011–dc23/eng/20220310
LC record available at https://lccn.loc.gov/2022004159
LC ebook record available at https://lccn.loc.gov/2022004160

ISBN: HB: 978-1-3501-6052-1
PB: 978-1-3502-2679-1
ePDF: 978-1-3501-6053-8
eBook: 978-1-3501-6054-5

Typeset by Deanta Global Publishing Services, Chennai, India

Sitting Bull, the great Native American Chief of the Sioux tribe, is reported to have said, 'Inside of me there are two dogs. One is mean and evil and the other is brave and good, and they fight each other all the time.'

When asked which one would win, Sitting Bull answered, 'The one I feed the most.'

Contents

List of Tables	viii
Acknowledgements	ix
Preface	x

Part I A Background of Inaction and Complexity

1	The Need for a New Model of Educational Leadership	3
2	Educational Leadership and the Threat of Inaction	24
3	Educational Leaders in an Age of Complex Problems	42

Part II Covert Threats

4	Covert Processes: Unmasking the Threats	63
5	Planning for the Future by Scanning the Deep Past	82
6	Educational Leadership in an Uncertain Political Future	102
7	Understanding and Preparing for Tipping Points	123

Part III Leadership Responses

8	The Prevention of Tipping Points: The Educational Leader's Role	143
9	Future Threats: Covid-19 as an Aid to an Educational Leadership Response	162
10	The Ethical Commitments of Steward Leaders	182
11	New Frames for Accountability and Inspection	198
12	Educational Leadership for a World of Covert Threats	220

Afterword	236
Appendix 1: Surviving and Prospering as an Educational Leader in an Age of Uncertainty	237
References	240
Index	255

Tables

1.1	The Nature and Impact of Five Different Codes of Education	10
3.1	Different Levels of System and Implications for Leadership Style and Behaviour	47
3.2	The Jumee Window (after Stern, 2021)	52
3.3	Complexity and Leadership Approaches in an Age of Covert Threats	58
7.1	Covert Processes and Tipping Points in Three Areas	128
8.1	Covid-19 and Potential Health Service Collapse	149
8.2	Global Temperature Rise Tipping Points	151
8.3	The Threats to Educational Leadership Sustainability	153
8.4	Using Levels of Leverage Points to Prevent Covert Threats and Their Tipping Points	157
9.1	Threat Qualities and Concerns – Comparing Covid-19 and Global Temperature Rise	174
9.2	Increasing Awareness of Global Temperature Rises	177
10.1	Minimum Requirements for Human Well-being and Indicators of Unacceptable Deficits	190
11.1	Three Different Models of Accountability and Inspection: Aims, Structures and Consequences	200
11.2	The Varying Nature of Accountability under Three Different Systems	208
12.1	Building Relationships, Building Trust	231

Acknowledgements

There are a number of people I want to particularly thank for their help in my writing this book. I would like to thank Alison Baker at Bloomsbury for her invaluable advice and support throughout the process but particularly at a couple of difficult moments in time during the book's writing. Second, I would like to thank Julian Stern for the huge amount of time he spent in reading individual chapters and then the full manuscript. He managed to be unfailingly positive and constructive. I would also like to thank Nigel Wright and David Oldroyd, who read individual chapters, and Chris Sink for not only reading material but also providing very valuable feedback on some of the calculations. Finally, I would like to thank Chris and Sarah for more than tolerating my idiosyncrasies, and to Oliver and Max, for giving me such pleasure as a grandfather.

Preface

We live in an age of great complexity and uncertainty, and yet at the same time increasingly feel the need for action to prevent or slow down a number of highly threatening events. Two at the time of writing are centre stage. The first has been the sudden appearance and global impact of Covid-19, a virus which has undermined a great deal of what has been considered as 'normal' social, political and economic activity. Globally, most governments have enforced social isolation on individuals and families, have ordered the closure of many businesses and yet paid the income of their workers, some of whom have had to learn to work from home. Whilst the development of vaccines is increasingly seen as the best strategy, it still remains in doubt whether these and further responses to the virus can return societies to previous functioning or whether more permanent changes will be needed in order to prevent even worse effects.

Yet, in future years Covid-19 might well be seen as a precursor of something even more threatening: the mounting concern over climate change. If unlike Covid-19 this threat has been around for decades, it is only very recently that the scientific argument for fossil fuels increasing atmospheric levels of carbon dioxide, and thus leading to increased global warming, has now very largely been won. This, of course, is only the scientific argument, and action on climate change still faces some formidable opponents, who now focus on three main issues. First is the reluctance of countries with large fossil fuel reserves to agree to radical changes by the adoption of more renewable and less polluting forms of energy. It then came as little surprise when the leaders of China, India and Australia (with huge reserves of coal), Saudi Arabia, similarly with oil, and Russia, with gas, all failed to attend the 2021 COP 26 in Glasgow. A second issue is that whilst many major energy companies now accept that global warming is a reality, they argue that this is not happening as quickly as scientists claim, and therefore a more gradual movement from fossil fuels to renewables is that historically richer, mostly Western countries have been the major exploiters of fossil fuel reserves and that these wealthier nations, because of their present wealth and their past behaviours, should therefore be the major funders of such change. With so many key nation-states facing in very different directions, whilst the scientific argument may have been very largely won, it is by no means clear whether there is currently sufficient unanimity for substantive global action on climate change to become a reality.

So living in an age of great complexity and uncertainty, and with threats like Covid-19 and climate change, few can be confident of forecasting what kinds of adjustments will be needed, which of these will actually take place, by whom and by when. One thing about which we unfortunately *can* be more confident is that the world of the future will almost certainly be less predictable and controllable than it has seemed previously. Both Covid-19 and climate change have forced us to realize how complex are the processes underlying them and their impacts, and in such a world we will – or should – be less confident about the outcomes of our judgements and decisions. Now some will claim that they know what will happen and will ask others for – or simply take – the power to sort out such uncertainties in ways which don't ask for too much deep thinking about the nature of the problems in this uncertain future. Yet by refusing to face the range and depth of complexities facing us, they will not resolve such problems but only muddy our understanding of difficult and shadowy developments, and, by under-describing such threats, may well exacerbate their impacts.

So where does a book on educational leaders fit into this picture? It is a book about an educational leadership role in a world characterized not just by overt threats but also by complexity and covert threats. It argues that such threats should not be seen as only the concerns of governments and supranational bodies but need to be seen as issues to which all can and should respond. Educational leaders can then have a pivotal role in helping their students, communities and societies to understand such present and emerging threats, and the education they advocate should be one which recognizes and accepts the reality of a complex world, and in so doing they can help others to learn how to live in an uncertain future. This then is a book which is highly critical of neat and simple solutions, and instead advocates an education which enables present and future generations to be critical and rational members of societies, which demand evidence-based solutions to problems rather than being swayed by fact-free, fear-based demagoguery. It then advocates an educational leadership role which looks beyond a focus on the nuts and bolts of big ideas, and focuses on the big ideas themselves. If the educational leadership role for some decades has largely been seen as one of the implementation of other people's ideas, there is now a critical need for educational leaders to help existing populations better understand present and future uncertainties, and to provide them and future generations with better ways of dealing with these. It argues that educational leaders then need to develop a strong stewardship role and that by working in more collaborative teams underpinned by the values of cooperation, care and trust, benign human values and the actions following from them can be genuine forces in countering more malign ones. It is not a book which promises certainties, but it is one which argues that educational leaders should assist others in understanding the nature of emerging and covert threats, and that by helping these others to develop stewardship frames of mind themselves, they can act in ways which better negotiate an uncertain and unpredictable future.

Part I

A Background of Inaction and Complexity

1

The Need for a New Model of Educational Leadership

Introduction

The first draft of this chapter was written in early spring 2020, when life across the globe was undergoing extraordinary changes. Areas of China and European countries like Italy, Spain and France were in complete lockdown. The UK was starting to enter the same situation, whilst North America, Russia, the Indian subcontinent, South America and Africa still had to experience this threat. Many governments affected by Covid-19 began ordering their citizens to self-isolate for weeks and sometimes months at a time, either because they displayed coronavirus symptoms or simply to stop them from catching and spreading it. Covid-19 didn't seem to have the virulence of the Spanish flu of 1918–19 (Spinney, 2017), but it seemed at least as infectious, and with a mortality rate of somewhere between 1 and 5 per cent, and much higher for the elderly, and those with underlying medical conditions it needed to be taken extraordinarily seriously, even if tragically for many, it wasn't. Now, two years on, most countries have felt its effects, many have gone through a number of waves of the disease, and new variants have added to global anxieties. Even as vaccines have come on stream, conspiracy theories about the non-existence of the virus, and of the supposed hidden intentions behind vaccine provision, have all added to the confusion, concern and uncertainty.

Yet in the years before the outbreak, warnings by epidemiologists about the development of similar diseases were ignored or downplayed in many countries, as either preparations were made for an influenza epidemic or other issues distracted politicians' attention (e.g. *Guardian*, 22/10/20). Yet concerns over some kind of outbreak were very real and for extremely good reasons. First has been the extraordinary rise in the global population over the last century, from one billion to nearly eight billion, which has increased people's proximity to one another, so facilitating the disease's transmission. Second, the globalization of trade has meant that businesses have become producers of individual parts of consumables like cars and televisions, which are then assembled elsewhere, and so more travel and greater connectivity have increased. Finally, as more exotic holiday destinations have become possible, so the globalization of leisure has promoted diseases from being parochial to becoming, like their human hosts, international travellers. The spread of Covid has then largely been an effect of globalization, even if a covert one.

The effects of globalization upon educational leadership are reasonably similar, even if educational leaders have given them much less attention. This is perhaps unsurprising: many school leaders began as class teachers focused on student care and instruction, and a great many still experience an ethical compulsion to make a difference to their students' prospects (Bottery, et al. 2018). So when Covid-19 arrived, Thornton(2021) suggested that educational leaders' responses were going through three different phases – an immediate crisis phase, a phase of adaptation and a final 'opportunity' phase. In the UK, the picture was one which Beauchamp et al. (2021) described as headteachers spending much time providing clear information and communication to teachers, parents and students on a variety of change and response issues. These included things like the best strategies for avoiding the disease, understanding the latest and often confused and contradictory government directives and working out how best to apply these to their institutions and its members. They also needed to work out how to accommodate socially distanced students, teachers and other school employees. In addition, there were interesting affective and strategic responses. Beauchamp et al. (2021) then also describe the perceived need by many headteachers to develop greater personal resilience, and to develop flatter and more distributed forms of management and leadership, with greater levels of care, trust and staff collaboration. In similar manner, Thornton (2020) in New Zealand also described how secondary principals quickly prioritized individual well-being over learning issues.

Now if Thornton's three-phase model is correct the leadership role will probably continue to change. Immediate responses followed by periods of adaptation are then likely to be followed by reflection upon longer-term changes. Such movement has also been seen more broadly, as new Covid variants have produced a number of different second and third waves, and there has been much societal concern that new vaccines might need creating if variants of Covid-19 become more resistant than earlier versions. If populations then did gain greater immunity, some thought that the disease might come to resemble influenza – as potentially life-threatening to the elderly and those with underlying medical conditions and as requiring a vaccine variant probably every year. Such adaptations, however, are still largely second-phase responses and perhaps the most important question long term is how any third 'opportunity' phase will be used, both societally and educationally. At this moment in time, such developments are still largely speculation, but it seems quite possible that this third phase may only be seen as the opportunity to relaunch the economy or to stockpile more vaccines, and then attempt to return to the previously existing state of affairs, with the educational leadership role reflecting the same very limited degree of change.

However, this would be a seriously wasted opportunity, as Covid-19 is not the only crisis to which societies and its educational institutions will have to respond in the next few years. Globally, many people are having to adapt to environmental conditions which were previously thought as 'once-in-a-lifetime' events but which are occurring on a much more regular basis. Global increases in the regularity and severity of storms have led to the flooding of homes and properties, mudslides and the stripping of topsoil from agricultural lands; higher temperatures are also leading to more regular episodes of drought, wildfires and creeping desertification (Wallace-Wells, 2019). Such events not only decrease food production but also pose serious health risks for many people, particularly the elderly, as well as threatening the extinction of many land-based and aquatic species. There is also increasing concern that pandemics caused by other zoonotic diseases – those which can jump from one species to another – may swamp health systems and then threaten a society's very foundations. If such events were to occur, the educational leadership role would need to expand beyond such traditional duties as staff management, curriculum development, financial administration and policy implementation, and their role in a crisis would need to transcend that of low-level communicators of government instructions, managers of institutional social distancing measures, organizers of online teaching and of school closures and their reopening.

The need for educational leaders as macro-level stewards

In such circumstances there are a number of ways in which the role of an educational leader may need to change. If pandemics, local flooding or heat waves become more frequent, their role will likely need to evolve into one of developing a better understanding of such events before they recur and also of helping communities, parents and students to respond in ways appropriate to the local context. Some of this is already implicit in the role, as educational leaders are

– by definition – stewards of their students' welfare. So in better understanding damaging events and their causes, and in helping to inform and better prepare both present and future populations in their schools and communities for the emergence of such threats, their stewardship role will need to expand.

Such a notion of stewardship – in not only taking on but also educating others into a stewardship role – whilst currently not a central function, has certainly been discussed in the business and educational leadership literature. Hernandez (2008, p. 121), for example, talks of stewardship as 'an outcome of leadership behaviour that promotes a sense of personal responsibility in followers for the long-term well-being of the organisation and society'. Similarly, April (2013) talks of the need for a form of leadership which 'focuses on others, the community and society at large, rather than the self'. This is an idea which links well with the kind of magnanimous leadership which Aristotle (1976) talked about in leaders working for the good of others, whilst Sergiovanni (1996) and Greenleaf (1997) have both advocated a stewardship element in their discussions of servant leadership, in which the leadership role is viewed as serving the needs of members not only of their own institution but of their community as well.

Such writers then take the concerns of a 'steward' leadership beyond that of leading others in institutions and develop it into one which urges others not only to contribute to the betterment of their fellow members but also to consider how they can help towards the care of their community and the wider society. This is the start of a much-needed movement from focusing almost completely upon micro- and meso-concerns to considering larger macro-issues. This resonates with the kind of thinking by Singer (1981), who argued that human beings need to expand the area of moral and ethical concern beyond the purely human to embrace concern for the natural environment and all those, human and non-human, who share it. This then leads to a broader, more important, stewardship role, which is reframed to more greatly emphasize broader issues of sustainability.

Now there has been some coverage in the educational leadership literature on the subject of leadership sustainability. However, this has tended to focus upon the kinds of threats which globally have reduced the number of individuals applying for leadership posts and of leaving or retiring early because of stress and ill-health (Davies, 2007; Hargreaves and Fink, 2007; Doyle and Locke 2014). This literature then largely discusses the micro- and meso-level effects on leadership sustainability and borrows heavily from macro-level concepts about environmental sustainability, even if it does not make global ecological concerns a focus for the kinds of sustainability which leaders need to help develop. The omission of such ecological sustainability in leadership literature looks to be really quite dangerous, for despite a decades-long emphasis by most governments on economic prosperity, the real bedrock of societal sustainability, and therefore of educational and leadership viability, lies in the sustainability of the complex relationships of life on this planet (Dasgupta, 2021). If these are destroyed, then human societies and their economic policies also become unsustainable. Given such pivotal importance, failing to extend the stewardship role to embrace such concerns might well come to be seen as an abnegation of leadership responsibility.

However, this book is not suggesting that educational leaders should have some kind of oversight role for global sustainability. There are many better-qualified macro-level experts to take on such a role. But it *is* being argued that in accepting an ethical commitment of care and well-being to others, this cannot be limited to focusing on only individual human sustainability nor just upon micro- and meso-level concerns. Educational leadership needs to expand its stewardship focus beyond the personal, interpersonal and institutional, in order to understand the threats generated at macro-levels to all species, not just human beings. Educational leaders then need to enable students not only to become more personally sustainable but also, as they reach maturity, to embrace a societal role with respect to such concerns and responsibilities.

Educational codes

So how can educational leaders develop a stewardship role in their institutions? One strategy would be to review an institution's ultimate educational purposes, content and values, and examine the extent to which stewardship concerns are included. Such ultimate purposes – such 'educational codes' – normally underpin the choice of curricula, pedagogy, the roles of teachers and educational leaders, and the kinds of citizenship felt most appropriate to that society. In previous writings, I have argued (Bottery, 1990, 1992) that four particular educational codes have normally been used in most societies. A first code – a *cultural transmission code* – is concerned with transmitting to students what are regarded as the best elements of a national and cultural past – the key events, issues and values. In so doing, students are then taught to embrace a selection (by others) of the content and values of their cultural heritage. Such content is often taught as matters of objective fact, even as it is a code which celebrates a particular version of the history of the past, steering students into celebrating this interpretation.

A second code, a *child-centred code*, has been employed when it has been believed that the interests and needs of the child should be paramount, and that their choices should dictate the selection of facts, issues and values. With a child-centred code, then, students are likely to be allowed to choose the topics they wish to study, students should be active in making sense of their learning and because maturity can only come about through the early exercise of responsibility and freedom, institutional management should reflect the importance of the student voice in more democratic institutions.

A third code, a *social reconstruction code*, has normally been employed when there is a perceived need for major societal changes. When this happens, particular issues are selected for discussion, and students are usually empowered into believing that they are capable of turning such discussion into action when they reach adulthood. This code would then very likely see as unacceptable any attempt to transmit bodies of knowledge established in a previous era which thwarted such empowerment. Educational institutions would instead be seen as a major way of changing society, where learning would be seen as a principal means of change. It would be an active process, guided but not dominated by teachers, who would help students to understand and critique materials, so that when older they could help to change social norms and institutions.

A fourth code, an *economic code*, is often promoted when the economic growth of a society and associated consumption and production are seen as paramount issues. Some of the important issues for this code in educational institutions are that schools should be important in furthering the economic prosperity of that nation, that they should produce a well-trained motivated workforce which not only competed in international markets but also provided students with the skills to earn a good living when they left school and that discussion, criticism and creativity should all be linked to the promotion of such economic goals.

Now whilst most educational systems incorporate emphases from all four of these codes, given the nature of many current and emerging threats, it is surprising how little they deal with the need for a greater environmental stewardship. Even the social reconstruction code, which emphasizes the need for greater social change, tends to focus more on problems within human societies than in dealing with external issues and forces which impact on a society. A *stewardship code* is then currently an outlier, even as there is now substantial need for it. Whilst, as already argued, a micro-level embrace of the concept of 'stewardship' is implicit in an educator's role, a broader stewardship role must look beyond care and concern at personal and interpersonal levels, and make centre stage the adoption of stewardship attitudes of care and concern with respect to the ecological relationships on this planet, arguing that if the ecosphere is not sustainable, then neither is humanity. Finally, and to ensure that sustainability is *inter-* as well as *intra-*generational, it would need to embrace the view that the needs of present generations should not compromise the ability of future generations to meet their needs.

Each of these codes then is illustrated in Table 1.1, demonstrating different links between schooling and society, the type of knowledge valued and the roles allotted to students, teachers and school leaders.

Such views are well rehearsed in the environmental literature, but there are a number of other issues in this broader 'ecological' vision of a stewardship code which have been much less emphasized in education systems and which are currently lacking in most educational leadership literature. The following six issues are then argued as being essential to an educational stewardship code.

The need for a more prominent macro-frame to the leadership role

The need for a more prominent macro-framing of the educational leadership role is partly addressed by a 'critical' educational literature (e.g. Rizvi and Lingard, 2009; Ball, 2012; Spring, 2014; Gunter, 2016), which argues that major global and national influences affect the purposes and manner in which educational institutions are run, and how the role of educational leadership is used. However, the macro-level location of many influences is not always recognized. A number of these influences will be described here, to be developed more fully later in the book.

So, a first influence is the global interlinking and increased speed of financial transactions, underpinned by a neoliberal ideology. This is often called 'economic globalization' and has had far-reaching competitive and private sector influences upon public sector institutions over the last half-century, as well as profoundly affecting the way in which educational leadership has been steered and practised (Ball, 2003, Raworth, 2017, Maroy and Voisin, 2017, Brown et al., 2016).

Another macro-event is the movement of power away from smaller to larger political entities and of reactions to such movement by those at lower levels. This has placed educational leaders at an existential crossroads which asks: for which level of political authority should educational institutions and their leaders inculcate political loyalty? From schools in many countries historically being utilized as the principal method of indoctrinating individuals away from identity

Table 1.1 The Nature and Impact of Five Different Codes of Education

Code	Links between schooling and society	Type of knowledge valued	Role of the student	Role of the teacher	Leadership role
Cultural transmission	Objectivist, semi-permanent, values transmitted internalized and practised	Objectivist facts and values transmitted hierarchically – a banking concept of education	Passive imbiber, usually one of many to be graded in stratified society	Transmits knowledge and values reinforcing status quo	Guardian, elitist, hierarchical, conservative, passing on given truths
Student-centred	Valuing of student interests over either school-driven or societally driven values	Based on student's experience, choices and interests	Active, involved, constructor of personal curriculum and learning style	Facilitator and constructor of situations perceived beneficial for and by the child	Facilitator of student experience and interests
Social reconstruction	Schools critically analyse societal values in terms of validity and social utility	Topic/problem centred, focused on resolving pressing social and ecological issues	Active, critical and empowered identity gained through interaction in social groups	Facilitator and constructor of relevant problems and materials	Leader of rational criticism and change; democratic and probably communitarian
Economic code	Values conducive to utility and economic growth. Obedience is to be fostered in lower ranks; creativity and discovery in higher ones	That which furthers personal and national wealth, mostly with a technological, scientific emphasis	To be trained to fit into an economic machine. Initiative and creativity encouraged if this dovetails with ultimate occupational destination	Trainer, constructor and transmitter of values and practices, lower-order member of hierarchy	Blend of hierarchical utilitarian with some creative emphases if relevant to economic growth

| Stewardship code | Considerable emphasis on values of interdependence, sufficiency and intergenerational sustainability encouraged and practised | Knowledge of covert threats that could critique excessive human consumption and move to actions for greater sustainability. | Informed, active, critical of the impact of behaviours, customs and policies on ecological sustainability | Facilitator of sustainable thought and practice, linking micro-, meso- and macro- for intergenerational consideration | Raiser of global existential issues, exemplar of sustainable practice, facilitator of critical systemic 'big picture' thinking |

and loyalty at the local level and towards the level of the nation-state (Green, 1997), powerful supranational bodies now lay similar claims. At the same time, subnational levels are trying to reassert local power and identity, whilst free-market advocates suggest that educational leaders are only individuals in charge of institutions competing for student numbers against other similar producers (Bottery, 2003, Heater, 2004, Davidson and Rees-Mogg, 1999).

The genesis of global markets has also led to the paradoxes in what is popularly called 'cultural globalization', for as one set of pressures moves societies and schools towards a greater cultural standardization in terms of forces like consumerism or religious orthodoxy, another set of pressures steers schools and their societies towards greater cultural diversity, and experimentation, aided by faster communication and a greater consumer choice (Ritzer, 2004, Sennet,1998, Rorty, 1989).

There is also now a much greater awareness of macro-pressures on local and regional ecologies from global climate change, and of human demands on global resources. The effects are varied but worrying: as noted, increased flooding or desertification, bush and forest fires, and an increasing lack of agricultural land are all products of these pressures, whilst the Covid-19 outbreak has demonstrated how externally introduced change can happen very quickly and make dramatic differences to human social and economic life.

Finally, the effects of macro-force are also to be seen in the threats to educational leadership sustainability (Young and Szachowicz, 2014, Starr, 2015, Bottery et al., 2018). A number of personal threats – increased workload, role complexity and surveillance, for example – are often 'downstream' effects of larger 'upstream' macro-events, such as national governmental use of low-trust, high-stakes testing and accountability policies. If leaders are then to better combat the sustainability pressures which they increasingly experience, a more developed understanding of such macro-forces will be essential.

The need to understand the linkages between the macro-, the meso-, and micro-levels, and how they can threaten or enhance sustainability

Unsurprisingly, then, a further change in re-framing the leadership role is for a better understanding of how macro-changes can affect meso- and micro-level activity. Some of this is already apparent in the way that different forms of globalization affect educational legislation, which in turn affects the choice of curriculum codes; the treatment of issues of class, race and gender;

the management of school finances and how and why schools are tested and inspected. Indeed, much personal leadership sustainability is threatened not only by the kinds of macro-changes demanded but also by their sheer quantity. As Penny, a UK headteacher (in Bottery et al., 2018), said, she had to deal with 'countless, countless, countless initiatives . . . and sometimes you come in and the desk is a heap, and I'm desperately toiling away'. Susan, a Hong Kong principal, thought the quantity was stressful, but so also was the pace of imposition: 'it is too many things, and also a lot of changes, something done in this way, tomorrow another thing comes out . . . I can do things very quick, very fast, but you see coming a lot of papers, circulars . . . and the rate of change that is demanded.' Such macro-level demands then have clear and worrying effects on those working at lower levels.

As problematic, however, is when macro-values and legislation don't create practice, but the practice demanded creates new micro-values. When this happens, as Fergusson (1994, p. 113) argued, the effects of macro-legislation on both teachers and their leaders can be manipulative and covertly role-changing:

> As sceptical teachers submit to force majeure and comply to National Curriculum programmes of study, test their pupils, accept appraisal, as reluctant heads sit on sub-committees of governing bodies to apportion the school's budget, etc., they come gradually to live and be imbued by the logic of new roles, new tasks, new functions, and in the end to absorb partial redefinition of their professional selves, first inhabiting them, eventually becoming them.

If educators then don't see the macro-drivers of such legislation, they may also fail to see its underlying long-term intentions and effects. Changes in practice may at first seem tedious but relatively harmless, even as they steer individuals with an unseen hand towards new value positions and actions. Some may then celebrate such change, but others may find them difficult to live with; whilst others may attempt to subvert such macro-intentions, some may simply decide to leave (see Chapter 12 of Bottery et al. 2018). Those in a leadership role then requires a strong understanding of how the linkages between all three levels can affect personal sustainability.

A number of under-recognized processes currently threaten multi-level sustainability

Many modern-day threats are underpinned by a number of processes which are insufficiently recognized. Four of the potentially most damaging are:

- Positive feedback. Positive feedback is probably best understood if it is recognized that much of the stability in human life is provided by its opposite – that of negative feedback. Negative feedback is observed when equipment like air conditioning detects rising temperatures and returns this to a more desirable level. The threat of positive feedback comes from the fact that it increases a process rather than reverses it. Thus when temperatures in the Arctic rise above freezing, ice and snow melts, and as the resulting water is darker in colour than ice and snow, it absorbs more heat and so raises temperatures further, which then melts more ice. The resultant greater mass of water then absorbs more heat, which melts more ice, and so the process of positive feedback continues. If nothing happens to prevent this, a region may become ice-free and remain that way. Over the last few decades there has then been considerable shrinkage of ice at both North and South Poles, due to increased greenhouse gas emissions, and if this continues, higher sea levels can be expected, as may the flooding of major cities and the increasing salinity of arable land (Ward, 2010).
- Exponential growth. Many critical processes don't develop in a linear arithmetic manner. They don't then expand from 1 to 2 to 3 to 4, but rather in an exponential manner – from 1 to 2 to 4 to 8 to 16, or from 1 to 3 to 9 to 27, and so on, depending on the rate of growth. However, if exponential growth is mistaken as arithmetic growth, then numbers will expand much faster than planned for. Recently, exponential growth has received considerable publicity through the growth of Covid-19, whose increase is exponential in nature. The 'R-number' for Covid-19 indicates the number of people who are likely to be infected by one person with the disease. An R-number of 1 means that only one other will be infected, but an R number of 2 means two more will be infected, each of whom is likely to infect two others, and so on. Covid-19 has then demonstrated how dangerous a rise above R1 can be. Exponential growth also applies to other critical issues, such as human population growth and the increased consumption of resources. These examples are discussed further in Chapter 4.
- Connectivity. This is a process which has become familiar through increased digital connectivity, which has facilitated many social and business processes during Covid-19 outbreaks. Yet whilst many may think digital connectivity is highly beneficial, there are those who claim we are moving into an era of damaging over- or hyper-connectivity (Goldin and Mariathasan, 2014). In addition, other forms of connectivity and their impacts are at least as important. 'Social' connectivity – the degree to

which individuals feel part of the community in which they live – is critical to social and mental well-being. Another, 'environmental' connectivity, is concerned with the nature of relationships between living things, and particularly of human relationships with other species, and here there is a real danger that, if we fail to appreciate how interconnected we are with other species, we may endanger other species and ourselves, as we damage the environment within which all species live. These issues are also further developed in Chapter 4.
- Tipping points. Finally, we may reach a moment when a process becomes irreversible – when a 'tipping point' occurs. This is the phenomenon of the straw breaking the camel's back, and macro-examples of potential tipping points are increasing, and worryingly so, as rising temperatures in the Arctic are beginning to trigger a substantial release of methane hydrates from the ocean floor or from frozen tundra, which then turn into the gaseous form of methane, a highly potent greenhouse gas (Ruppel and Kessler, 2017). Its release could substantially accelerate warming processes, and positive feedback processes would then result in the release of even more methane, which might reach a 'tipping point' beyond which new, unpredictable and highly threatening conditions could emerge.

Now, if such processes remain largely unrecognized, their highly dangerous effects may not be taken as seriously as they need to be. Educational institutions and their leaders are well positioned to facilitate a better understanding. Development of such a role is covered in Chapters 4, 8 and 9.

The need to better understand the implications of living in a world of great complexity

A further issue essential to a broader stewardship perspective lies in the need to understand better the complexity of the world in which we live. The Covid-19 pandemic has produced great anxiety, much stemming from the wide range of unanticipated concerns which were generated. These included:

- What will happen if I get the virus and hospitals are overwhelmed?
- How do I avoid infection when the virus infects so easily?
- What will governments do to help a small retailer like myself with cash flow problems due to the disease?
- What will be the psychological effects of social isolation on me as I live on my own?

- Are some vaccines more effective than others? Do some have dangerous side effects and would it therefore be better to not have the vaccine?
- How successful will the vaccine be with new variants of the disease?

Some concerns can be resolved easily (Where do I go to get a vaccine injection?). Others might change as new problems arise:

- 'Will the vaccine I've been given deal with new strains of the disease?' Importantly, however, other concerns may never be fully answerable. Questions like
- 'Can the disease be completely eliminated, or do we have to learn to live with it?'
- 'What is the correct balance between shielding people from the disease and re-energizing the economy?'

are the kind of questions which require highly contextualized and complex responses, and, to make matters more problematic, there seem to be a number of different kinds of complexity at work here.

A first kind – *systemic complexity* – refers to how actors within systems (animals in an ecosphere, individuals in schools and populations in cities and societies) all act and interact in multiple and complex ways, which can make it virtually impossible to understand and predict the effects of interactions within a system, and one is then likely to only understand events as they emerge from the interactions of complex systemic events. Little wonder that prediction and control can be so difficult.

A second kind – *epistemic complexity* – focuses on what we know and what we don't know about the external world. Whilst many may feel confident about some 'known knowns' – Which season follows spring? – there will be much more concern about 'known unknowns' (Rumsfeld, 2002) – things we know that we don't know enough about. Many issues surrounding Covid-19 initially belonged to this category, though some of these were resolved through better understanding of how the virus infects people. However, we can be wrong about what we think we know, and there are likely to be many, many issues which we don't know that we don't know. So there undoubtedly exist a huge and changing category of emerging complex problems, and people tend to worry more about what they don't know than what they do.

A third kind of complexity is the human side of epistemic complexity – what will be called *relational complexity*. This focuses on what individuals know or don't know about themselves, about others and about the relationships between them. There is much that many may feel they know about themselves, but there are almost certainly things they don't know. Moreover, as much of a person's life is spent in communicating with others, this means that these others may know things about the individual which the individual doesn't know and also things that neither party recognizes but still influence how an individual acts and interacts. So if individuals cannot be sure of the quality and the quantity of the information they receive, and if they send signals to others which they don't know they are making, then this creates even greater relational complexity.

A final kind of complexity will be called *wicked complexity*, after the work of Rittel and Weber (1973). With wicked complexity, many problems are difficult to understand and resolve, in part because they are unique problems to which a unique solution is required and in part because people may disagree over whether a problem is actually a problem. Many issues may then only become problems when people *believe* they are problems. Covid-19 and its vaccines are good examples of these, with a significant minority of people worldwide denying the threat or even the very existence of the disease, with others believing that the vaccines have been produced with sinister governmental intentions (Subbaro, 2020). This doesn't mean that Covid-19 isn't a real threat or that the vaccines don't prevent Covid-19 from making people ill. But such disbelief affects the way in which people act with respect to the virus, and its vaccines, and this can have large ramifications for a society if the existence of something highly dangerous is denied.

Now some highly complex threats may be products of combinations of different kinds of complexity and, if true, then the profound uncertainty experienced with Covid-19 may not be a particularly extreme example but is still more likely to be a portent of problem complexity in the future. This then is a critical issue to deal with: how can educational leaders and their institutions be better prepared to help others deal with a future of such radical uncertainty?

The need to be informed about the incidence of past macro-threats

One way of preparing for such issues is by framing the leadership role in such a way that they are more informed about previous macro-threats. Now arguing for the need for such understanding of the past may not persuade those who believe that educational leaders need a much greater focus on present-day problems and future threats. Yet the role needs to be better informed about past macro-events because there is much to be learnt from them about the probable nature and effects of present and future threats. Whilst some major impacts upon life on this planet – such as the five previous great extinctions – occurred before human beings evolved (Benton, 2003, Brannen, 2018), all of them were the result of different natural disasters which could well impact on human beings once more, whilst a probable sixth global extinction event seems almost completely attributable to human activity (Klare, 2012; Kolbert; 2014; Brannen, 2018). Moreover, the collapse of some early civilizations (Diamond, 2006, Cline, 2014, Middleton, 2017) seems to have been in part due to natural climatic changes, even as humanity contributed to such collapses through population increases, inter-societal conflict, deforestation and soil exhaustion, and such challenges have not gone away. Finally, much can be learnt from the nature and spread of previous diseases in better understanding the effects of Covid-19 – and the spread of future diseases as well.

Species extinctions, societal collapses and pandemics should then all be of concern to present-day educational leaders, because the possibility of these in the near and deeper future is no longer a subject restricted to archaeologists, historians and science fiction writers. Their possibility as genuine threats to ecological and human sustainability then needs to be within every educational leader's frame of reference. Chapter 5 examines this issue in further detail.

The need to have a longer time frame into the future

If the leadership role requires a longer time frame into the past, there are also very good reasons for acquiring a longer time frame into the future. If a central role lies in providing students with the best possible experience and preparation for adult life, then this needs to include a preparation for future challenges and will require a deeper understanding of the development and treatment of particular threats, greater personal resilience and the ability to live with such uncertainty (Johnstone, 2019, Zolli and Healy, 2012, Kay and King, 2020). A further reason for a longer future time frame stems from the need to recognize that present student generations need a greater appreciation of the macro-contexts within which their lives are being played out and which looks beyond this to the concerns of future generations. As the Brundtland Commission (1987) said in its seminal definition, the only way to ensure a continued sustainability is to recognize that it

> 'meets the needs of the present without compromising the ability of future generations to meet their needs'.

This inclusion of intergenerational equity may seem something of a surprise to those first reading the Commission's Report, as the problems of *intra*generational equity could be viewed as more pressing. Yet concerns for existing generations are already intergenerational, with three or four generations often alive at the same time. However, Brundtland was referring to generations still to be born, and a call for their sustainability may seem the more difficult to answer the further into the future one goes: how do we know what people ten generations from now will need? Much has been written and argued on this (Heilbronner, 1975, Hardin, 1977, de-Shalit, 1995, Partridge 2003) and it is easy to get distracted by minutiae and to neglect the larger picture: human beings, until they evolve into another species in tens or hundreds of thousands of years' time, will still require fresh air and water, nutritious food, caring families, social networks and fulfilling purposes – and readers will probably add their own future 'essentials' to such a list. If humanity acts in ways which prevent the passing on of conditions within which such necessities can be achieved – by polluting the ecosphere, or by creating overly competitive and selfish societies (and again readers will add other 'pollutants' here) – then we fail those in the future. The need to educate others into leaving the world at least as sustainable as they found it (and likely *more* sustainable than the present generation leaves it) then becomes an essential educational leadership focus.

So what kind of leadership would then be most appropriate for the issues described here? Potential answers to this question are now examined.

Creating a leadership style appropriate to conditions of uncertainty and threat

The Covid-19 pandemic was unknown and unexpected, and it therefore created many unanticipated problems, as well as having far-reaching impacts upon people's lives, which had little or nothing to do with the physical effects of the disease. Who had fully realized its effects upon people with dementia in care homes? Or on those individuals running businesses in the service industry? With such an entrance and with such effects, it was unsurprising that profound uncertainty was generated. As individuals, groups and governments tried to understand and counteract its effects, some realized that their understanding was unlikely to ever be complete. Moreover even where extensive research was undertaken, little certainty was guaranteed: individual researchers, research groups and policymakers did not always choose the same data, or give equal weight to the data they did choose. Even when they did, they sometimes didn't always reach the same conclusions to inform policy recommendations and personal actions. This was very largely because virtually all human decisions are based on selections of facts and values, simply because there are so many facts to choose from, and so many remain unknown. As Simon (1956) rightly suggested we have little option in many situations but to 'satisfice' – to work towards an acceptable combination of 'satisfy' and 'suffice'. This then is often the best human beings can do, particularly when many threats are so complex and challenging, and the ways forward so uncertain.

Now if many situations are highly challenging and uncertain, and constantly changing, what does this imply for the leadership role? This is one of the critical questions to be addressed throughout this book, and some initial ideas will be sketched out here. First, the role needs to be peopled by individuals who can cope with the challenges of such complexity, unpredictability and uncertainty.

Second, such individuals must also possess the 'negative capability' that Clarke (2015) talks about or which Webster-Wright (2009) refers to as 'authentic reflexivity' – the ability to not be rushed into action but to stand back and reflect upon a situation, as often this will be the wiser choice.

Third, they must also be able to accept that different people may well understand a problem in very different ways and that they may then need to work with these others to arrive at the best way forward.

Fourth, such leaders will also need the humility to recognize that however gifted they are, they only possess one person's view of such problems, and that whilst they may be well informed, they remain singular, contextualized and limited in their capacity to understand, and so will on many occasions need the help of diverse others.

One final important element of an appropriate leadership style will then be one of working out how to reduce the profound uncertainty which accompanies the appearance of complex threats. This uncertainty is exacerbated by the dynamics of the kinds of processes already covered in this chapter, many of which may be largely covert. Without a strong understanding of their nature, and of how to prepare for their impacts, societies will be much less sustainable. By then discussing these issues within frameworks linking the macro with the meso and the micro, educational leaders will be better equipped to interrogate previous case histories of damaging experiences and so be better prepared for future instances of uncertainty.

Now given these kinds of requirements, some traditional leadership approaches will be much less suited to dealing with issues of such complexity and uncertainty. Transactional leadership, widely used in both business and education, was the dominant Western approach for much of the last century and was underpinned by a tacit belief in business certainty: Western countries, particularly the United States, dominated the world economy, and the business environment was largely seen as predictable, predominantly conducted by large bureaucratic organizations, which placed employees in 'boxes' with highly specified roles to deliver on tightly defined objectives by those senior in a role hierarchy. Relationships were similarly fairly basic and predictable, normally based upon the use of rewards and/or punishment to shape actors' thoughts and behaviours through things like promotion and appraisal. Seldom were relationships between those in such hierarchical organizations developed beyond one of role specification to one of care and trust. In addition, seldom were the views of those lower in hierarchies consulted with respect to the overriding nature of a problem, even though such alternate perspectives might have been extremely useful. This form of organizational leadership – based on stasis, hierarchy and rigid work specification – would then be highly unsuited for dealing with issues of profound uncertainty, when many ideas might need generating, and probably by individuals with different roles, from different contexts and with different positions in a hierarchy.

Transformational leadership approaches may then seem an improvement. Indeed, they were widely adopted as appropriate business responses to the unstable and unpredictable market conditions in the 1970s and 1980s brought about by Japanese and 'Asian Tiger' business competition which undermined the dominance of Western bureaucratic approaches. The driving idea of transformational leadership – to have more charismatic and innovative individuals leading teams in an uncertain business climate – was transferred into public sector institutions by policymakers convinced that public sector leaders needed to think and lead in a more creative and entrepreneurial manner in an age of declining state revenues. However, this approach still makes a fundamental error when dealing with problems of profound uncertainty, for much of the business literature from which it derives paints picture of individual 'hero' leaders, which suggests that 'leadership' is an individual quality and that individual leaders should lead others through their personal visions or by espousing the visions of others more senior to them in some hierarchy. Yet what is most often needed is an approach where problems and answers are refined and then defined through an equality of consultation with other stakeholders, other points of view. Moreover, the notion of transformational leadership is strongly linked to the Western (and predominantly US) belief that extroverts have got much more to offer leadership than introverts. Yet as Cain (2013) argues in a delightfully entitled book *Quiet: The Power of Introverts in a World That Can't*

Stop Talking, a 'quiet' introvert approach has strengths neglected in much business – and then educational – leadership literature. The idea of the necessity of transformational leadership can then place immense and unnecessary pressure on individuals who are not particularly extrovert or charismatic but who may be very effective in a much quieter way.

Such concerns have then led to a movement away from the espousal of transformational leadership in national colleges of leadership and more towards notions of leadership which are less individual and more shared. Unsurprisingly, then, 'distributed leadership', which Bush (2019, p. 11) described as 'the normatively preferred [educational] leadership model in the twenty-first century', has been the most popular form of leadership in educational literature over the last couple of decades. Were it to be underpinned by a focus on the kinds of problems described earlier, were it to be informed by the kind of stewardship code argued for in this book and, finally, were it to make use of different stakeholder and expert views to reach agreement on problem definition and potential solutions, then it could be an appropriate leadership approach to the present and future problems described in this book.

However, 'distributed leadership', like many other fashionable terms, has generated a wide range of views on what it means, and with what it should be concerned, and therefore has a number of under-voiced problems. It might be used as a means for developing greater social justice through a school's decision-making structures (Woods and Roberts, 2016), but whilst praiseworthy in itself, such a concern is unlikely to be sufficiently focused on dealing with the kind of macro-issues of profound uncertainty addressed in this book. It might also be used at institutional levels as a managerial device to reduce formal leadership workload (Crawford, 2019), which again could be very useful but which doesn't specify the kind of workload being discussed, nor the qualities that individuals receiving such leadership power should possess. Finally, and as Western (2019) points out, distributing leadership means distributing power, and this can feel very risky to those distributing this power if they personally still remain formally accountable to others. He is also right, as we shall see in later chapters, in suggesting that distributed leadership works best when there are high levels of trust and a strong consensus on leadership objectives.

Conclusions

This chapter has examined the variety of threats that humanity can expect to face in the coming years and has suggested that not only are many societies unprepared for many of these but so also are their educational institutions, and much leadership practice, as demonstrated in traditional and some currently espoused models, is largely inappropriate to the challenges to be faced. Educational leaders then need to become macro-level stewards in a world of great complexity, where conditions of considerable uncertainty are likely to operate. To become effective stewards, they will not only have to be much more cognizant of the nature of approaching threats but also of how to work with others in an era when control and predictability are much more difficult to attain. It is then highly important to consider why such developments have for too long been areas of inaction. The next chapter then examines the reasons for this and suggest ways these may be overcome.

2

Educational Leadership and the Threat of Inaction

Introduction

The previous chapter began by noting how we are living in times of increasing uncertainty and that this limits the time of much of what can be said or suggested on many emerging threats. Take, for instance, the changing nature of Covid-19 and the responses to it. As this chapter was being redrafted, Covid variants were in their second and third waves in some countries, whilst others had yet to experience their full effects. At the same time, and usually in richer ones, there was considerable coverage of populations by vaccine injections, but many other countries were so poorly provided for that it was possible that more variants might emerge in such under-protected countries, which might be immune to current vaccines, and a new global wave might then begin. This, it would seem, may depend less on medical interventions and more upon the degree – or lack thereof – of political cooperation globally. Now there were some positive signals here: the newly installed US president Biden appeared to recognize the seriousness of the situation after a radically disorganized period of office by his predecessor, and he also responded positively to the need for action on climate change. Further, there was talk about the possibility of the taxation of large tech companies globally, which could make a huge difference to the funding of threats generated at the macro-level; and whilst the Climate Change Conference (COP26) in Glasgow in October/November of 2021 failed to deliver many hard promises, it still reflected a growing awareness by public and politicians alike of the need for urgent coordinated action on climate change.

Yet, at the time of writing, despite such developments, little has actually changed, and so asking the question 'Why has there been such delay in facing up to and acting on many emerging threats?' still remains highly relevant. Indeed, Covid-19 is not the only threat facing humanity and in the long run probably not the most important. Ord (2020) provides a catalogue of different global threats, including asteroids and comet impacts, super-volcanic eruptions, artificial intelligence and nuclear weapons. However currently, the most dangerous threat is probably that of climate change, because of its reach, its multi-varied causes and effects, and the lack of attention and response to it over the past few decades. This chapter then focuses on this threat when discussing the lack of response, as much of the analysis can be utilized when considering other threats. Levin et al. (2012), for example, describe climate change as one of a small but highly dangerous set of 'super-wicked' problems which have four main characteristics:

1. Short-term mindsets prevent their seriousness and future impact from being taken properly into account.
2. Those trying to resolve the problem are also those causing it.
3. There is an insufficiently agreed and coordinated global response to the urgency of the threat.
4. Whilst difficult to set precise dates, virtually all the scientific evidence points to the fact that the time to resolve the particular problem is running out.

The current and likely future effects of climate change upon habitats, food supplies, sea levels and human health have been tracked and recorded in considerable detail over the last twenty years, and there is no authoritative scientific body which now opposing the view that the global climate is changing for the worse, as global temperatures are rising, and these are then producing a series of unprecedented threats to humankind and most other species.

In a book examining how the role of the educational leader needs to change to address an increasing number of evolving threats, it is important to ask why a threat as serious as climate change has until very recently not received the recognition it deserves – neither in society at large, nor in educational institutions, nor in the educational leadership literature. Why has climate change for so long been seen as a relatively minor issue on public, government and leadership agendas? There seem to be a number of different causes for such inaction which have high relevance to the lack of reaction to other threats as well.

The first problem is that whilst the basic science of global warming and climate change is generally well understood, the processes by which it occurs are much less so. Without such understanding, it is argued that the potential rapidity of climate change and therefore the need for much greater speed in preparation for its impacts will not be fully appreciated.

A second problem stems, a little surprisingly, from existence as hunter-gatherers in prehistoric times, as we are still using thought patterns and risk behaviours from that time in reacting to present-day challenges. Whilst sometimes these strategies are effective, they can also contradict each other and may be inappropriate to the nature of present-day challenges.

A third problem stems from a tendency to frame climate change issues from one perspective and in so doing to prescribe single-level responses to issues. In many countries, this has led to the issue being framed as either a problem deriving from personal consumption or a macro-level problem which downplays the importance of individual actions. It will be argued that a merging of micro-, meso- and macro-understandings is needed in order to understand the full impact of climate change and its remediation.

Fourth, in using personal understandings of problems, individuals may experience feelings of frustration and powerlessness, and such single-level solutions can lead to individuals then disengaging from forms of action which might reduce such threats. Such issues are better understood and resolved when using a number of different levels of analysis and action.

Responses to such inhibitors can be facilitated by a new model of educational leadership, which is grounded in notions of complexity, problem sharing, a larger future orientation and a greater contextualization. There is, however, a fifth issue which needs attention – that of the lack of awareness or unwillingness of nation-states to engage in the kind of global-level cooperation required to produce really effective responses. Coordinated action might then be obstructed by a number of current tensions, including that between the United States, China and Russia, and their respective allies. All such impediments to action then need consideration.

The facts of climate change

We then begin by looking at the science of climate change. Whilst this can seem a densely complex area, Read et al. (2004) and Norgaard (2011) argue that there are really only two relatively simple facts that people need to know in order to understand how climate change occurs. A first is that the current increase in global warming is due to an increase in the amount of carbon dioxide in the earth's atmosphere. The second is that the most important contribution to such carbon dioxide increase comes from the human burning of fossil fuels, primarily those of coal and oil. Now both of these statements are true, but on their own they may fail to convey the seriousness of the threat of climate change and may also fail to convince the newcomer or the sceptic of the dangers in this area. Rather more needs adding.

One might then need to point out that the science on climate change is not a recent area of study but goes back nearly 200 years. Tyndall in 1859, for instance, noted that gases like carbon dioxide and methane were 'greenhouse' gases, in the sense that they prevented heat escaping from the earth's atmosphere. From this, in 1896 Arrhenius concluded that if the percentage of these gases in the atmosphere rose, so would the global atmospheric temperature. Then, in 1938 Calendar took this analysis further by presenting evidence to show that the human burning of fossil fuels was the primary cause of this rise in temperatures. Sadly his results were either ridiculed or ignored. However, the exhaustive record of rising temperatures by Keeling over the last fifty years (Kunzig and Broeckner, 2008) has now established beyond any reasonable dispute the remarkable and worrying rise in the concentration of such gases in the earth's atmosphere, and there is no longer any other serious contender to the anthropogenic burning of fossil fuels as the major contributor to this rise. Humanity and particularly its more affluent nations have been the principal causes of such increases.

Yet, despite such solid scientific foundations, it is remarkable how subdued has been the public response to the concerns generated by such data over the last few decades. A number of explanations have been provided to explain the lack of urgency and action by policymakers and the general public, as well as those in other positions of leadership and authority who, one might have thought, would have urged greater consideration of, and action towards, this threat. Yet, whilst there are pockets of strong and informed practice, progress has been much slower than anticipated, and remarkably little has been written about the role that educational leaders might play with respect to this threat. So why have responses been so muted?

It is worth noting that in the United States in 2010, Reynolds et al. compared responses of well-educated laypeople to climate change questions with responses by a similar group in 1992. They found that in the more recent group there was better appreciation of climate change causes, and a better understanding of some of the basic science, yet there still continued to be a lack of the two key facts mentioned earlier: that increases in global warming were very largely due to increases in atmospheric carbon dioxide and that the burning of fossil fuels was the major cause of such increases.

In the United States and other wealthy Western countries, part of the reason for this lack of understanding and action almost certainly stems from the widespread disinformation over the last few decades by those extracting carbon-based fuels (see Washington and Cook, 2011, Oreskes and Conway, 2012) and also from anti-intellectual influences with respect to the nature of evidence and the validity of the scientific method (Jacoby, 2018). However, even with such impediments, there still remains a distinct lack of understanding of some of the key processes underlying climate change, and whilst disinformation or simple ignorance can be a block to progress, the lack of understanding of the processes described in the previous chapter (positive feedback, exponential growth, connectivity and tipping points) constitutes *covert* threats, because societies have tended to focus upon other concerns and, in under-appreciating the dangers that such processes can pose, have probably exacerbated their long-term damage.

However, it is important to flag up one final issue here, which is the manner in which problems may be viewed, because such adoption can have profound effects upon personal beliefs in what we can understand and change. This importance stems from the fact that human beings over the past few thousand years have had fairly stable and continuous experiences of the world's climate, which can lure many into thinking that the world runs on simple, 'tame' processes, which may also seduce one into thinking that this is essentially a world which human beings can understand, predict and control. Unfortunately, as Rittel and Weber (1973) suggest, many problems are much more complex than actually thought. Not only are many difficult to anticipate, predict and control; they are also distinguished by people differing in their judgements as to whether they are problems at all. A much-used example of this is the nature of the humble dandelion – gardeners may see it as a real problem in their carefully manicured gardens; children may see them simply as nice yellow flowers. Many other people don't even think about them. This personal dimension of what constitutes a problem then adds an extra layer of complexity to the identification of many problems. In terms of issues like climate change, to assume that you have control over processes when you actually don't, or that there isn't a problem here at all, is an increasingly dangerous position for humanity to take.

The problem of solving problems: Inheritances from prehistory

If some of the processes underlying climate change are covert threats because their lack of recognition can lead to sudden, unexpected and damaging effects, another area of concern can be found in the strategies we take in assessing such threats. Some approaches were developed in prehistoric times, to our origins as a distinct species, when our brains evolved to better assess challenges, and practices were refined to enable us stay alive in a dangerous world. These are inheritances which have helped us to survive through hundreds of thousands of years but which, Marshall (2015) argues, could now lead us to ignore rather than respond to threats like climate change. In terms of brain evolution, two distinct parts of it have developed very different strategies. One part, the older, emotional brain, situated in the amygdala and the hippocampus, uses past experiences to generate near-immediate responses to threats, whilst the newer, more rational part of the brain, located in the cortex and neocortex, tends to use more analytical, logical and symbolic means of encoding issues before then responding.

The assessments and reactions to potentially dangerous events by our prehistoric ancestors then seem to have been prompted by both parts of the brain, and current habits and assumptions have then been inherited through experiences in the long past. It is a very long past: *Homo sapiens* has existed as a distinct species for about 300,000 years, but current research strongly suggests it is only in the last 10,000–12,000 years that the vast majority of the population has adopted fairly static pastoral and agricultural ways of life, before then building larger communities, city states, nation-states and empires. For the first 97 per cent of our existence then we have lived within small hunter-gatherer groups of between fifty and seventy individuals (Cummings et al., 2018), which mostly moved around within particular geographical areas, using intimate knowledge of their surroundings to travel from location to location to exploit the food and resources at appropriate times of the year (Brody, 2002). Now a degree of natural selection of both individuals and groups would have taken place over this vast amount of time, with those behaviours being selected which helped acquire the most resources and which helped avoid predators. Other behaviours which were not as productive, or which did not reduce predatory threats, would likely have led to the extinction of their practitioners. Commentators like Gardner (2009) and Marshall (2015) have then suggested that a number of rules of thumb would have been adopted in assessing potential threats. Some of these were probably:

- *If it looks like a lion, it probably is a lion.* In other words, assume that your first identification of a threat is correct, as there is no loss if you are wrong in this assumption; so give less importance to things that don't look like threats.
- *If it's new or unusual, then pay it attention, and prepare a threat response*; if it isn't new (and isn't something like a lion), you don't need to take as much

notice of it as when it is new. Things you are accustomed to are much less likely to be threats than things that are new and unusual.
- *If it's very close, assume it's more of a threat than something that isn't so near.* Things that are very near need quicker responses than things that aren't.
- *If it's suddenly very close, then react even more quickly.* In other words, things that are sudden and unexpected need treating much more as potential threats than things that appear gradually.
- *If a threat exists now, then react more quickly to it than a threat that will be a problem only in the future.* Things that may be problems in the future don't need the same immediate attention as current problems.
- *If a threat is highly visible, then pay attention to it.* In other words, things that are clear and distinct need more attention than things that are obscure or diffuse.

Now virtually all of these are examples of reactions to sudden threats and are largely quick emotional intuitive reactions of fear, surprise, novelty, shock or repellence. They would have been very sensible responses to possess if you were trying to exist on the African veldt, where many other species saw you as a tasty meal. Nevertheless, they need to be seen, on their own, as rather limited survival mechanisms, for on many occasions, a little more reflection might produce a better assessment of the degree of risk and a more reflective response might well save your life. Thus, reacting to things that are near makes strong sense, but it doesn't always pay to ignore a more distant object, for the extra time spent examining it might well improve your chances of survival. Again, the more time that is spent gathering different views about the threat potential of something, the more likely you are to form a more accurate picture of the nature of the 'threat' and therefore of the most appropriate response. Finally, ignoring something that is slow-moving and obscure may turn out to be a very poor move: lions stalk their prey by moving slowly and then pouncing at the last moment. One can well imagine that many hunter-gatherers would have employed both sets of rules, but others, probably now extinct, didn't.

Now when it comes to the current threat of climate change, commentators like Marshall (2014) suggest that our approach is stacked against a full consideration, because we initially react to most threats as our predecessors did: when potential threats are new, near, sudden and/or highly visible, we are likely to initially react with emotions of fear, surprise and/or shock. Many dangers are sudden, clear and easily identified; they are 'now' events, like people struggling for breath having contracted with Covid-19. Climate change, however, doesn't always consist of sudden events; often, as with warmer summers, it's more of a gradual, rather diffuse, development, where the ultimate impact is still some way down the road and therefore may be something which doesn't provoke much alarm.

Yet when we come to examine the nature of climate change, we find that in many cases climate change hasn't presented itself as a sudden global threat, but more as a series of episodes of extreme weather in different parts of the world. So whilst some climate change events, like hurricanes or heat waves, can be very damaging, similar events have been experienced in the past and usually at particular times of the year. Moreover, even if geological data suggest that present climate change is happening comparatively quickly, in tens or hundreds of years, in a human time frame these will likely be seen as happening rather slowly.

Recent events may then be extreme, but such events have occurred before, and predecessors did not attribute global climate change to them. Moreover, many events reported as examples of climate change may happen far away from those who hear of them, and this prevents them from being seen as global scale threats. Finally, threats are normally defined as such because of the dangers and the damage they produce; yet whilst some effects of climate change can be genuinely alarming, many effects can on occasions feel quite beneficial, as when countries in temperate latitudes experience particularly sunny weather over a period of time.

The problem then seems to be that we have built-in wiring which alerts us to sudden, close threats, but which discounts those which are more gradual and more distant. The result is that our old emotional intuitive brain can prevent us from taking the issue of climate change as seriously as we need to. This, it is claimed, explains the limited response and action.

However, I'm not sure this is the full explanation. It is hardly as if our newer more rational, reflective brain has not been given plenty of practice in reflecting upon climate change effects and the evidence for its existence over the last few decades. If there is any balance between these two differently functioning parts of the brain, one would expect that the decades of exposure to this threat would be a good length of time for such reflection. Yet the fact remains that there is much less emphasis and much less action here than one might expect from just the old brain/new brain hypothesis. We may need to conclude that humanity is not going to stop using the sometimes contradictory and inappropriate inheritances from our deep past when attempting to assess levels of threat, as these prehistoric inheritances can be crucial tools, honed over many generations, to keep us alive. However, we have to recognize that after about 290,000 years of living as hunter-gatherers, humanity's principal way of life has drastically changed to a more sedentary, more agricultural and then to a more industrial base, before very recently moving into an age of information technology. Hunter-gatherer risk assessment strategies may then not always be appropriate for these other ways of living. A more conscious understanding of how we have changed during this time would almost certainly help avoid inappropriate old-brain usage. Educators and educational leaders could have a pivotal role here. They employ the same apparatus in assessing risks as everyone else, and in a 24/7 world, the demands from senior levels of hierarchies for immediate responses to potentially threatening instructions, circulars and 'advice' can lead to such threats also being judged more by the older, more emotionally responsive part of the brain, rather than the more recent reflective and rational side. A better appreciation by educators of how our brains tend to work could then help their students and communities to be aware of the need to make more considered, more appropriate judgements in times of stress and pressure.

In sum, whilst prehistoric inheritances may still be useful in some situations, perhaps the major conclusion here is of the need to be aware of the old brain and its behaviours, and to help others in the present day to make much greater use of the functions of the new brain. The threats from modern-day climate change are infinitely more complex than facing a lion on the veldt. However, there may then be other more contemporary reasons for inaction which need incorporating into explanations of the lack of action. We then move to look at some of these.

The problem of solving problems: Contemporary explanations

Over the last two or three decades, as noted earlier, some climate change commentators have suggested that the dominant reason for the subdued interest in climate change has been an information gap, where people didn't know or didn't understand the causes behind climate change. The appropriate strategy has then been seen as one of raising awareness through providing the relevant facts in the area, of the kind already described, in the belief that once these were well known and understood, then rational, intelligent and caring individuals would become more engaged and more active in dealing with these threats.

A large body of writing has then been produced by environmentalists over the last couple of decades, as well as hugely authoritative reports by the IPCC (e.g. 2014, 2018/19, 2020), demonstrating how solid has been the scientific consensus on the causes of global warming. Yet the evidence still suggested that the anticipated raising of the level of interest and response very largely didn't occur. Further, and more worryingly, there has also been evidence (Krosnick et al., 2006; Kellstedt et al. 2008; Norgaard, 2011) that in some cases the extra information actually reduced people's interest and commitment. In sum, whilst numerous reports, books and articles have been written on the science, impact and dangers of climate change, the subject has failed to reach anywhere near the level of interest and action that might have been expected.

The nearest some have come to taking it seriously has been through using such concerns as metaphors for problems in their own areas of practice. If one googles 'educational leadership' and 'climate', for example, the vast majority of 'hits' refer to the problems of educational leadership in creating the right school ethos or climate. Further, concerns about climate change have often been transmuted from concerns about environmental sustainability into ones about leadership sustainability (Hargreaves and Fink, 2007, Davies 2007), with few or no links being made between the causes of leadership sustainability – largely the problems behind lowered leadership recruitment and retention – and the kind of leadership responses required to address the much wider and more serious global environmental threat. There have been a few exceptions – such as the special edition of *Management in Education* (2016), but the issue of climate change has either been largely ignored or has become little more than an analogy for more immediate personal, professional and institutional concerns.

So, providing more information hasn't had the level of impact one might have thought it would. Perhaps this isn't *that* surprising: individuals are not tabula rasa, on which a desired mindset can be inscribed. They come to issues with pre-formed ideas, values and opinions, and tend to choose materials which fit with such previous orientations. This is why Marshall (2015, p 44) argues that we approach new information dynamically, because

> our views are constantly being shaped through the negotiation between our own identity, our group loyalty, and our relationship with wider society. We are active participants at every stage, influencing those around us as much as we are influenced by them.

This suggests a much more complex view of human learning than concepts like a 'banking' concept of education suggests, where knowledge is deposited in a student's brain, for them to 'spend' later. Such simplicity may seem appealing to some but is actually very unhelpful, for most people assess others' proposals with degrees of scepticism and criticality. This is the point that Stern (2020) makes with respect to the relationships between leaders and followers – these do not consist of the simple transmission of thought and action from one leading individual to other people following that person, but are in fact deeply interactive encounters, where both sides need each other and both sides are changed, to such an extent that the two terms 'leader' and 'follower' become increasingly unhelpful in describing the status of the parties involved. In addition, and importantly, part of this critical interrogation is viewed through a person's conception of themselves. As Gecas and Burke argue (1995, p. 50-2),

> the self is not simply a passive sponge that soaks up information from the environment . . . rather it is an active agent engaged in various self-serving purposes . . . perception, cognition, and retention of self-relevant information are highly selective, depending on whether the information is favourable or unfavourable to one's self-conception.

As Stern (2021) points out, such self-conception adds complexity and difficulties to relationships, as individuals never fully know themselves, and neither do the people with whom they are interacting. However, whilst needing to acknowledge this addition to complexity, we also need to move beyond individual experience to fully understand the origins of an individual's views, as the dynamics of learning and assessment take place within meso- and macro-contexts, the influences of which can strongly shape individual beliefs. Thus, in an age of neoliberal ideology, individuals may be viewed (and may come to view themselves) as self-interested and competitive consumers, who are then prevented from focusing upon larger issues by being inducted by the macro-culture into a micro-consumerist lifestyle, where satisfaction of present personal wants supersedes all other concerns. Such individuals may then not have – or may not want to acquire –the kinds of longer-term macro-foci needed to appreciate how such consumerist effects can impact the planet's climate and resources. Perhaps unsurprisingly, then, findings by Zahran et al. (2006) suggest that citizens in US states having high levels of greenhouse gas emissions are less likely to support climate change policies than states with lower levels. Moreover, at the national level Sandvik (2008, p. 333) has also found that 'the willingness of a nation to contribute to reductions in greenhouse gas emissions decreases with its share of these emissions'.

Such findings might, at first blush, suggest a lack of care about climate change effects, as higher levels of income and consumption seem to either prevent individuals from or seduce them into only looking to their own short-term satisfaction. However, research by Norgaard (2011) provides numerous examples of people in Norway and the United States. who, despite having very high standards of living, not only recognized the dangers of climate change but also clearly cared about its effects. Yet, importantly, many of these same people didn't want to engage in conversations about these threats, even as they recognized how much their own countries and their own lifestyles were exacerbating the problem. Norgaard then suggests that this combination of high concern and low action most likely stems from a combination of feelings, in particular of fear, guilt and powerlessness, and she quotes numerous individuals who recognized the culpability of their culture and society (and therefore themselves) in the increase of greenhouse gases, but also their lack of belief in their ability to make any difference to this threat.

This analysis fits well with the description of 'super-wicked problems' (Levin, et al. 2012) described earlier, and in particular, the short-term mindsets of consumerist societies which prevent climate change future impacts from being taken sufficiently seriously. Such consumers are very aware that they are the causes of problems they should be trying to resolve, but they doubt the strength of will or interest by their governments in committing to radical action; and as they recognize these elements, they experience a chill of fear as reports increasingly suggest that time is running out for essential solutions

Norgaard (2011) then argues that when you see a problem and know that you are at least in part to blame, but see no way of personally preventing the problem's development, then finding ways of ignoring the problem or finding small justifications for your behaviour is likely to be adopted in order to avoid constant confrontation with your fear over the future, your guilt at your contribution and your powerlessness at doing anything about it. Importantly, this combination of feelings was also found by Norgaard in the views of educators, who, whilst also being aware of climate change issues, suggested to her that it was imperative for educators to convey an optimistic 'can do' attitude to their students, which led many to avoid discussions on a topic which they believed would only create negative feelings and ultimately depression in their students.

These findings, I think, suggest a theory of inaction with respect to climate change which is rather more complex than simple 'genetic inheritance', 'information deficit' or 'self-interested' models suggest. Whilst these models have their part to play, more central is understanding why people perform displacement activities to avoid discussion of climate change. To do this, one needs to better appreciate the contexts within which people live and act. Bulkeley (2000, p. 315–16) therefore argues that people should not be described as 'individual agents acting "rationally" in response to information made available to them'. Nor should they be portrayed as 'stable, coherent, and consistent' in ways which abstract them from their context. Rather, the lack of individual action on climate change needs to be framed within a more considered account of the meso- and macro-forces acting upon these individuals, which then induces them to engage in strategies of avoidance when confronted by such issues. However, the nature of such events can then be interpreted more optimistically: if macro-level discussions on climate change generate genuine reforms at this level, it could then be the case that meso- and micro-level forces could be released and so reduce personal feelings of fear, guilt and powerlessness, and instead could impel, perhaps even unleash, highly positive actions by individuals, for they have then come to view their personal actions as capable of making a significant difference. In short, a multi-level understanding of action and inaction is required for a better appreciation of why climate change as a threat has been so relatively neglected.

Multi-level understandings of action and inaction

A good place to further develop such understanding of inaction – and of the possibility of its reversal – comes from Norgaard's (2011) work on rural Norwegians' views on climate change. This may seem a rather parochial focus, but paradoxically it demonstrates well how multinational are the reactions. Rural life in Norway is seen by most Norwegians as having the admirable qualities of being outdoor, healthy, egalitarian, honest, environmentally responsible and self-reliant. This seems to most Norwegians to be a good life, one to be treasured. Yet there is an internal contradiction here which many Norwegians know of but try to avoid talking about. As Hovden and Lindseth (2002, p. 163) noted:

> Norway, an already wealthy and highly developed country, built a very significant fortune in the 1990s from the very activity that has made stabilisation of CO_2 emissions next to impossible.

The situation doesn't seem to have changed much: the '*I*' (13/4/21) reported that six environmental organizations were calling on Norway to stop plans to open ocean areas to deep-sea mining, which would very likely cause great damage to the ocean bed and species living there.

Norwegians are, of course, not alone in this contradiction: plenty of wealthy countries declare a commitment to environmental issues, yet continue to utilize natural resources in ways which substantially harm the environment. In so doing, individuals then have to maintain two contradictory sets of values. When, for instance, Hillary Clinton visited Norway to negotiate US access to 900 trillion dollars of Norwegian Arctic oil reserves, she was still able to refer to climate change as 'the chief threat of the 21st century' (Marshall, 2015, p. 169). Yet, of course, it takes two sides to make a deal, and Norway agreed to let the United States have access to these huge reserves of oil, whilst still trying to project itself to the rest of the world as a clean, environmentally friendly and socially just nation. Yet, as Norgaard (2011, p. 88) remarks,

> For Norwegians information on global warming contradicts their sense of being environmentally responsible. And as a problem generated by wealthy nations, for which people in poor nations disproportionately suffer, knowledge of global warming also challenges Norwegians' sense of themselves as egalitarian and socially just.

How is such simultaneous holding of incompatible values possible? Lifton (1993, p. 210) has suggested that it requires a 'psychic numbing' of at least one side of such concerns. Such behaviour is demonstrated by individuals at different levels of society in a number of ways. One in Norway is for policymakers to acknowledge that they belong to an oil producing country but also claim that they make only a small contribution when compared with countries like the United States and Saudi Arabia. Another way is for local politicians to label climate change as a national and international issue rather than a local one and so not requiring discussion at their level of involvement. Further Norgaard (p. 117) talks of a 'collective backward focus' by many citizens, as they celebrate Norway's history, rather than adopting a greater future focus towards problems to come. In so doing, she argues (p. 131):

> ideas of traditions and links to the past serve as an anchoring point in changing times, and provide a sense of security that, at least some people believe, helps them deal with the larger world.

Such 'backward focus' is seen in many other countries. In the UK, for example, there is constant referral to and celebration of the Second World War, as it takes people back to a time when Britain was a pivotal global force in defeating the Nazis and one that gave many a sense of national pride, when many present politicians and much policy today seem to do the opposite. Britons, like Norwegians, then also tend to focus on the everyday things of life, on the good old days and less on the larger issues, particularly if concerns are raised about climate change, which up until the immediate present have been very largely seen as a problem of the future. Norgaard also found that when she tried to involve others in such discussion, this was not viewed as a polite topic of conversation, that it would instead contribute to negative feelings, and the conversation was quickly moved to other topics.

Whilst Norgaard argued that Norway's context – a rich country contributing to CO2 emissions but wanting to see itself as environmentally responsible – led to a variety of attempts to avoid thinking about or discussing this issue, it nevertheless seemed clear to her that the US context made discussion and action on climate change even more difficult there. There are certainly many parallels between these two countries, which probably apply elsewhere. Thus, US educators also didn't want to depress or scare their students by dwelling on this subject, and local politicians framed it as a national or international issue, thus excluding it from their focus. Finally, she also found that in social situations, most people didn't want to make conversation about it because of the negative feelings it induced.

Nevertheless, there are also substantial contextual differences between the two countries. To begin with, the United States is currently the world's second largest contributor to greenhouse gas emissions, and the majority of its citizens are much more wedded to forms of conspicuous consumption than Norwegians are, and have historically shown little desire to elect leaders who would lower the use of carbon-based energy in the production of goods. Indeed, the United States has had a succession of presidents over the last few decades who have either expressed profound scepticism or denied the reality of global warming and have withdrawn from global emissions treaties for not being in the interest of the United States. Whilst Obama and Biden seem notable exception here, Jacoby (2018) argues that such historic presidential scepticism and denial are probably rooted in a national culture of anti-intellectualism, allied to a loud fundamentalist religious voice, as well as being influenced by well-financed groups of energy providers wanting to continue extracting oil and coal (Oreskes and Conway, 2011). However, in June 2021 President Biden suspended the licenses granted by Donald Trump in the last two weeks of his presidency to energy companies to explore Alaskan natural resources. The decision here may be a bellwether of the direction of US policy over the next few years.

Nevertheless, before this account moves into greater optimism, there is one very important contextual impediment to US policies on climate change and that is the supremacy of individualist politics. Bellah et al. (2008, p. xiv) have argued that 'individualism is the first language in which Americans tend to think about themselves', and, whilst often seen as one of the cornerstones of the American concept of liberty, individualism has a number of qualities which hinder climate change action. Its primacy as a political doctrine can then reduce the influence that united groups of individuals can bring to bear on issues, and therefore allows better-organized groups against climate change to have much greater persuasion on policymaking than would otherwise be the case. Further, the easy translation of individual citizenship into forms of individual consumerism (Barber, 1984) also deflects people away from properly understanding issues that are created and need resolving at larger meso- and macro-levels. Individualism as a dominant social, political and economic frame can thereby prevent individuals from understanding the kinds of action which needs to be taken at the macro-level with such problems, as too often the response is a rejection of notions of big or intrusive government. Rather than wanting to hear more about the issue, then, some individuals in the United States may react by simply refusing to listen. The situation in other countries which have more communal approaches is likely to be very different and much more positive.

It is clear then that in order to fully understand inaction on climate change, one needs to understand the national, local and personal contextual impediments to action. Only then will one be in a position to understand the extent to which macro-changes can impact individual behaviours, and then the extent to which it is possible to identify the best leverage points (Meadows, 2008), and so apply pressure for change through such understanding. If the importance of context is not recognized, then the necessity of climate change may in some places not be embraced, and individuals will then continue to use 'psychic numbing' to avoid such discussion. This makes the role of education that much harder, but at least it makes clear the cultural challenges that educators need to face. Indeed educational leaders, knowing their institutions and their communities, are usually very well placed to adjust such messages to the contexts involved.

So educational leaders then need to understand the various levels of context, and then focus beyond individuals, institutions and communities with which they work, and to understand the macro-contexts within which these micro- and meso-contexts operate. The evidence from Norway and the United States then strongly suggests that people have avoided talking about these issues because of the fear of what is coming, the guilt felt as their countries contribute to the creation of this macro-problem and the feelings of powerlessness they live with because they think micro- and meso-level actions can do little to remedy this threat. Yet there are strong indications that macro-level change can have strong influences – both positively and negatively – on individual inaction. So possessing a strong understanding of the dynamics and the possible interventions derived from local, cultural and national contexts then seems essential if educational leaders are to personally impact upon such events. As Clarke and Dempster (2020, p. 3) argue, we need to move

> from the pessimism of the intellect to the optimism of the will, an optimism built on exercising personal agency.

Conclusion: Facilitating and impeding at the global level

The reasons for inaction discussed in this chapter – the lack of understanding of climate change processes, the inheritance of inappropriate risk-assessment strategies, the debilitating presence in individuals of fear, guilt and powerlessness, and the tendency to neglect multi-level contextual influences – then all need addressing. At the present time, probably the most unpredictable area is the nature of the relationship between nation-states. The increase in tensions between the United States and China, and their respective allies, over the recent past, the disputes between China and countries like Japan and Indonesia over dominance in the South China Sea, the imperial ambitions of Russia with respect to its neighbours and the growing disputes by nations bordering the Arctic over the exploitation of natural resources there all contribute to a situation where global competition seems to be more pronounced than does increased cooperation (Klare, 2012, Smith, 2012). Yet the kind of threats described in this book which are emerging at the global level all require concerted global cooperation if they are to be remedied. Such high-level competition and unpredictability could then lead to unexpected and unanticipated political situations which dramatically limited global cooperation over measures reducing carbon emissions. Such competitive actions would then likely prevent the possibility of global temperature reduction and climate stabilization. This subject of nation-state competition and cooperation is examined in greater depth in Chapter 6.

Such observations once more point to the uncertainties generated by events at the global level which can then affect outcomes at lower levels. It is not necessarily a dystopian warning, because such events could lead to positive outcomes for remedying climate change, just as much as they could lead to much darker outcomes. Moreover, such influences are not just one-way: movement at lower levels can also impact higher levels, just as much as the reverse. Responses to the first four causes of inaction, as well as local and national pressures for increased political action on climate change, can combine with the perception of the national benefit gained from such cooperation to persuade political leaders that greater cooperation on climate change policies is the preferred option. It also raises for educational leaders the question of what kind of educational leadership is most appropriate in such an age of complexity and uncertainty, which will be the subject of the next chapter.

3

Educational Leaders in an Age of Complex Problems

Introduction

On 28 June 1914, seven young Serbians decided to assassinate Archduke Ferdinand, heir to the throne of the Austro-Hungarian Empire. He was in Sarajevo on that day to commemorate a Serbian defeat by the Ottoman Empire in 1389. Armed with bombs and loaded revolvers, with explosives strapped to their chests and with cyanide to commit suicide after the act, the Serbs positioned themselves along the well-publicized route of his drive through the city. The first attempt was an abject failure: the bomb missed the archduke's car and hit the car behind; the would-be assassin threw himself in the river, only to find the river was too low to drown himself, and his cyanide didn't work. The archduke refused to abandon the drive, but for safety's sake, it was decided to change the route. However, the drivers of the first two cars were Czech, and nobody bothered to translate the new orders from German into Czech. So before long they made a wrong turn, which by chance took them right past where another of the would-be assassins, Gavrilo Princip, was standing. The car even slowed down as it came towards him, and he simply stepped out and shot dead the archduke and his wife Sophie. This action by an individual Serb led Austria-Hungary, increasingly threatened by nationalist uprisings within its empire, to declare war on Serbia a month later. Serbia then called on its long-time ally Russia to support it, and when Russia began to mobilize troops, Austria-Hungary then called on Germany to back it up. Russia then invoked an earlier alliance with France and Britain to support it against Germany and Austria-Hungary. France, still seeking revenge for the humiliating defeat by Germany in the 1870 Franco-Prussian War, began to mobilize its troops, and when Germany invaded France through Belgium, Britain, which had an alliance with Belgium, joined in. The Great War – the war to end all wars, in which seventeen million people died – then began due to the interactions between a number of unrelated, unanticipated and apparently random micro- and macro-acts. The war changed the political, economic and social complexion of countries worldwide, the consequences of which are still being experienced today. One lesson from this is that the world is infinitely more complex than is usually conceived, and radical uncertainty and the totally unexpected are much more common than is normally recognized.

Different kinds of complexity

This chapter revisits and develops the four different kinds of complexity described in the first chapter. As suggested there, the four kinds of complexity are *systemic*, *epistemic*, *relational* and *wicked* complexity. They are examined in detail in order to arrive at conclusions as to the most appropriate leadership approach for dealing with these kinds of problems.

Systemic complexity and emergent structures

Systemic complexity stems from the fact that many causes and their effects occur within systemic webs rather than linear chains. In the real world simple linear sequences of cause and effect do occur, where, for example, A causes B which causes C (I drop my pen, I bend down to pick it up, I bang my head on the corner of the desk). More often, however, cause and effect are embedded within systems where A causes B, which then impacts L, Y and R, which then affect V, S and T, which may then return to affect A and C. The introduction to this chapter is a good example, for it illustrates how a lone gunman can be provided with the opportunity to assassinate a high-ranking dignitary through a series of unanticipated problems and decisions, and how the reverberations of this single act led not only to the deaths of millions of people in the First World War but also to the emergence of a great deal of unexpected world history afterwards (Clark, 2012). For example, much of the current conflict in the Middle East With can be traced back to the division of the Ottoman Empire after the First World War by two civil servants, Sykes and Picot, into British and French spheres of influence, with no regard to the tribe, ethnicity or language of the people living there (Hourani, 2005). It is a tragic example of a simple action in a large system leading to unanticipated and unpredictable causations, where many effects can be difficult or impossible to understand, predict or control. Indeed, because of this, as Levy (1992) argues, so many variables are at work in a system that its overall behaviour can only be understood as an emergent consequence of the holistic sum of all the myriad behaviours embedded within.

If this is the case, then we need to recognize that the beginning and the consequences of the First World War were but two examples of how systems can and do evolve in unexpected, unpredictable and potentially highly damaging ways. So whilst belief in a world of simple linear causality may be reassuring, because it promises the ability to predict and control much that is faced, such confidence will very often be badly misplaced. In reality, identifying chains of linear causality at only one level may be little more than the extraction of a single causal chain: the archduke's car slowing down was the micro-event allowing Princip to kill the archduke and his wife, but it should not be extracted from larger webs of causation, such as the macro-reasons for Serbian hostility to the Austro-Hungarian empire, and the subsequent reactions by the European Powers. The micro-parts can be fully understood only when seen as elements of a much larger picture, which may be insufficiently considered or understood. But then you can't understand the macro-situation of Serbian hostility, or the reactions of the Great Powers, without knowing the micro-events which contributed to them. All are parts of systems composed of micro-, meso- and macro-events which interact and create new events in many simultaneous and unpredictable ways.

Now Clark (2012) described the great powers as 'sleepwalking' into the First World War, and one can understand what he meant by this: individuals, institutions and countries (the micro, the meso and the macro) all seeming to react to unexpected stimuli into taking actions, which acted as further stimuli provoking actions from others, until formal declarations of war led to actual bloody conflict. However, such unthinking actions do not comprise all that intelligent actors are capable of. Indeed, it seems possible to describe four different kinds of system structures and behaviours, within which only some intelligence and awareness are demonstrated.

A first kind or level of system is that which is purely physical in nature, such as weather patterns and landscape changes, producing impacts caused solely by the interplay of physical forces. No intelligence or awareness is demonstrated here. A second level, however, is one which contains low-level actors, like ants, whose behaviour and understanding are limited almost entirely to genetically programmed behaviours. However, this does not mean that the systems within which their behaviour is embedded necessarily work at a similarly low level: one highly surprising example is the description of harvester ants (Johnson, 2001), which are genetically programmed to perform a number of actions which preserve the health of the colony. Notice that I don't say 'to preserve' the health of the colony, for ants don't have this level of intelligence or systemic understanding. Nevertheless, one of their actions is to get rid of the detritus accumulating in and around the nest; another is to remove the bodies of dead harvester ants. This genetic programming also determines at what distance from the nest the ants dump the detritus and dead bodies, because choosing a site too close to the nest would foster disease and might ultimately eliminate the colony. The result is that the simple genetically induced actions of individual ants lead to – indeed structure the emergence of – a higher-level colony, even though no members of the colony (including the queen ant) have any individual understanding of this higher level. The whole is then greater than the sum of the parts, and whilst there is nothing conscious about such individual behaviours, they do lead to the adaptive behaviour which makes the species more sustainable.

A third level of system still exhibits the genetically induced behaviours of individuals which lead to emergent structures; but in addition individuals are also able to adapt through reacting to and changing behaviour in response to either positive or negative stimuli in their environment (Skinner, 1972), by copying the behaviours of others (Bandura, 1977) or by using rationality to reflect upon and then learn to repeat behaviours to avoid negative stimuli or to seek out positive ones (Piaget and Inhelder, 1956). Such behaviours are a step forward from those based purely on genetic inheritances and are the beginnings of educational activities.

However, there remains a fourth level of capacity which human beings, and probably higher-level animals like apes, dolphins and octopi, possess. This is the ability to be conscious of and remember events and their responses to them, and then of being able to reflect upon, and form, new interpretations of this reality. Then, using prediction and anticipation, they are able to frame pictures of possible futures, permitting a degree of control and steerage of new instances not seen at lower system levels. Whilst this is clearly a major step forward in interpreting and attempting control of the external world, such interpretations also add an extra layer of complexity to understanding reality, because these are *subjective* interpretations, and as Lincoln and Guba (1994, p. 107) argue, any given interpretation or paradigm is then

> simply the most informed and sophisticated view that its proponents have been able to devise . . . the sets of answers given . . . are all inventions of the human mind and hence subject to human error.

Whilst actors working at lower system levels are also engaged in responding to an external environment, as Bryman (1992, p. 79) points out, those with abilities at the higher fourth level are 'engaged in interpretations of other people's interpretations'. This extra layer of complexity to human systems creates more sophisticated frames and interpretations of cause and effect than those governed by lower-level interpretations, as such conscious framing permits actors to frame scenarios for past, present and future events, which then facilitate the creation of entirely novel and possibly more adaptive behaviours. In doing so, however, they also add an extra layer of complexity to such understanding. Actors at lower levels may be maladaptive in their behaviours due to a mismatch between genetic programming or behavioural conditioning to external events, but human beings may do all of these things and also be maladaptive in their interpretations of what they think they can understand and predict. Complexity is then a valuable addition to human adaptability, but it creates new challenges through its inclusion.

Such descriptions of behaviour and decision-making at different system levels directly relate to the work of educational leaders, because the manner in which individual leaders 'frame' their understanding of the actors and the organizations within which they work then determines the kind of leadership style they are likely to adopt. Table 3.1, then, suggests that educational leaders can adopt very different leadership styles based on different system levels.

Now whilst few leaders are likely to assume that other human beings function at level 1, the actions of level 1 systems remain important because they suggest the need to incorporate into a leadership approach an appreciation of the immensely complex and huge quantity of interactions involved in any physical system which are very difficult to predict and control. Educational leaders need to recognize such contexts, and their impacts appreciated, not only because of their potential for creating damaging threats to many areas of the globe but also because their complexity and unpredictability should induce in leaders an ethic of personal humility as to what they can control and predict. Such humility then becomes an essential quality of a global stewardship role.

There is certainly more room for leadership choice and action when encountering genetically determined patterns of behaviour, even if these are clearly not the only determinants of human behaviour; instead, they are but more sets of flexible parameters constricting or determining a range of options depending upon the nature of the variables encountered. However, genetic endowment should not be treated too lightly: the recognition of inherited qualities usually plays some part in informing the selection of individuals, even

Table 3.1 Different Levels of System and Implications for Leadership Style and Behaviour

Type of system	Examples	Implications for leadership style and behaviour
1. Physical systems	Weather systems, climate change, volcanic activity	Recognize the nature of the force and the context, and adapt behaviours to these
2. Systems composed of actors relying solely on genetically adaptive traits	Plants, ants, bees, bird flight formation, bats' use of echolocation	Recognize, adapt and steer genetically endowed actors towards objectives
3. Systems containing genetic and environmentally conditioned adaptive actors	Most species of animals learn from positive and negative conditioning	Select and steer actors through behavioural learning techniques towards objectives
4. Systems containing consciously framing adaptive actors	Human beings, probably dolphins and apes, possibly octopi	Recognize individuals' capacity for conscious creative framing and facilitate group creative synergy

if environmentally determined behaviours and skill acquisitions are often seen as more dominant and important.

The third system level is that at which actors are able to adjust their behaviours through operant and classical conditioning, and social learning processes. This might well induce some leaders (If they believe that this is how other human beings normally operate) to believe that the use of forms of transactional leadership – essentially management by rewards and punishments – are the most appropriate. Certainly, people are in part motivated by negative and positive stimuli, and many programmed learning techniques, as well as behavioural modification programmes, rely on such understandings. Transactional leadership tends to adopt the same assumptions and continues the same approaches through its use of positive conditioning of others to follow their lead. However, such leadership approaches fail to appreciate and utilize the highest levels at which human beings can operate, and by so doing, they fail to recognize the sophisticated manner in which human beings can understand and frame the world, and therefore radically underestimate individual potentialities and the complexities of human relationships and systems.

So when considering the leadership of systems which contain consciously framing adaptive actors – the fourth system level – one needs to recognize how much more complex these will be than those containing actors functioning at lower levels. Nevertheless, it is important that such higher levels of ability are nurtured, for whilst handling such abilities may be complex and demanding, it is also the level which develops individual sustainability and stewardship. Equipping students to understand not only their own levels of understanding but also the complexity of the systems within which they will operate as adults should then be essential.

Epistemic complexity

If systemic complexity derives from the highly complicated manner in which forces and actors interact and impact within a system, epistemic complexity asks: given our sensory, interpretative and contextualized natures, how much data, how much information, can we be certain of, and how much do we actually miss – or misinterpret? If systemic complexity dwells on the complexity derived from multiple and often un-trackable causative events, epistemic complexity examines not only what we think we know but also the sheer quantity of material we don't know of or don't really understand.

The first obvious but important point about epistemic complexity is that human beings, like all other living things, can only understand the world in which they live through limited sensory apparatus. But they only pass this on to a brain which is dependent on them for what it receives, and if that data is limited, distorted or incorrect, then the brain can only make limited or incorrect judgements about its external environment. A first conclusion is simple if a little alarming – we can never be certain that the understanding that our senses and brain make of our environment is ever completely accurate. Now, even with his suspect politics, Rumsfeld (2002) helpfully suggests that our understanding of the world then needs dividing into a number of different categories. He was keen to show that even though it was a 'known unknown' whether Saddam Hussein had weapons of mass destruction, there might be other 'unknown unknown' weapons which still justified invasion. Few I think would now agree with the plausibility of his analysis, but it nevertheless provides a helpful categorization of human understanding. So a first category is that of the 'known knowns': those things we know that we know and from which we expect and normally experience predictable impacts. For most people, 'known knowns' occur at personal, interpersonal and local levels, the 'known knowns' of educational leadership probably including things like staff roles, school rules and routines, other people's likes and dislikes, and possibly knowledge of significant forces impacting on the school, though here there are likely to be things their knowledge of which individual leaders will differ in their certainty.

But even 'known knowns' do not provide a very strong base: some assumptions of certainty may be misplaced, or simply wrong: you were certain that half term was in a particular week, but in fact it was in the one after. You may think you know the main reason for a principal's retirement, but in fact you didn't know about his illness. You may think you know a national inspectorate's principal goals but have misunderstood what has been written about this. There is then a second category of understanding: that of 'unknown knowns', where we may think we know something but are mistaken in this. If, then, a national inspectorate's goals are misunderstood, plenty of room is created for problems further down the line if you act on or even simply believe these 'facts'.

A third kind of understanding suggested by Rumsfeld (2002) makes detailed understanding of situations even more problematic. The category of the 'known unknowns' comprises things we know that we don't know (or at least think that we don't know), and here it becomes really difficult to predict what might happen as a result of such ignorance. Many kinds of activities which might be valuable to individual leaders – the details of much educational legislation, the intentions of policymakers, what will be the principal effect of a combination of events – are all examples where leaders may realize that they don't know things that would be useful to them. Nevertheless, the fact that we know we don't know something leaves a little room for optimism and action, for we can then begin to try and work out ways in which we might gain knowledge about such an event. Educational leaders, for instance, who think that climate change might affect educational thought and practice but do not know how it might, can at least begin to research this issue and consider how this might affect the present conception of their role.

A fourth and final kind of understanding is very obvious but much more problematic. This is the category of 'unknown unknowns', which includes all those things which we don't know that we don't know. Of course, no one can say how many such 'unknown unknowns' exist, even as it seems highly likely that some of them, because of our lack of knowledge of them, may impact in surprising and unpredictable ways. At one time humanity did not know of the existence of bacteria and viruses, or of the way they infected human beings, and this meant that many treatments were a mixture of quarantine, misplaced religious beliefs and guesswork. Today, those who do not know that many diseases are zoonotic

– that they can jump from animals and birds to human beings – are more poorly placed to prevent their own infection than those who know of this. There will very likely be many other examples where no one (yet) knows of something or its impact. Whilst this is obvious, it raises currently unanswerable, but worrying, questions about what educational leaders will not be able to 'know' or anticipate with respect to their role.

Bottery et al. (2018) provide an overview of Rumsfeld's categories applied to three different levels of educational leadership work: the micro-level – personal and relationship activities; the meso-level – activities and relationships conducted at the institutional level); and the macro-level – those which constitute communal, cultural, national and global actions and relationships. What is particularly notable is that the 'known knowns' and the 'unknown knowns' of leadership were located mostly at the micro- and meso-levels. This is perhaps unsurprising – as already noted, these are the educational levels to which most educators are attracted, and the levels to which most leaders' attention is focused, and in which most probably feel they have the greatest expertise. However, like many other professions, over the last few decades, the practice of educational leadership has experienced many impacts from the macro-level, as supranational bodies, national governments and large organizations have tried to create more consistency and exert greater control over institutional, relationship and personal roles and activities. It is at this level that most educational leaders are likely to locate the most 'known unknowns' and 'unknown unknowns'. The development of problems at these levels has then constituted real challenges to many who entered the profession seeking to practice education and enjoy personal fulfilment at the micro- and meso-levels, yet who have had to develop expertise in areas for which they may have had little previous training, or perhaps interest.

Such lack of expertise or training very likely applies to issues of sustainability created at the macro-level, and not just to headline issues like climate change and environmental damage: the impact of global financial dealings, intercultural clashes, political disputes between global and national bodies, and the huge increases in access to global information systems all need taking into consideration. If one adds to this the sheer speed of such change, and of many educational leaders' unpreparedness and lack of knowledge concerning such macro-change, then further pressure is placed on them as they try to monitor, understand and adapt their practice to these new forces. When professionals are only properly equipped for dealing with problems at micro- and meso-levels, then epistemic complexity – the complexity and problems derived from a limited understanding of the world that surrounds us – becomes all the greater.

Relational complexity

Relational complexity, like epistemic complexity, is concerned with the range of our ignorance, but whilst epistemic complexity is focused on our knowledge of the external world, relational complexity is focused on what we know and don't know about ourselves and our relations with others. It might be thought that 'personal complexity' would be a better descriptor of such complexity, but personal complexity is wrapped up inside relational complexity because all are engaged in relationships which begin from what we know and don't know about ourselves, and then extend to what we know and don't know about those with whom we are trying to form relationships. Furthermore, as this book has started to advance the argument that leadership in times of covert threats needs to more strongly focus upon a macro-stewardship agenda, it is also being argued that this is best provided through a series of collaborative relationships. It should then be clear that relational complexity and collaborative leadership are strongly linked: collaborative leadership is highly necessary, even as relational complexity makes it that much more difficult.

So what is the complexity displayed here? Whilst epistemic complexity focuses upon our understanding of an external world as consisting of 'known knowns', 'known unknowns' and 'unknown unknowns' (Rumsfeld, 2002), relational complexity begins by focusing upon our understanding of ourselves, and what we communicate to others, what Luft (1963) calls the 'Johari Window'. This suggests that each of us possesses four different elements: *an open self* (an area of ourselves we know and are happy for others to see); *a blind self* (aspects of ourselves we disclose to others without realizing it); a *concealed self* (those parts of us we know about but we don't want to reveal to others); and finally *an unknown self* (those parts which neither myself nor others realize exist). If then there are parts of us we know, parts we are happy to reveal, parts we want to conceal and parts few including ourselves realize exist, then communication and the relationships formed from them are made that much more complex, because, for example, others may well misinterpret the accidentally disclosed for the deliberately disclosed and form the wrong conclusions as to my intentions.

Yet this is only one half of the problem. In a solipsist world, everything may revolve around me and my understanding of this world, including my understanding of other people, but strangely enough, everyone else sees the world through their own senses. This means that the complexity that I experience in my understanding of myself and of relationships with others

Table 3.2 The Jumee Window (after Stern, 2021)

	What I know	*What I don't know*
What other people know	Known knowns – what both I and other people know	Unknown knowns – unknown by me, known by others
What other people don't know	Known unknowns – known by me, unknown by others	Unknown unknowns — unknown by me and by others

is complemented by the same complexity that they experience in their understanding of themselves and of their relationships with me and others. This is why Stern (2021) talks not of a Johari Window but of a Jumee Window (see Table 3.2).

Now whilst there are some differences in the meanings of the terms between Rumsfeld and Stern, Stern's 'Jumee Window' expresses very well the situation that we find ourselves in when conducting or developing relationships. Not only does Table 3.2 suggest an equality of knowledge in such relationships – and thus equalizes the contributions of 'leaders' and 'followers' – but it also suggests that the complexity of relationships is greater than that of personal knowledge, which contributes only a part to that relationship. So if one comes to the conclusion, as this book is moving towards, that leadership is best conducted in times of complexity through the development of higher levels of relationships, then paradoxically this adds to the complexity of such development even as it adds to the possibility of solutions. Finally, this book will also come to argue that if the leadership relationships for complex times need to be of a higher level than those described for transactional and transformational models, then engaging in relationships and then raising them to higher levels are both essential moves to the solving of complex problems, even as they may add to such complexity. This may, of course, explain why some leaders prefer simpler models of leadership – they are not nearly as complex or demanding.

Wicked complexity

The final form of complexity, wicked complexity, is composed of problems which may have similarities to systemic and epistemic complexity, but it also has an important feature which gives it some similarities to relational complexity: the problems deriving from it usually are not entirely distinct from the individuals who are concerned about them. With wicked problems, often issues are seen as problems because individuals define particular issues as problems. So when a number of people are involved in a situation, both definition and resolution of a problem are going to need sufficiently good relationships between them to agree on what the problem is and what is the best way forward of resolving it. An absence of flies in your house is likely to be a problem only if you are a house spider. Rittel and Weber (1973) contrast such wicked problems with tame problems, which can usually be solved by following a simple linear plan (the door is locked; it needs a key to unlock it; if I put the right key in the right lock, I will be able to open the door).

The complexity of tame and wicked issues was first proposed by Rittel and Weber in 1973, and has been developed by a number of writers (Conklin, 2006; Rayner, 2006; Head, 2008: Bore and Wright, 2009; Wright, 2011; Verweij and Thompson, 2011; Bottery, 2016, and Creasy, 2017). The seven major differences between tame and wicked approaches to dealing with problems seem to be:

1. In terms of the nature of how a problem was caused, tame approaches tend to assume single-level, linear and simple causations, whilst wicked views see most problems as more multi-level and multi-causal.
2. When it comes to how unique the problem is, tame approaches tend to believe that most problems are capable of being fully understood, in part through comparison with similar problems. Wicked views see problems as much more unique in nature, largely because of the unique contexts they inhabit and their complex and multi-causal nature.
3. When it comes to the accuracy of the framing and definition of a problem, tame approaches tend to think that these can be definitive, whilst wicked views will argue that no one has the correct answer, and so framings and definitions are going to need negotiation within a group, and are likely to be provisional.
4. So when it comes to the truth or falsity of definitions and solutions, tame approaches will believe quite strongly in the possibility of arriving at the one best definition and therefore the one best solution. Wicked approaches will normally use many different framings and a number of trial and error attempts to resolve the problem, and then will likely once more see most attempts as no more than provisional.
5. It follows from the aforementioned that tame approaches to solutions are likely to be single-focused, led by talented individuals, and normally will then be successful 'silver-bullet' solutions. Wicked approaches will normally see the need for a multi-focused dialectic within a team and the likely generation of many different suggestions for what are at best no

more than 'clumsy' solutions – which, even if they have some success, are unlikely to completely resolve the problem.
6. The degree of belief in the certainty of any proposed resolution will then also be predictable: tame approaches will think that full resolution of a problem is at least probable, whilst wicked approaches will believe this to hardly ever rise above the possible.
7. Finally, tame and wicked approaches will have very different views on how long the problem process will normally take, with tame approaches assuming clear linear structures and solutions, which then shouldn't take very long at all, whereas wicked approaches will argue that because of the difficulty that comes from the generation and nature of a problem, and the dialectical processes involved in definition and resolution before any (provisional) attempt is made, one should assume that the full process will take much longer than someone adopting a tame approach would imagine.

Now there are currently many pressures reinforcing the belief that 'tame' problems and solutions constitute the majority of the problems that we face, and therefore comprise the majority of the kinds of solutions required. Current political and economic pressures increase demand for 'fast' policies, and for quick results which are easily understood by a non-specialist audience, as well as pressures from a 24/7 media to explain problems simply and quickly. All combine to pressure people into adopting a 'tame' framing of issues.

Yet, as H. L. Mencken once said, to every complex problem there exists a solution which is neat, simple and wrong, and many problems, and much of the work of educational leaders is not neat and simple. Most educational problems are not accompanied by booklets with instructions permitting the application of off-the-shelf solutions. Unlike 'lock and key problems' there are no infallible rulebooks for creating the good society, for enhancing creativity in learning, for boosting standards in schools, for raising staff morale, or indeed for creating better leadership, even if there are plenty of views on these issues. The more awkward problems – Rittel and Weber's 'wicked' problems – are then very different from tame ones.

So as already noted, many of these problems are not necessarily 'problems' in any objective sense: they are defined as problems because the personality, values and experience of an individual predispose them to classify an issue as such. Indeed, not only does a 'wicked' issue require that someone defines it as a problem before it becomes a problem; it is also highly unlikely to have any definitive set of rules for its solution. Many variables and many values may be involved in resolving such problems, and if so, 'tame' standardized solutions, which often fail to sufficiently consider contextualized elements, are very likely to be ineffective or damaging – or both. Further, because of the complexity of 'wicked' problems, a problem may be treated, but it may only be symptomatic of a deeper underlying issue or problem (a student may not be lazy but bored by the lack of demand in the work given). Finally, the nature of a wicked problem may be impossible for a group to agree upon, as well as an appropriate solution, because it is only seen as a problem by a limited number within this group. Indeed, it may be impossible to prescribe the kind of 'silver-bullet' solution that might completely resolve the issue. Because of this, some problems may never be fully soluble, and the best solutions then will be 'clumsy', 'messy' or 'silver buckshot' approaches (Rayner, 2006, Grint, 2008) which employ a combination of different resolutions but which are likely to only ever be partially successful. All major wicked problems and solutions then need to follow the first rule of rock climbing – that at any time one needs to keep at least three points of contact with the rock being climbed; in the current context this emphasizes the need to use a number of varied solutions in dealing with such problems.

Of course, if some educational leaders accept as true that the world is largely composed of tame problems, and if they then believe that it is possible to solve the problems given to them in this way, then they may well feel that governmental blame and feelings of guilt at their lack of success will be justified, which could have major implications for their personal sustainability. If however, there is better understanding of the difference between tame and wicked issues, and that many issues deemed tame may actually be wicked in nature, then the kinds of qualities required by educational leaders in approaching wicked problems can be developed. So, if we take the seven major differences between tame and wicked approaches used in dealing with problems outlined earlier, then leadership qualities needed for dealing with wicked problems become apparent.

First, the complex multi-level and multi-causal generation of problems will require leadership qualities of being able to organize groups for collective discussion and decision-making on potential wicked framings of the problem.

Second, the fact that each wicked problem probably comes with unique properties and context requires that leaders have the qualities and skills of 'bricoleurs' (Grint (2008)) who work from the presentation of the problem rather than imposing plans or solutions from the beginning.

Third, because it is not possible for anyone to have a 'correct' view of a wicked problem, they must recognize that better views are made by developing group relationships, not by driving through personally preferred views or solutions.

Fourth, because many framings rather than just one or two are likely to be needed, the need to encourage others to develop and propose a larger number of approaches will be very important.

Fifth, understanding that a group needs to arrive at a provisional 'clumsy' definition and solution is less about leading through providing good answers than it is about having the ability to frame good questions for the group.

Sixth, by also understanding that wicked problems will be best resolved by a group dialectic between varied interpretations of a problem and its resolution, another essential leadership quality will be understanding that most solutions will be political in nature, and leaders will need to diplomatically enable progress through 'clumsy' negotiations towards common agreed ground.

Finally, they not only need to understand and accept that framing useful conceptions of problem and resolution takes time, but they also need to cultivate the ability to remain comfortable with uncertainty, to pause and reflect rather than be rushed into action.

This description of such leadership qualities reinforces the understanding that some leadership approaches may be essential for dealing with wicked situations, but others, by their nature are much less suitable. *Transactional approaches* based on punishment and/or reward not only tend to assume leadership by an individual but are unlikely to encourage or use others' contributions, as the approach is largely based upon the shaping of participants' behaviours towards pre-planned forms of action through positive and negative conditioning, rather than by incorporating others' views, experiences and values. *Transformative leadership* approaches make much the same kind of mistake, as they assume that leaders should have singular visions in order to lead others to solutions and actions already decided upon. Wicked problems instead require leaders with intelligence, empathy and political acumen to bring together and blend a variety of views, in order to generate a settlement on the framing of a problem and its resolution. *Distributed leadership* could be underpinned by the kind of qualities described for dealing with wicked problems, but it does not have to be. As noted in Chapter 1, it may simply be a device to reduce single leadership workload; it might be used to develop social justice in a school (Woods and Roberts, 2016), which, whilst praiseworthy, is insufficiently focused on the stewardship issues raised in this. It may also be underpinned by the belief that many or most problems are tame in nature, and so may simply devolve tame problem definition and resolution to individuals lower in an educational hierarchy, and thus abnegate the kind of leadership needed to acknowledge, understand and act to resolve wicked and complex problems.

So when the kind of complex issues discussed so far present themselves, then a different and distinct leadership style is required. The kind of leadership required to deal with problems of wicked complexity can now be extended to include the three other kinds of complexity, as summarized in Table 3.3, thus providing a more complete view of the kinds of leadership needed for engaging with such challenges. If we begin by examining the nature of leadership in a world of systemic complexity, it will be remembered that such complexity is created by the interaction of events and actors at numerous levels within and between systems, which then lead to limited understandings in emergent systems of events, actors and impacts. Western (2019, p. 257) suggests that the complexity of today requires an understanding that organizations are 'ecosystems within ecosystems'. He suggests then that the quote from Western

> Internally, organisations are webs of connected and interdependent networks, and externally organisations function within wider ecosystems, as the external environment impacts on their internal dynamics and vice-versa.

'Single-vision' approaches to leadership will then capture much less of this complexity than approaches based on a sharing of frames of understanding, even if they cannot guarantee certainty in either frame or resolution. In such situations, then leadership qualities which encourage diversity and inclusivity through the development of creative group synergies are very likely to be the most appropriate. An acceptance of the different forms of complexity will then be critical.

Epistemic complexity is that complexity which recognizes how limited our knowledge is of this world and what happens within it. Like the other forms of complexity, it suggests that the best forms of resolution are going to be those where many approaches are discussed and debated, and where status and hierarchy are not used to determine which approach is finally adopted, as such decisions are too often based on the embedded assumptions of those in senior positions. A stronger acceptance of human limitations then helps reduce approaches which make such exclusive assumptions and instead helps champion leadership qualities facilitating forms of interpersonal dialectic, whilst embracing a humility of approach which promises no more than provisional decisions. The location of the best decisions may then be as surprising as the uniqueness of the problems being considered.

Relational complexity firms up such belief in the need for a diversity and inclusivity of opinion, and expands these by arguing that diversity and

Table 3.3 Complexity and Leadership Approaches in an Age of Covert Threats

Complexity type	Problem type	Best forms of resolution	Inappropriate leadership approaches	Appropriate leadership qualities
Systemic complexity	Complexity formed by numerous unpredictable linkages	Shared, inclusive, contextualized	Those advocating only one point of view based on standardized responses	Inclusive, intelligent, contextual awareness, creating group synergies
Epistemic complexity	Complexity created by our ignorance or misjudgements of much that occurs	Formed by group discussion, with the provisional nature of outcomes accepted	Those exhibiting the hubris of certainty coming from the conviction that one leadership view is the one for others to follow	Facilitating a dialectic process amongst the group, provisional, humility, facilitative
Relational complexity	Complexity created by ignorance of our own and others limitations and knowledge of self	Personal reflections and deeper more honest and trusting relationships with others	Those advocating certainty in fully understanding themselves and others, and therefore of the need for only a one-view leadership	The development of rich relationships of trust and care and where status barriers are reduced
Wicked complexity	Based on unique problem contextualization and by human judgement on what is the problem	Shared definition, contextualized, time-dependent, resolved by silver buckshot, not silver bullets	Advocating only one view (usually theirs) of the nature of the problem and its resolution by standardized means	Facilitates discussions; change achieved by relationships, not power; a bricoleur, comfortable with uncertainty

inclusivity have to be based on forms of relationships which rise above the logical or manipulative, and move into the ethical for if the views of others are to be properly listened to, the relations between the parties will need to be respectful, trusting and caring, because it is only at this relational level that rich and nuanced discussion will take place.

Finally, wicked complexity is that which accepts a background of systemic and epistemic complexity, but adds to these by pointing out that problems are many times created by human judgements on whether something is or is not a problem. Moreover, not only will many problems be unique due to individual framing and context, but considerable comparison and discussion will be needed within a group over the validity and viability of such different individualized 'frames'. Leadership approaches which recognize the need to encourage the voicing of differences, and of the need to facilitate discussion and an ultimate agreement on most likely problem definition and resolution, are going to require leadership qualities which also enable and facilitate strong relationships, and which are able to keep such discussions 'hanging' until an appropriate agreed solution can be found.

Conclusions

This chapter has suggested that in a world of turbulence and covert threats, the combination of four different forms of complexity makes the educational leader's role much more challenging than in a world assumed to be largely tame and linear. In trying to frame the most appropriate kind of leadership for such complex times, a leadership approach is beginning to emerge, one which is inclusive and facilitative, which understands the need to appreciate a problem's uniqueness and the importance of context. It is also the leadership approach which facilitates rather than leads and dictates discussions on the definition of problems and their resolution, and which is comfortable with the provisional nature of most conclusions and therefore of having to live with uncertainty. Finally, this analysis is beginning to suggest that the appropriate form of leadership for complex situations is not a singular role, for the problems to be faced will need to be resolved by teams rather than individuals, and as the relationships in such teams need to be at a level where genuine trust and care are emphasized, and hierarchy and status are not, then a form of *relational leadership* is likely going to describe the process by which stewardship leadership is realized. Stewardship may then be the focus of leadership work, but relational leadership may be the most appropriate style for achieving this work.

Part II

Covert Threats

4

Covert Processes

Unmasking the Threats

Introduction

This chapter continues the argument that educational leaders need to adopt a much more pronounced stewardship role than has so far been generally accepted and that part of this should involve much greater awareness of threats which derive their danger from their lack of general recognition. The subjects of complexity in general, and of 'wicked' problems in particular, were covered in the previous chapter, and this discussion now continues with an examination of other covert threats, because any lack of their recognition can lead to radical underestimations of their threat. This chapter then moves to focus on the threats from three other processes: (i) positive feedback, (ii) exponential growth and (iii) degrees of connectivity. These processes have all tended to be under-recognized and so actions to prevent or mediate them can be very slow, or simply not taken, which can then result in highly damaging consequences. All of them can have significant effects upon levels of human and environmental sustainability, through creating less predictability and control, increasing the speed of change and the likelihood of various forms of system collapse. Moreover, because these processes often act interdependently, in unpredictable and uncontrollable ways, end results can be even more uncertain and unforeseeable than if they had acted independently. Therefore, as Meadows (2008, p. 7) argues,

> the behaviour of a system cannot be known just by knowing the elements of which the system is made.

If the threat of the sum of these processes is a greater threat than such processes acting on their own, then understanding this interdependence will be an essential part of an educational stewardship role. However, it is important to note that these processes can have benign as well as malign impacts and therefore that such stewardship and sustainability will be enhanced by the cultivation of the benign aspects of such processes. We then move first to examine the nature of positive feedback.

Positive feedback

Positive feedback is not another name for the kind of complimentary remarks often made upon hearing a particularly good talk or piano recital. As suggested earlier, it is often easier to understand the process of positive feedback by contrasting it with its opposite, negative feedback, which is often thought of as the 'good guy' of the two, the one which increases sustainability by maintaining the stability of existing beneficial conditions, whereas positive feedback is more often the bad guy because it reduces such stability, as in the end a positive feedback process can cause yet more of the same action to occur and thus reduce any desired stability.

Negative feedback is normally seen through actions such as those of central heating. With this, a desired room temperature is set, and if the room gets too cold, the central heating kicks in to return it to a desired temperature. Where stasis is desired, then, mechanisms which utilize a negative feedback process are employed. *Positive feedback* is a very different beast – and in many conditions, a more dangerous one, as the effects that are created in positive feedback make it more likely that these effects will increase. It can then be centrally involved in creating new macro-climates through global warming or cooling. For example, the 'Snowball Earth' of about 650 million years ago (Brannen, 2018) was created by extreme variations in the earth's orbit which reduced temperatures and, with increased snow and ice cover, led to the reflection of heat back from the earth's surface, which reduced temperatures even further, which increased ice cover, which reduced temperatures further and so on. It seems that only a large slice of luck in the form of a large series of volcanic explosions moved the climate back towards temperatures which allowed life on earth to flourish once more. Currently, however, positive feedback processes are now creating the reverse of a snowball earth, as a man-made increase in greenhouses gases like carbon dioxide and methane is preventing heat from escaping from the atmosphere and is therefore raising temperatures globally. Indeed, the warmest six years have all been since 2015, with 2016, 2019 and 2020 being the top three. With such temperature rises, vegetation becomes much drier and increases the likelihood of grassland and forest fires, which then release even more greenhouse gases into the atmosphere, which then raise temperatures further . . . and so on, to a point where the process may be unstoppable, threatening most life on the planet.

The same processes occur in the human world as well. Financial crises like the Dutch Tulip mania of 1637, the South Sea Bubble of 1720, the great financial crash of the 1930s and the financial crisis of 2007–9 were all generated by positive feedback processes. In the first two examples, when particular stocks became very popular their prices rose, and this led others to invest in them as well. This persuaded newcomers into the market, who also bought stocks until the product became vastly overvalued. Yet people still kept buying the stock, gambling they could sell before prices began to fall. In many cases, though, many held on too late and, when the market collapsed, were left holdings virtually valueless stock.

In education, trust relationships between policymakers and professionals are good examples of both negative and positive feedback processes. The sustainability of trust relationships may well depend upon an equality in feelings of such trust (Bottery, 2004), and when there are problems in the relationship, it is often the case that negative feedback techniques are used to try and return the situation to its previous stability. So, when one party complains of a lack of trust, the other may try and demonstrate or increase their trustful behaviour. However, if one party displays strong distrust of another, as when governments adopt low-trust policies towards professionals, the recipient of this perceived insult may not try to repair the relationship but may instead respond with similar feelings and actions of distrust and dislike. The danger then is that the relationship may switch from one where negative feedback is employed to one where positive feedback processes come into play, and an increase in distrust by party A of party B then increases B's distrust of A, which then reinforces the unfavourable opinion by party A of party B and so on. This positive feedback effect can be seen when governments use 'naming and shaming' tactics with respect to school performance, as happened with the New Labour government of England in the early 2000s, which Bangs et al. (2011, pp. 23–7) observed had marked effects not only on teacher morale but also on educator–government relationships.

However, it is important to point out once more that the creation and effects of malign and benign processes may be heavily dependent upon a complex of personal and contextual variables. Potentially malign occurrences may not happen because variables prevent these processes from developing further, suggesting that if one were able to identify particular events which encourage or discourage a process, these might be used as 'leverage points' to prevent a situation from getting out of hand. This issue will be discussed further in Chapters 7 and 8, when possible 'tipping point' consequences of these processes are examined.

Exponential growth

Like negative and positive feedback, exponential growth can be a highly useful or a highly dangerous process. From a standard Western business perspective, where a central objective is to increase the growth of the company – in size, in turnover and in profits – then a company's exponential growth is usually viewed as a very 'good thing' – as exemplified by a quick visit to the *Amazon* website, where this positive meaning of the term has a virtual monopoly in most business books on the subject. Yet for those more concerned about the environmental impact of the increased use of resources by such companies, and of the impact on the environment of their consumption by the general public, growth is a much more problematic term, and the process of exponential growth therefore needs to be viewed much more critically.

Not only is the process of exponential growth often insufficiently understood or under-recognized but so are its effects and the reasons for its effects. Educational leaders therefore need to have a strong grasp of the concept if they are to better perform a full stewardship role. Like positive and negative feedback, exponential growth also has a related activity, that of arithmetic *or linear* growth, which is commonly observed at micro- and meso-levels, and which is then simpler and easier to understand. This kind of growth occurs when things increase by the simple addition of one extra amount; progression then occurs from 1 to 2, 2 to 3, 3 to 4 and so on. It is a process that virtually anyone can see and understand, and probably feel that because of its relatively slow increase, it is a process which is easily measurable and hence predictable and controllable.

Now exponential growth has been known for thousands of years, but oftentimes by only a minority of a population. Many people probably know of it through stories which make the impact of the process the point of the story. The ancient Indian story of the prince wishing to give a reward to one of his advisors is one example: the advisor asked if he could have 1 grain of rice for the first square of a chess board, doubling it to 2 grains for the second, doubling the 2 grains to 4 grains for the third, to 8 for the fourth and so on to the 64th and last square. So the story goes, the prince readily agreed, thinking that this was a request easily fulfilled, only for him to realize on further reflection that the end square would require more grains of rice than existed in the whole world. Many people still question whether that is actually true, because the answer is such a surprise. My personal calculation suggests that this amounts to well over eight billion trillion grains: the advisor did rather well in one sense but of course could never collect his full reward. The moral of the story is simply this: be aware of how quickly numbers can grow, and how large they become, when they are exponentially doubled.

The other story often told about exponential growth, and reproduced by Weisman (2013), produces a similar kind of surprise, but this time the surprise comes with the speed of the process rather than the quantity created. In this story, a question is asked: if a single bacterium were placed in a bottle at 11 pm, and if it divided into two every minute, and an hour later the bottle was full, at what time would the bottle be half-full? As with the rice grain and the chess board, many people initially have difficulty with this question and are usually astonished when they realize that the bottle would be half-full at 11.59, only one minute before the hour is up. If this is true – and it is! – then something alarming is happening, and this once more is existential growth. The second question which Weisman (2013) asks crystallizes this worry: if you were a clever bacterium, at what time would you realize you were running out of space in this bottle? Would you realize this at 11.55 pm, when the bottle was still 97 per cent *empty*? Unless you were a particularly prescient bacterium, which had also been tutored in exponential growth processes, the proximity of this time to midnight would almost certainly not initially occur to you.

Covid-19 and exponential growth

We are now living in times where one particular problem of exponential growth is a matter of considerable public interest. This is the kind of growth that Covid-19 demonstrates, and its highly infectious nature means that if appropriate measures are not taken, it may spread very quickly. With an R rate of 2, the original virus could spread from one person to two others, and these two could then spread it to four, who would then spread it to eight and so on. Of course, the reality is not likely to be as precise: two other people may be infected but sometimes only one more, and sometimes three more, but the average R rate for the original Covid-19 virus hovered around 2 (just as, amazingly, for measles it hovers between 15 and 20). That is why policymakers are so concerned about R rates, and why they have been even more concerned about Covid variants, like the Indian, the Delta, and particularly the Omicron variant, which all seem to have a higher R rate than the original strain. A major aim then is to reduce the R rate to below 1, for then each infectious person will pass the disease to less than one other, and the R rate would then decline until the virus was no longer a major threat.

Now most of humanity has taken heed of the spread of Covid-19 because this is not a theoretical concern but a very real threat: many people will now know of someone who has suffered or died from the disease, and most will have reflected on the danger to themselves. Perhaps if the exponential nature of the disease was grasped by more people, precautions taken might then be more stringently followed, and when its R rate declined, people would still be very careful because they would realize it could return to spread rapidly one more. The increased understanding of the R rate during the Covid pandemic then possibly makes the existential growth of Covid-19 a little less than a covert threat, even though the complexities that have emerged from its impacts make it a highly difficult threat to manage.

Exponential human population growth

If the exponential growth of Covid-19 is a recognizable and dangerous global threat, the exponential growth of the human population globally is rather like the problem of climate change discussed in Chapter 2 – it is a huge problem, but one which has largely been under the public radar, which has made it even more of a threat. There are two additional factors which make this threat even more wicked. Neo-Malthusian commentators like Ehrlich (1971) and Meadows et al.(2004) argue that the world is a place of finite resources, yet large sections of the human population are growing exponentially and sooner or later the result will be widespread famine, with other disasters following closely upon such a calamity. Even though the date of the appearance of this global catastrophe has kept being pushed back, the core of this concern has not gone away: with the world's population in 2020 standing at over 7.8 billion and rising, and with, as Cain (2020) points out, a planet currently only able to sustainably support 1.6 billion people living at current US consumption levels, ethically acceptable perspectives on population growth then need to include questions about global equity in the distribution and consumption of resources. There is then substantial criticism of over-simplistic talk of global population growth (e.g. Monbiot, 2009, Dorling, 2013, Cain, 2020), it being argued that *total* human numbers should not be the principal focus of such concern but rather comparisons between the quantity of resources consumed by individuals in wealthier and poorer countries. Further, much talk about human population growth is talk about human needs, and yet for anyone taking a macro-stewardship perspective, the impact of human population consumption and utilization of resources upon other species and the wider environment requires their inclusion in any discussions on such global equity.

The result is that exponential human population growth is more a regional phenomenon, even if it remains part of a global problem. For where exponential growth is no longer prevalent, a new problem of ageing populations has emerged which not only in itself but also in areas which still experience exponential population growth poses new kinds of covert threat.

So it is both damagingly simplistic and misleading to talk about human population growth as if it were a mathematical equation, for currently some human populations are expanding and others are declining. In many developed countries, a more immediate concern has been the experience of declining birth rates at the same time as populations are living longer (Munz and Reiterer, 2009). When this challenge is placed in a global context (e.g. Demeny, 2003), wealthy nation-states, with ageing, declining and conservative populations, are now living alongside poorer nation-states with younger expanding populations who need and want a greater proportion of the world's resources, which their wealthier counterparts have historically been very slow in providing.

The internal problems of nations with populations of increased longevity but reduced fertility then generate a number of other concerns. One is the decreasing percentage of populations able to pay taxes to sustain core welfare institutions like education and health. The situation is made more difficult by the fact that ageing populations suffer more from chronic, rather than acute, medical conditions, and more expensive health care is then required at just the time when the ability to raise such funding becomes an increasing problem. Many of these wealthier counties have then begun to introduce electorally unpalatable reforms such as delayed retirement ages, reductions in state pensions and movement to private ones, whilst countries as diverse as Denmark, Japan, Singapore and Italy have all introduced a variety of incentives to increase family sizes, including tax breaks, and increased family allowances. In June 2021 China, often still thought of as economically developing rather than economically developed, tacitly acknowledged its own looming problems of an ageing population by permitting couples to have three children rather than two.

So lack of exponential population growth does not necessarily eliminate problems, but for those countries still with accelerating rates, such as many sub-Saharan African countries, they still have to contend with this challenge. Indeed, by the end of this century, Vollset et al. (2018) note that projections indicate that

Nigeria will have the world's second largest global population with 791 million. At the same time, to make predictions that much more problematic, the same authors suggest that, contrary to previous thinking, a much quicker transition to lower fertility rates – and hence shrinking numbers – is now occurring, due in part to increased 'demographic transition' (Bongaarts, 2009). This is happening partly because of more readily available contraception but, most importantly, through more women being able globally to access education and employment, and hence make more independent decisions, including the number of children they wish to bear. Education systems can play a critical part in this process, even as their leaders will need to consider what education can contribute to stabilize societies facing dramatic downturns in population.

A declining global population might then mitigate some of the problems caused by former exponential growth, such as resource consumption, and of increasing national concerns about food, water and energy security, as well as, perhaps, putting less pressure on the environment and on biodiversity. Yet one needs to be very careful here: this is only a projection, and not a statement of fact, and even if it were correct, the global population is still projected to peak at 9.7 billion by 2064, before declining to 8.8 billion by the end of the century (Harvey, 2020) – still higher than today, and with all the problems in this area currently being faced.

Educational systems and their leaders will then be working in a great deal of unknown territory. Not only will there likely be a greater degree of cultural mixing, as countries with ageing populations seek to employ younger people from poorer countries, with all the possibilities and problems inherent in such a move. But in addition, both immigrants and the elderly in wealthier countries could help in developing new forms of intergenerational education, partly to help the young, and partly to give an ageing population greater meaning and purpose to their lives (Bottery, 2016). Such movements would put considerable pressure on current frameworks, aims and curricula of schools but could also release much creative energy and greater intercultural and intergenerational understanding, and thereby produce much greater social sustainability. Human exponential population growth remains a complex but highly important issue, particularly as expanding poorer populations interact with declining richer ones.

Connectivity

A third covert threat is that of connectivity. Now the notion of 'connectivity' processes is not new: despite current popularity through a focus on 'digital connectivity', a wider stewardship focus needs to understand other forms as well. One such process goes back thousands of years, as prehistoric cave paintings and the cultures of hunter-gatherer communities demonstrate a deeply ingrained respect for both the environment and the creatures within it. Such *inter*-species connectedness is paralleled by an *intra*-species social connectedness, with different levels in both human and animal species. This section then begins by examining environmental connectivity, before moving to social and digital connectivity.

Environmental connectivity

There is now good evidence to suggest that with respect to human connectedness to the environment, many societies have now become under-connected. Over the millennia, *Homo sapiens* has moved from hunter-gatherer to agricultural forms of subsistence and from there to city dwellers and internet communicators. In the process, many have lost the sense of being members of interconnected systemic ecologies and have instead assumed the role of little more than of environmental exploiters. Boulding (1968) suggests that such under-connectedness has been the basis of a 'cowboy' approach to the environment, where little thought is given to the conservation and sustainability of resources in an area, and instead, when such resources have been exhausted, they have simply been extracted from somewhere else, with little or no thought to their long-term sustainability. This has now led to growing concerns about large areas of resource and environmental degradation, and of resulting climate change and wholesale species extinctions. Boulding instead urges a change in human habits and values, embracing a deeper understanding of our interdependence with other species, and instead of acting as if we lived in a cowboy world, he then suggests that we need to see ourselves as living on a spaceship world where

> the measure of well-being is not how fast the crew [of this spaceship world] is able to consume its limited stores, but rather how effective the crew members are in maintaining their shared resource stocks, and the life-support systems on which they all depend.

The need to maintain the quantity and quality of resource stocks is further developed by Princen (2005), who argues for a movement from a frontier world with dominant values of consumption and growth, through to an environmental protection world, where a dialogue takes place between consumption values and environmental well-being, and then finally to a sustainability world, where environmental health is seen as the determining factor trumping human consumer desires, for without a healthy environment, there can be no healthy human society. Princen then argues that humanity needs to nurture a very closer interconnectedness with the environment and, instead of being its exploiter, becomes its principal steward in order to protect the long-term needs of its own species and that of all other living things.

Princen's (2005) sustainability world might then be seen as a form of connectivity which attempts to reach an optimal state, involving a complex, highly interconnected, systemic relationship with other living things, where it is recognized that the parts interrelate and depend upon each other, where other creatures have rights to existence just as we do, and where human well-being is largely determined by how well such systems are understood and nurtured. The maintenance of such a sustainable spaceship world is almost certainly more difficult to understand and support than a cowboy world, as it is not a world of simple exploitation, but one of complex stewardship and care, constantly working towards an optimal connectivity. The complexities involved may never be fully understood, and may never be fully mastered, as once again this is not a 'tame' world which is being described, but a highly complex one, and which needs approaching with an ethic of intellectual humility. If human beings approach it primarily as exploiters and consumers, problems are likely to be created which are not recognized and then may become irresolvable. It is then a formidable but highly necessary role for educational leaders.

Social connectivity

Connectivity is then a vital part of individual, group and inter-species sustainability, and in a chapter on covert threats, connectivity becomes a threat when individuals, groups or species are under-connected, such that bonds are not strong enough, or when they are over-connected, when bonds are too pressing and too intrusive. Whilst it is then possible to talk of attempting to reach levels of optimal connectivity, any case of such connectivity will depend upon the following contextual factors.

First, it will depend upon the degree of integration of the species one is discussing – the highly social and integrated communities of ants have very much more intense forms of connectivity with other members of their own species than do, for instance, tigers or polar bears, who for much of their lives are solitary creatures, usually coming together only for mating purposes.

Second, it will depend upon the function of connectivity within a species – the connectivity within herds of zebra, for example, is in large part for protection from predators, and this is very different from the short-term connectivity of individual male and female black widow spiders for reproductive purposes. In evolutionary terms, human beings seem to have formed social groups partly to avoid predation but also to increase the chances of success when hunting (see Cummings et al. 2019).

Finally, it will depend on the kind of qualities a species brings to such connectedness. So, whilst ants are highly social, most of their behaviour is based upon strongly laid-in genetic traits. Animals higher up the phylogenetic scale, like zebras, can learn new behaviours from classical and operant-conditioning, and thus possess a degree of learned flexibility in their social behaviour. However, primates take social connectedness to higher levels of intimacy, with complex expressions of thoughts and feelings concerning others of their kind. Now there may be something of a chicken-and-egg situation here: did the development of a large brain permit primates to develop more complex social relationships and connectedness, or did the need for such complex relationships encourage the growth and selection of larger brains? Whichever is true – and it is likely that both are to some extent – human beings have taken this sophistication to a level where they display different kinds of connectedness with different *numbers* of individuals. Dunbar (2010), for instance, has demonstrated that the average number of people an individual can normally think of as close friends, which involves deep levels of intimacy and support, averages only 3 and 4 individuals, the principal reason for this very small number being, Dunbar suggests, one of time: it takes a great deal of work and effort to maintain such levels of connectedness. However, when it comes to a level of connectedness associated with personal acquaintances, where such deep levels of intimacy are not required, the number tends to hover around 150, and Dunbar (2012) points out how surprising it is that many human groupings approximate to this number. This being the case, 'optimal connectivity' may not only be a matter of what species you belong to, but how large your brain is, and what function you want this connectedness to serve. The nature of the threat of under- or over-connectedness in humans would then seem to be determined by the functions of a particular level of connectedness. In terms of educational leadership, this book proposes that the nature of leadership needs to change to embrace higher-level forms of relationship involving care and trust if a rich and complex form of stewardship is to be attained, and so the threat of under-connected social relationships needs to be seen as a very real challenge for the development of such higher-level relationships, which are seldom seen in single-person or transactional forms of leadership The damage to limited number groupings in leadership groups would then very likely come from impairment in the quality of such close relations, whilst with larger grouping the damage might well come from the sheer quantity of information bombarding an individual from too many sources. This latter form of threat currently seems to stem principally from a third area of connectivity, digital connectivity.

Digital connectivity

Currently, 'connectivity' is associated by many with the massive expansion – and widespread approval – of human digital relationships. Commentators like Fredette et al. (2012) talk of such digital connectedness as 'arguably the single most important trend in today's world'. Not only does it increase the speed of access to data and information, but it also provides a greater constancy and convenience of such access. Moreover, as such data come from a greater number of sources, it provides an increased richness, a wider geographical reach and more substantial access to present and past information, suggesting that such expansion in digital connectedness presents a new and different league of possibilities for human beings. Diamandis and Kottler (2012 p. 9) graphically illustrate its potential by noting that

> a Masai warrior . . . on a smart phone with access to Google has better access to information than the President [of the United States] did just fifteen years ago.

In educational terms, Sheninger (2014) argues that digital media can be paradigm-changing in motivating students, in connecting them to problems of the real world and hence to engaging them in more 'authentic' learning. Not only does he suggest that this greatly motivates learning, but that it also improves leadership practice through facilitating better communication, support and access to the kind of resources which facilitate personal and school development. Sheninger (2014, p. 104) then enthusiastically concludes that

> Today, any person, any age, anywhere at any time can connect with any person, any age, anywhere, at any time to share thinking and create, and the outcomes are 'going viral'. We are truly no longer 'I' but 'we'.

Now Covid-19 has given a considerable boost to such connectivity. Two of the disease's initial effects were enforced social isolation and the disruption of business activity. In both cases, digital connectedness came to be seen as an essential resource. As ways of maintaining social networks, emails, Facetime and Skype were rapidly expanded into group communication systems like Teams, Zoom and Webex, with families creating online quizzes and engaging with others in ways both more extended and more regular than many had experienced pre-Covid. For those with underlying health conditions, as self-isolation required the online ordering of food and other supplies, digital connectivity became essential and also helped address their social under-connectedness. In so doing it became a major prop for many people's mental health, well-being and sustainability.

For businesses whose employees could not come into work, many reported that whilst they enjoyed office banter, they saw great benefits in home-based working, and it remains to be seen how many businesses will decide that they have no need for previous expensive office space. In both schools and universities many teachers have had to up-skill in online teaching to an extent unlikely without Covid-19. Once again, Teams, Zoom and Webex have become standard forms of group meetings, involving less travel and time, and as universities have successfully conducted doctoral *vivas* online using such systems, the reduced cost, time and effort could lead to this becoming the 'new normal' for such examinations, in the process also opening up the possibility of using experts at far greater geographical distance. Covid-19 is then once more creating challenges which are changing many social and economic practices in surprising and unexpected ways.

However, there is a downside to connectivity which Covid-19 may also have ramped up. Before Covid-19, there was an increased concern, as Davidow (2011) has argued, that such connectedness could all too easily translate into a hyper-connectivity, where the sheer quantity of data increases pressures on those in a leadership role, with the result, as Goldin and Mariathasan (2014) argue, that individuals may be unable 'to manage these growing complexities and interdependencies'. Once more this demonstrates that optimal connectedness is a matter of degree, where both reduced- and hyper-connectedness can be major threats to individual and group sustainability.

The subtitle of Sheninger's (2014) book is *Changing Paradigms for Changing Times*, and he is correct in arguing that a changing paradigm is needed for changing times, but this cannot be one based solely upon greater digital connectivity. Whilst it may help re-frame the nature of learning, motivation and educational roles, it needs to be accompanied by other paradigms which better appreciate the increasing complexity and wicked nature of many problems faced by educational leaders, and which also demonstrate how they might be better dealt with.

Potential process effects

Now the widespread presence of these under-recognized processes – positive feedback, exponential growth, degrees of connectivity – and the wicked problems discussed in this and the previous chapter – produces a number of concerns for many, including educational leaders.

Increases in the speed of change

A first and most obvious effect of these processes is the increased speed with which things change, and sometimes faster than many can adapt to. In the case of the environment, there is now highly persuasive evidence that temperatures, climates and habitats are changing faster than many animal and plant species can adjust to (IPCC, 2018; Kolbert, 2014; WWF, 2008; Wilson, 2003). Moreover, even were species capable of such adaptation, other species upon which they depended might not, and their long-term survival would still be threatened. As we shall see in the next chapter, the same can be true for human societies as well (Diamond, 2006, Cline, 2014).

In many human occupations, including education, speed of change in policies and practice can also threaten work and career sustainability (Starr, 2015). Such speed may produce a dangerous combination of overwork, and a lack of preparedness for new challenges, resulting in reduced numbers of those applying for and taking on the role, heightened stress for those already in it, and more people leaving or taking early retirement. At the same time, the necessarily individual and contextualized nature of adaptation may go unrecognized: forty years ago, Lipsky (1980) showed how most 'street-level bureaucrats' attempted to provide adequate provision to their 'clients' through personal calculations and allocations of time and energy resources, which new policy initiatives may ignore or of which they may be unaware, and which then threaten an individual's sustainability.

Increased consumption and pollution of resources

A second effect comes directly from this increase in speed. When processes combine to speed up change, resources like fresh water and fossils fuels are normally extracted and consumed faster as well, with the concurrent danger that they cannot be replaced. Moreover, because the environment is largely constituted of complex interdependent systems, the effects on one resource can have considerable effects upon others, the result of which may be unpredictable and potentially irremediable. In the human world, resources may be 'human resources' which in times of increased speed and pressure may also be 'consumed' by 'greedy organisations' (Gronn, 2003) with little concern for their personal welfare, leading to individuals leaving before their number and quality can be replaced. The effects upon those remaining, and upon institutions, as high turnover of staff creates greater unpredictability, are then also likely to be problematic (Fuller, 2012). When increases in speed and resource extraction occur, pollution will likely grow proportionately. Environmentally, the burning of fossil fuels, subsequent increases in greenhouse gases and the increased production of industrial by-products damage both air and water quality. Institutionally, 'pollution' may be experienced due to the physical, mental and emotional strains caused by overwork, and by pressures of time and continual audit, then leading to a situation where further 'pollution' cannot be tolerated, and individuals may then decide to either leave a leadership position or reject it as a career ambition. This is now being recognised in health services as an effect of the pressures brought on by the Covid virus.

Decreased predictability and control

The processes and their effects covered in this chapter can then lead to a third effect – a decreased ability to predict and control events. Positive feedback exacerbates rather than re-balances present trends. Exponential growth leads many to underestimate the rate of increase. Hyper-connectivity makes it increasingly difficult to track all of the changes impacting upon institutions and individuals, whilst a reduced connectivity lessens the strength of necessary links within a system. These processes can then lead to a decreased ability to estimate, predict and control processes and their outcomes, and then can produce the kinds of 'tipping points' more fully discussed in Chapters 7 and 8.

Cultivating the benign aspects of covert processes

Positive feedback, exponential growth, suboptimal forms of connectivity and the occurrence of wicked problems may then lead to increases in the speed of change, increased consumption and pollution of resources, decreased predictability and control of events, and the potential creation of 'tipping points'. However, it is also important to recognize that these processes can have benign as well as malign consequences, and so their cultivation may be extremely useful in preventing the emergence of tipping points. There seem to be four such benign aspects.

A *first benign aspect* is the cultivation of a variety of possible responses to problems in complex systems – especially social systems – which can be highly unpredictable in their outcomes because they are composed of different contexts and different actors, which produce unique interactions and impacts. Yet the answer to such diversity and contextualization is not to attempt large-scale standardization but to appreciate how unique people, institutions and policies are. Over a hundred years ago, Sadler (in Higginson ed, 1979, p. 6) warned that we need to be immensely careful when borrowing educational ideas from other countries, arguing that

> We cannot wander at pleasure around the educational systems of the world, like a child strolling through a garden, and pick off a flower from one bush and some leaves from another, and then expect that if we stick what we have gathered into the soil at home, we have a living plant.

Such caution is also the basis for Bassey's (1999) claim that one should not venture beyond making 'fuzzy generalisations' when exploring an incident in an educational setting, for in contextually complex situations, one should only look for the degree to which situations are similar, and one should not assume that they will ever be exactly the same. This then cautions against attempts to generalize beyond individual instances of change in order to implement macro-level standardized procedures. Implementing policies, without full and proper consideration of the effects produced by different actors and contexts, can then be very damaging. Any attempt by a government to then create 'designer leaders' (Gronn, 2002) is a dangerous move precisely because it prevents an individual leader's personal appreciation of the contextualization of a problem, as well as inhibiting a needed variety of response.

Indeed, and importantly, standardization is one of the worst ways of ensuring sustainability, for the natural world is created from the experimentation generated by the existence of a complex diversity of species, where those most equipped and well adapted to particular contexts survive. Standardization prevents this necessary experimentation. Similarly, in an era of rapid change and challenge in the social world, adhering to standardized models (of, for instance, educational leadership) makes more likely the probability that any major 'flaws' inherent in a standardized model will lead to less system sustainability, as these flaws can then be transmitted throughout this standardized range. Diversity through greater contextualization, and leadership diversity in particular, is almost certainly the best means of ensuring overall adaptability and sustainability. The cultivation of different kinds of responses to particular contextual challenges and supporting, rather than suppressing, leadership responses based at least in part on personality and lived experience rather than on policy standardization provide much better ways of generating sustainable responses

A *second aspect* lies in radically reducing reliance on the effectiveness of tame problems and solutions for complex problems, and instead embracing the 'silver buckshot' of wicked resolutions rather than the 'silver bullet' responses of tame approaches. As many solution failures are underpinned by simplistic assumptions about the nature of a problem, 'silver bullet' solutions are likely in many situations to be ill-suited and context-deficient. If tame assumptions are adopted and failures occur, blame may be wrongly attached to implementers, which then becomes another threat to their personal sustainability. Instead, approaches which recognize that many problems are highly complex build from the understanding that the best solutions are unlikely to be single or one-off solutions and are more likely to be a cocktail of 'clumsy' or 'silver buckshot' responses (Rayner, 2006, Grint, 2008, Verweij and Thompson, 2011). Moreover, it should not be assumed that such responses will always work: they are 'best guesses', derived from the available evidence and a range of opinions, and their use should be seen as informed and justifiable attempts, from which further experimentation may be needed to get nearer a workable solution.

A stronger understanding of how the concept of 'wicked problems' can re-frame the leadership role is then needed. Instead of believing that a major leadership function lies in the individual resolution of intractable problems, the leadership role needs to be seen as more about creating the right conditions for working with others in framing informed and justifiable responses to problems. As Marion and Uhl-Bien (2001, p. 394) suggest, a leader's role is then more about 'creating transformational environments . . . than in creating the innovation itself'. This may be hard for some stakeholders and some leaders to accept, as it runs against many traditional models of leadership. However, a greater recognition of individual limitations, and of the strengths of others, means that those occupying a formal role need to welcome the contributions that others can bring to defining and resolving problems, and in many cases lead on this aspect. Designated leaders then need to engage as much in the creation of the conditions for dealing with wicked problems as in attempting their personal resolution.

A *third aspect* lies in recognizing the need for an epistemology and ethics of humility, which are both underpinned by acceptance of our highly limited personal understandings of the world. From a sensory apparatus, feeding into a brain which never actually 'sees' this world, through to the individual differences generated by genetic inheritance and many environmental impacts, individuals have necessarily unique but highly restricted perceptions of any 'reality', and therefore no matter how talented, they are poorly suited to taking full personal responsibility for leading others in dealing with such a complex world.

Such epistemological humility would, as noted earlier, need to '[bring] us to terms with our own limits' (Grenberg, 2005, p. 6–7). This is an epistemology which, despite some people's fears, would not reduce personal and system sustainability. Instead, by recognizing personal limitations and acting within such knowledge, they are more likely to increase it; it is the working with tame assumptions in a wicked world which is much more likely to reduce such sustainability. Failing to recognize the wicked nature of many situations, and our own limitations in understanding them, then prevents the adoption of states of mind which better fit the reality faced. Such humility also helps to point up the unnecessary hubris of those forms of leadership where the work is seen as like throwing stones – calculated, rational, controllable and predictable in its outcomes. Some leadership work may be like this, but as Plsek (2001) argues, leadership work is often more like the throwing of birds, with conflicting intentions between the thrower and the 'thrown'. Those leaders who think of themselves as 'stone-throwers' are then likely to have much less control than they think they have, their role ultimately being less sustainable through this lack of recognition of their limitations. In a world of the complex and the wicked, the leader who believes they are throwing birds rather than stones is likely to be the more sustainable of the two, underpinned as they are by an epistemological humility rather than hubristic certainty (Schein and Schein, 2018).

A *final aspect* stems from the nature of wicked problems itself, for a greater awareness of the surprising ubiquity of wicked problems in organizations and society in general could help change the manner in which leaders view their work. Instead of aspiring to some magisterial understanding of organizational functioning, a more rational and sustainable position would be one which acknowledged that leadership is necessarily full of surprises, and leaders should then not be too surprised by their occurrence. Instead of accepting that policies are created at the top, to be implemented at the bottom, they and policymakers need to view policies as drafts of ideas which have to be worked through by different groups of people in the contexts in which they will be implemented. Instead of assuming that most problems can be conclusively resolved, individual and institutional sustainability would be strengthened, not weakened, by acknowledging that some problems may only be partly solved, some may return later in a different guise and some may not be immediately resolvable, but, for the time being, may need to be lived with.

Conclusions

This chapter has argued that educational leaders, acting in a stewardship role, need to see a large part of this role as demonstrating to their students how to develop an attitude of global stewardship. Part of such education needs to be a grounding in a much stronger awareness of the existence of a number of covert processes, many times not recognized, often misunderstood and yet all, given the right conditions, capable of causing great damage at micro-, meso- and macro-levels. Without a stronger understanding of such processes, there exists the real possibility that they could generate dangerous and unpredictable situations. But they are not the only threats that a stewardship role needs to take on board, as there are other threats, and other lessons to be learnt in preventing damaging end results. One further area of threat is that of events first located in humanity's deep past. Some of these have only recently been realized, whilst others have simply been neglected, but critical to their better understanding is the use of longer-term thinking, and the next chapter will therefore examine what lessons educational leaders can learn from our prehistoric and ancient deep past.

5

Planning for the Future by Scanning the Deep Past

Introduction

This book argues that in a world which is changing much more rapidly than most find comfortable, it behoves those taking on leadership positions in education to reflect on whether their role needs framing differently to better respond to such changes. A critical move here is towards a greater recognition of an extended stewardship role which needs to include values and practices concerning a number of macro-issues, particularly environmental ones, rather than locating their focus primarily at personal, interpersonal and institutional levels. This is not to say that micro- or meso-level activities are not important: they are, because they remain the principal arenas within which leadership is practised and without them, the realization of any educational aims is not possible. But a stewardship role encompassing a vision of global change must not be ignored; nor should one which takes such a vision into the long term, because their students will need the understanding and abilities to cope with macro-level changes occurring which may not present themselves fully for some time to come but which now need understanding and preparing for.

Now, the educational leadership role has always existed within a macro-context, which, if not properly recognized, may make educational leaders susceptible to invisible steers from this level, rather than their being able to critique such influences. Indeed in many Western countries over the last seventy years, there has not only been a general lack of recognition of the challenge of approaching environmental problems, just as the direction of much public education has moved educational leaders further away from notions of student and environmental stewardship. After the Second World War, for instance, many nation-states embarked on welfare state agendas which saw the state playing the major role in providing the structures and materials necessary for public health and education, and appointing leaders in these areas to devise ways of implementing these areas. The public sector was then seen as needing to both steer and row the boat of nation-state policy (Osborne and Gaebler, 1992), and welfare values and concerns tended to focus educational leadership around four issues: the reduction of societal inequalities through the state provision of critical services, like health and education; education as a 'public good', a means of furthering societal cohesion as well as for personal benefit; concern for individual well-being and for individual personal growth; and, finally, education based on the dominance of state provision, where in relationships between professionals and governments, professionals acted as gatekeepers to such provision.

However, largely due to a combination of financial problems, an increasingly critical literature on professional monopolies and a need in times of financial constraint to rein in government spending, new governments were elected with a very different – if still nationally focused – political platform in which the role of the state was reduced, and national and global market forces gained increased influence at these levels. Educational leaders were then re-directed by their governments towards strategies:

- of market competition as the natural and moral way of deciding choices;
- of professionals being 'on tap' to governments rather than 'on top' (Pollitt, 1993);
- of mixtures of hierarchical and market relationships between professionals and governments;
- of governments continuing to do much of the steering, but rowing increasingly seen as a private sector function.

Very little of either of these two political agenda examined a future where human population sizes and consumptions levels were growing, and which thereby placed great pressures on the natural world, nor did they look much beyond the concerns of the nation-state to examine the state of the globe. T-I-N-A – there is no alternative – was a Reagan/Thatcherite pro-market argument which few political opponents effectively countered (Varoufakis, 2020).

However, in 2020 the global arrival of Covid-19 brought about huge economic and political changes: many nation-states halted the market basis of much activity almost overnight, and many put on hold citizen rights of movement and activity, as they initiated a degree of surveillance of civilian populations not seen in any functioning peacetime democratic state. Nation-states then reasserted their dominance over other forms of control and steerage, demonstrating that in times of real crisis it was not only necessary but also highly possible for them to introduce very different forms of political and economic activity.

Now Covid-19 is an unexpected environmental, rather than a man-made, threat and demonstrates beyond doubt that political and economic issues do not constitute all the problems threatening global and national sustainability. Indeed, its appearance and effects now need to be seen as presaging the emergence of other environmental concerns, particularly that of a dangerously warming climate. This suggests the need to prioritize agenda which will move well beyond previous ones and instead formulate seven new global and national priorities, underpinned by the following seven beliefs:

1. If the global ecosphere within which all living creatures exist is not sustainable, then neither is the human race nor any other species.
2. The concept of well-being must be expanded beyond the level of the individual to the group, to that of national and global populations, and therefore must place much greater emphasis upon an ethic of global equity.
3. That given an expanding world population and decreasing global resources, current emphases on growth and consumption as principal objectives are unsustainable and need gradually replacing by a growing ethic of imperative sufficiency (Princen, 2005).
4. That because humanity is the only species capable of addressing the problems the planet faces (even if it created many of them), then it needs to take responsibility for a stewardship of this planet.
5. That educational leaders need to be contributors to such stewardship, educating future generations into understanding these emerging problems and the means of dealing with them.
6. As part of a developing stewardship role, educational leaders need to reflect not only upon events that are currently happening, or are likely to happen in the near future, but, as importantly, upon events that have occurred in the past and which are beginning to re-emerge as threats once more.
7. We therefore need to begin scanning the future by scanning the past.

The rest of this chapter then examines in detail the last two points, as there are a number of issues from the deep past which can and need to inform current educational leadership perspectives on the future.

A first issue involves re-examining the assumptions about climate stability and continuity, whilst the other focuses upon the surprising problems arising from when humanity moved from hunter-gatherer lifestyles to more static ones.

A second issue is the need to reflect upon a number of *Homo sapiens'* past mistakes and successes, in the first instance to avoid committing similar mistakes in the near future and in the second to learn from past successes. This will be undertaken through an examination of humanity's role in megafaunal extinctions at the end of the last ice age and by examining the changing picture of *Homo sapiens*' interactions with other close relatives in the deep past.

The third and final issue is that of understanding that major 'extinction events' can happen in the present just as much as they have happened in the past. One way is to reflect upon previous causes of global extinction events. The other way is through examining the collapse of ancient communities.

Such investigations may seem to some a long way from discussion of a needed change in the focus of the educational leadership role. Yet these issues have important implications for the threats that societies will very likely face in the coming century and so can help re-frame an educational leadership focus to better encompass a stewardship responsibility towards their students and the planetary environment. We begin then by examining assumptions about climate continuity which help conceal future threats to global sustainability.

Re-examining assumptions about the past: Climate continuity and stability

Few people recognize how extraordinarily lucky *Homo sapiens* has been in its evolution and recent geological history. It evolved on what Zalaziewicz J. and Williams M. (2012) term a 'goldilocks planet': a planet not too near but not too far from its sun, enabling it to experience climatic conditions which permitted a flourishing of life which most other planets were not fortunate enough to encounter. Humanity itself has also been remarkably lucky in the last 10,000–12,000 years, living in what most scientists now regard as an interglacial period – a geologically brief period of time of a few thousand years between two much longer ice ages, which over most of the last 2.6 million years have covered most of the Northern hemisphere in ice sheets. Indeed humanity, in living in this remarkably benign and stable interglacial period, has moved from being nomadic hunter-gatherers to static agriculturalists, then to state builders and onto being atom splitters and solar system explorers. However, there is little reason to believe that this current interglacial period signals the end of this much longer ice age: if previous ones are anything to go by – they have usually lasted between 10,000 and 15,000 years – then we are due for a return to further Arctic conditions before too long, geologically speaking, even if recent human actions in warming of the planet have contributed to the difficulty in predicting the precise timing.

The result of this benign 12,000-year interglacial 'holiday' then has been that human civilizations have experienced a remarkable degree of long-term climatic stability, and this stability has then been assumed to be the 'normal' state of affairs. The longer view – the return of new ice age – has then been downplayed because such experience occurred much earlier in human history. It has then been less well remembered and recorded, and therefore amounts to another form of covert threat. The experience of such stability and gradual change has been the norm rather than rapid movements towards tipping points (Lenton et al. 2013). At the same time, the stabilizing effect of negative feedback rather than the runaway effects of positive feedback, the more frequent experience of arithmetic rather than of exponential growth and the good fortune to live at a time when assumptions of simplicity and manageability rather than complexity and uncertainty have been more frequent have all then contributed to assumptions of climate stability.

Now prehistoric man came to assume this stability through considerable seasonal regularity: large stone constructions like those at Stonehenge in England, Macchu Picchu in Peru, Chichen Itza in Mexico and Newgrange in Ireland were all in part designed to capture the predictable and precise moments of either the summer or the winter solstices, stable indicators of what to expect in the coming months. However, humanity does possess generational memories through myths and legends of abrupt climatic events change, for which there has quite recently emerged strong confirmatory evidence (Weart, 2005; Kunzig and Broeckner, 2008; Flannery, 2015) of surprisingly rapid temperature variation. As Weart (2005) said in reviewing the conclusions of such research:

> Swings of temperature that were believed in the 1960s to take tens of thousands of years, in the 1970s, to take thousands of years, and in the 1980s to take hundreds of years, now were discovered to take only decades.

Now these abrupt temperature changes generally occurred in human prehistory as ice ages either arrived, and turned forest into tundra, and then to ice sheets, or as warmer interglacial periods arrived, leading to the break-up of these ice sheets, gouging out new landscapes, and inundating large tracts of low-lying land with floods from melting glaciers (Brannen, 2018; MacPhee, 2019). The latter were probably the origins of recurring stories from ancient civilizations of great floods, such as those recounted in the Sumerian epic of Gilgamesh, and repeated in the Christian Bible, formed probably from the sudden rush of billions of gallons of melt water from the Atlantic as it broke through the Straits of Gibraltar and engulfed large sections of the Mediterranean basin (Fagan, 2005,

2009). Other events, like the deposit of billions of gallons of cold freshwater from the North American glacial Lake Agassiz into the Atlantic 8200 years ago, likely caused the diversion of the Gulf Stream's warming waters away from Northern Europe, and produced dramatic drops in temperature and continuous heavy rainfall there, with resultant major crop failures and large-scale famines (Linden, 2006; Leydet et al., 2018).

Other sudden catastrophes were due to different kinds of natural events. The Minoan civilization on Crete (BC 2700 to BC 1450) seems to have come to an end due in large part to a huge volcanic explosion on the nearby island of Santorini, with consequent earthquakes and tsunamis weakening the island culture and reducing its food supply to such an extent that it became prey to Mycenaean conquest a little later (Middleton, 2017). More recent events, such as the Northern hemisphere's Little Ice Age, from 1300 to 1850, meant that whilst fairs could be held on frozen rivers such as those in London in 1638, with individuals also walking across the frozen Hudson River in 1780, the damaging effects on crops and the health of human populations were equally predictable. Finally, volcanic eruptions, like that on Krakatoa in Indonesia in 1883 led to crop failures worldwide as the dust ejected from the volcano caused low temperatures and subsequent crop failures on the other side of the world for years afterwards.

Nevertheless, in the long history and prehistory of humanity, such events have been the exceptions rather than the rule. Sheer good fortune seems to be a highly important if neglected factor in explaining our climate history. However, there is no reason to assume that such good luck will continue, particularly if *Homo sapiens* continues to rock this climatic boat. Changing the metaphor, as Broeckner (in Kunzig and Broeckner, 2008) suggested with respect to global climate, if you're living with an angry beast, you don't poke it with a sharp stick. The sharp stick currently takes the form of consumer lifestyles based on fossil fuel dependency, which have increased the percentage of greenhouse gases in the atmosphere. Our species, and particularly its wealthier members, have spent over two centuries poking very hard at the global climate with this stick. In sum, assumptions of continued climate stability are not supported by the evidence from prehistory, and, as we continue to jab this beast, it is imperative that educational leaders prepare their students for a much less predictable and less stable future. We are not talking 'geologic time' here, but only of a few decades into the future before present activities lead to temperature rises which kick-start such major changes. This then is not a long-term goal for educational leaders to consider: it is an understanding and an awareness which needs passing on urgently.

Re-examining assumptions about the past: The transition from hunter-gatherer to agricultural lifestyles

Whilst the assumption of climate continuity hides a genuine near-future threat to global sustainability, there is a further large assumption about humanity's past which also needs surfacing: the movement in human prehistory from living in hunter-gatherer groups to agricultural communities. The widely held assumption about *Homo sapiens*' transition from hunter-gatherers to agriculturalists about 11,000–12,000 years ago is that this was highly beneficial to our species, with most earlier writings seeing hunter-gathering as essentially the lowest level of human existence. Braidwood (1957, p. 122), for instance, suggested that

> a man who spends his whole life following animals just to kill them to eat, or moving from one berry patch to another, is really living just like an animal himself.

The transition from hunter-gatherer to pastoralist and agriculturalist has then been seen as a highly positive move, leading to the development of complex social, economic and political structures, and then to the creation of the post-industrial societies of today. Central to this belief is the assumption that moving from hunter-gatherer to agriculturalist created a more predictable and regular supply of food, and one which by taking up much less time provided the space for the creation and development of other activities. Indeed, the evidence (Scott, 2018; Cunliffe, 2012; Ponting, 2007) suggests that in a relatively small number of generations, agriculture spread across Asia and Europe to supplant hunter-gathering as the major form of subsistence, resulting in significant increases in population, a greater specialization of occupation, the creation of political, economic and legal systems, and, fundamental to these, the invention of literacy and numeracy. For much of recorded human history, then, this move to the modern state has been assumed to be an unarguable *good* thing, a move propelling humanity from savagery to civilized social beings.

However, history is normally written by the victors, and the deficits attributed to hunter-gatherer life are now strongly disputed, with the benefits of static agricultural communities better balanced by insights into their intrinsic problems (Scott, 2018; Barnard, 2018). Indeed, understanding the changes and challenges of 10,000 years ago is an important way of better understanding a number of present-day challenges threatening our current sustainability. Once more, the deep past can teach us a great deal about current problems and provide lessons for those who would equip future generations with the abilities to deal with them.

Now the term 'hunter-gatherer' is commonly taken to mean small family bands constantly on the move, finding food where they can, but always subject to the dangers of shortage and starvation. Prehistoric hunter-gatherers have then been pictured as dirty and unkempt, living in caves, constantly alert for other predators and functioning at a level of thinking one might associate with people living a day-to-day, hand-to-mouth existence. Yet current research makes it clear that hunter-gatherers have exhibited significant diversity, in terms of both size and complexity. Cummings (2018) has pointed out that the complex hunter-gatherer societies of Northwest America and the Ainu of Japan both demonstrate large groupings and highly complex social arrangements, whilst Spielman (2018) points out that Pueblo agricultural societies formed strong interdependent relationships with hunter-gatherer Plains Indians in the exchange of corn and buffalo meat. Finally, as Brody (2002) notes, many hunter-gatherer groups often remained within a defined territory, and still do, only moving around this to extract resources from a particular area during the appropriate season of the year.

Past hunter-gatherer lifestyles might then not only have been much more sustainable than has largely been assumed, but they may even have been enjoyable, and may explain why transitions between the two lifestyles took place at different times, in different places and for different reasons, and could well be reversed for a while. Darvill (2010), Cunliffe (2012), Scott (2018) and Cummings (2018) all point out that prehistoric wetlands like those in Mesopotamia and in the UK were stable and rich sources of food, and the evidence strongly suggests that hunter-gatherers chose to live for extended periods around such nutritionally substantive areas. They also developed practices normally assumed to be the preserve of agriculturalists. As Cummings (2018, p. 768) points out,

> hunter-gatherers invented farming . . . [through] subtle modifications by foragers in their wild plant gathering and management practices . . . along with new kinds of selective hunting, herding and taming strategies.

They were also not only adept at harvesting wild grain but capable of building substantial structures such as the massive construction of stone avenues at Carnac in France (Oliver, 2012), and the 60,000 timber post construction across marshland between two communities at Flag Fen near Peterborough in the UK (Cunliffe, 2012). These groups then were not composed of the shambling and stupid but were in fact clever, resourceful and highly organized communities who knew how to identify and exploit local resources.

Moreover, if hunter-gatherers remained at locations within fixed areas until those resources declined, their very mobility should perhaps be perceived as a strength rather than a weakness: an increasing literature on the static lifestyle of agricultural communities, which evolved into walled towns, cities and nation-states, led to a whole series of problems which still pre-occupy us today (see particularly Scott, 2018). Thus the need to plant crops and wait for them to harvest required a necessary inertia which often produces an increasing dependency on a small number of grain crops and domesticated livestock in that location. One rather surprising result then was of the decline in the variety and richness of their diet as compared with their hunter-gatherer neighbours. Evidence from prehistoric skeletal studies and bone density supports this: both Diamond (1987) and Scott (2018) cite evidence showing that the nutrition of static agricultural communities was in many cases nutritionally inferior to that of hunter-gatherers who had access to a much wider variety of foods.

Such problems for agriculturalists would be intensified if crops failed or if livestock died from disease. Furthermore, research has shown (Amyes, 2013; Wayne and Bolker, 2015) that when populations and domesticated animals are closely grouped together, they become highly susceptible to zoonotic diseases – diseases which jump from species to species. Indeed, this description of living conditions – static, cramped and zoonotic – fits rather well many of the contexts, thousands of years later, in which Covid-19 has spread. Present-day illnesses like measles, tuberculosis, influenza and malaria all became human diseases because of the proximity of agricultural communities to domesticated animals like cattle, pigs, chickens and ducks (Diamond, 1998). Hunter-gatherers, on the other hand, living in small mobile groups were much less susceptible and only because their communities have been moved to the margins has humanity lost this awareness. In the process, the covert threat of static communities is also forgotten.

There is one final downside to static communities. As Sahlins (1972), Diamond (1987), Brody (2002) and Oliver (2012) all argue, hunter-gatherer communities generally had – and still have – more limited hierarchies than static ones. Part of this is simply because the small numbers in mobile groups prevent any great degree of such human grading. Besides this, though, the problems such groups face tend to be age-old in nature, and as the elderly have the greatest experience in these, they therefore have normally taken the positions of most influence. By contrast, as agricultural communities expanded in size and number, becoming towns, then city states and sometimes empires, the increasing differences in ownership of land, property and livestock created greater occupational and social differentiation, and then in the possession of the most impressive and effective weapons. These might be used against incursions from other static communities, but they also facilitated the imposition of the will of the powerful upon the weaker and less fortunate within their own communities. The large differences in wealth and power in societies today in large part constitute another inheritance from earlier static communities.

Finally, not only are there sustainability lessons to be learnt from this discussion by present-day societies; there are also lessons for an educational leadership literature. Many descriptions of the transition from hunter-gatherer to agricultural lifestyles are highly inadequate, partly because the first studies of such transition were derived from European research, which was then extrapolated to other parts of the world without full confirmatory research. When this was eventually performed, it demonstrated very large differences in transition not only between different parts of the globe but also within much smaller contexts and for very different reasons. This explains why temporal and cultural divisions like Palaeolithic, Mesolithic and Neolithic, or the Stone Age, Bronze Age and Iron Age, are increasingly seen as categories far too broad to properly capture the reality of contextualized practice. The same can be said for many educational leadership studies: broad categories of leadership types, such as the transactional, transformational and distributed may also be far too broad to capture the essence of real leadership performance within a particular context, and may then prevent awareness of the significance of more detailed understandings. In both cases, what seems to be needed is a critical conversation between the general and particular, and appropriate adjustments made to produce more accurate descriptions of the realities encountered.

Learning from the past: Megafaunal mass extinctions and relationships with prehistoric cousins

The second issue from the deep past which has lessons for humanity today is the need to reflect upon past mistakes in order to avoid their future repetition The extinction of 'megafauna' – large animals and birds – in human prehistory is one example. Now whilst many earlier mass extinctions, considered later in this chapter, were not caused by human beings, largely because the human species had not yet evolved, evidence discussed here suggests that human beings played a significant role in wiping out a considerable number of large species between 50,000 and 10,000 years ago, actions we may be repeating today. These megafaunal extinctions have been well known from the fossil record for some time, but it had originally been thought that they were principally caused by climate change at the end of ice ages. However, Martin (1973, 1984) has pointed out the remarkably close relationship between the time when human beings first arrived in particular parts of the world, and the extinction of most large animals and birds in these same locations. In Australasia this occurred 50,000–40,000 years ago. In North and South America the same took place 12,000–14,000 years ago, and in New Zealand, where the evidence of human causation is particularly strong, about 800 years ago. Whilst the extinction of megafauna in Australasia, and later in the Americas is still contested, the circumstantial evidence is very strong: in both cases shortly after Homo sapiens appeared, the megafauna disappeared.

Now Martin (1984) claimed in his 'overkill hypothesis' that humans were responsible for extinction events in some contexts but not in others because of differences in 'prey naïveté' – where animals with no prior acquaintance of human beings did not recognize these small hairy bipeds as lethal predators until it was too late. Martin therefore suggests that these hunter-gatherers were suddenly presented with an apparently never-ending supply of fresh meat, which approached them with no sense of fear. In such circumstances, he argues, they unsurprisingly took what was on offer, and as Kruuk (1972) argued, even when they were satiated, they would still likely have continued killing and would have stored much of this meat for later, using techniques which are still seen in hunter-gatherer societies today. The fact that the same kind of extinction events did *not* happen on the same scale in African or Eurasia may well have been because the megafauna in these places had co-evolved with human beings, and were therefore well acquainted with their predatory behaviour, and would then have had the time to develop appropriate avoidance behaviours. In contrast, in areas of prey naïveté, hunter-gatherers would have wiped out the megafauna in one area, and then moved on to other places where megafauna had no experience of humans, and therefore had not learnt to avoid such predators. Such movement from killing site to killing site, claimed Martin, was the way in which many prehistoric hunter-gatherer groups made their way through North and then South America. As they did so, virtually all of the large megafauna disappeared.

Martin therefore argued that the remarkable temporal proximity of man's arrival in a new area and the extinction of the majority of their megafaunal species lend a high degree of circumstantial evidence to the overkill thesis. However, his thesis does not fully exclude other possible explanations. Indeed,

MacPhee and Marx (1997) have suggested that human transmission of zoonotic disease to megafaunal species might also have had a part to play, as they would have decimated megafaunal populations in the same way that European humans contributed to the deaths of untold millions of other human beings upon arrival in the Americas 500 years ago, the indigenous people having no defence against diseases like smallpox, measles and the common cold. In summarizing the arguments, MacPhee (2019) suggests that it was probably a combination of all these effects – climate change, human overkill and the transmission of zoonotic diseases – which caused the extinctions. To this might be added one final explanation, with respect to the extinction of bird species on isolated islands: that humanity did not kill these birds themselves but brought with them the animals that did – the rats, the dogs and the pigs which ate the birds' eggs. So whilst the jury is still out on the causes of megafaunal extinctions in particular localities, it still seems very likely that human beings played a significant part in most of these extinction events.

Some extinctions would then have been the product of deliberate killing, but many other extinctions may have been unintentional as when humanity spread disease, or when the animals they brought with them killed off indigenous inhabitants. This is an important point for the present day, because such past events may be precursors to what seems to be developing into a further great extinction event today, which – and this is the critical point – may be largely unnoticed if they are not cases of deliberate killing. Certainly, some deliberate killing does go on – whether for food, for trophies, or because these species compete with domestic animals for the same crops. However, it seems highly likely that as in the past, unintentional human activity may be the primary cause – as with the introduction of non-native species, of disease, the use of land for cultivation and changes in the temperature and environment within which species live. In such circumstances, the hidden (covert) complexity of an extinction process may often lead to an underestimation of the impact. Extinctions may then occur without an understanding or recognition of the processes causing them – or of humanity's contribution through generating these processes.

Of course it is highly difficult to determine the degree of intentionality by human beings tens of thousands of years ago. Nevertheless, the evidence from cave paintings and the viewpoints of early and modern hunter-gatherers (see Finlay, 2018; Brody, 2002) suggest that their world view was of a unity and respect for virtually all forms of life, as well as a profound and subtle understanding of the seasonal changes and behaviours of the animals and plants in their vicinity (Cummings et al., 2018), even if it is difficult to say whether these were framed within a stewardship ethic. Their likely role in megafaunal extinctions does not suggest this, and the highly limited, context-bound experiences of prehistoric humanity very likely limited such consideration. However, humanity today has the considerable advantage of being able to commit such thoughts to long-term reflection and scrutiny, and to amass evidence to judge the effects of their actions. Educational leaders then have the opportunity to play a major role in bringing such events to a wider consciousness and, in so doing, to develop a greater human stewardship of the planet.

Relationships with prehistoric cousins

Whilst the evidence for destructive relationships with megafauna seems increasingly convincing, the reverse seems to be the case with prehistoric cousins like the Neanderthals and the Denisovans. The traditional story, starting from when the first Neanderthal bones were identified in the middle of the nineteenth century in Germany, has been one of *Homo sapiens* being smarter, more adaptable, and more socially and technologically skilled than these and other hominids, and thereby of our out-competing Neanderthals and other variants. A description of the extinction of Neanderthals in Britain a decade ago by Cunliffe (2012, p. 45) suggested that they 'were no match for the twin onslaughts of clever rivals and bitter winters'. However, this ignores the fact that *Homo Sapiens* and Neanderthals had lived side by side in a number of western Eurasian locations for many thousands of years, and Neanderthals were actually physically better adapted to the cold than we were. Crucially, other recent evidence (Higham, 2021; Wragg Sykes, 2021) also suggests that they were not only capable of both artistic creations and music but interbred with humans, and the offspring lived to adulthood, suggesting a culture of care and compassion. As interestingly, Denisovans, who inhabited regions more eastward than Neanderthals but from Siberia in the north to Australia in the South, also interbred with both *Homo Sapiens* and Neanderthals. So rather than the latest evidence suggesting our superiority and domination over other hominids, and of our genetic predisposition to competition and violence against those different from ourselves, these three groups all seem to have been as predisposed to cooperation and care with other hominids as being competitive and aggressive. As Dunt (2021, p. 19) argues, this is important today, because it punctures beliefs by ideologies like neoliberalism that we are inherently hyper-competitive and should adopt social, political and economic practices in keeping with such a genetic predisposition. The reality is probably twofold. First, current evidence indicates that 'the range of human biological, cognitive and cultural variation encompasses the Neanderthal as much as the Andamanese islander or the Victorian gentleman' (Zilhau, 2014, p. 2016) – and that this almost certainly applies to the Denisovans as well. Second, our genetic predispositions were likely to have been at least as cooperative and caring as they were competitive and antagonistic – and today we have the choice to adopt either set of behaviours.

Understanding that extinction events can happen in the present as well as the past: Past causes of global extinction events

The potential for climate instability discussed earlier becomes even clearer as we move further back in time, for there is now much evidence to suggest that during the earth's long history it has suffered at least five periods of extreme climatic instability which have led to a similar number of mass species extinctions (Benton, 2006; Ward, 2008; Kolbert, 2014; Brannen, 2018). Most people are aware of the event sixty-five million years ago when all dinosaur species (except proto-birds), and 50 per cent of all other existing life forms, became extinct. The largely accepted explanation for this was a massive asteroid impact on the Yucatan Peninsula in Central America, first creating massive global conflagrations before then plunging the earth into an extended global winter.

The 'popularity' of this extinction event is not surprising given that dinosaurs have been a favourite school topic for decades. Many fewer have heard of 'snowball earth' about 600 million years ago, when as suggested by the name, the earth froze over even to the Equator, and it seems that it was only massive volcanic activity which prevented this becoming the earth's permanent condition. Indeed, after warmer times returned, the 'Cambrian explosion' about sixty million years after 'snowball' earth led to the huge diversification of life from which all existing life has evolved. But there have been other catastrophic global extinction events: the huge Permian extinction event of 130 million years ago eclipses the dinosaur extinction, as *95 per cent* of all species died out then, due to, it is believed, massive volcanic eruptions in the Siberian Traps, and the subsequent poisoning and overheating of the world's seas and atmosphere. The earth has also suffered from at least three other extinction events – at the Ordovician/Silurian geological boundary, in the late Devonian and at the Triassic/Jurassic boundary. They all tell much the same story – that major climatic changes (whether from asteroid impacts, volcanic explosions or the release of lethal gases) all led to climate changes which wiped out most species, including the dominant ones of those times – permitting a new dominant species to emerge.

Whilst some are coming to believe that humanity has now entered a new geological period, the Anthropocene, others believe that we have actually created it, and in the process have generated global climatic changes which are producing a sixth great extinction event (Wilson, 2003; Kolbert, 2014; Barnovsky and Hadley, 2015; Brannen, 2018). If true, we are then the only dominant species which has existed on this planet which understands its contribution to a mass extinction event, but also perhaps its contribution to its own extinction. Bets for the next dominant species currently seem evenly divided between cockroaches and rats.

Once again, mass extinction events may seem some way from the purposes of educational leadership, but this probably says more about the purposes to which leadership activity has usually been devoted, which very largely excludes discussion of this pressing existential macro-question. A strong argument can then be made that with the genuine possibility of a new global extinction event, issues of global survival should be at least as important to the focus of educational leadership as more parochial and speciest concerns. Now leadership foci should not exclude traditional issues, but it does strongly suggest that educational leaders need to frame their role at least in part by focusing on how human beings are currently changing the nature of the planet, and the consequences of this for those that live on it. Wallace-Wells (2019) describes how a 4- to 5-degree rise in global temperatures (not beyond the bounds of possibility) would take us into the same climatic conditions as when dinosaurs swam in the tropical waters of the Arctic Ocean. Before any of this were to happen, though, most major cities would be underwater, and probably much of human civilization (Ward, 2010). If educational leadership is at least in part a role tasked with the framing of responses to developing threats for future generations, and not simply with a role of compliant implementation to largely short-term governmental legislation, within narrowly focused hierarchies, then they need to reflect upon and develop the frames to better understand such past events, and to engage with the possibility of their repetition.

Understanding that extinction events can happen in the present as well as the past: The collapse of ancient communities

Extinction events can also be seen not only during the very deep past but also in the humanity's more recent history, with its creation of the first agricultural communities, subsequent city states and then the earliest empires. Some survived and prospered, but many did not, and the reasons for collapse of some and the survival of others remain highly relevant to societies today, as once again, humanity may be in danger of repeating similar mistakes.

So if we revisit the creation of early agricultural communities – probably somewhere between 10,000 and 13,000 years ago – the sites for them would have been chosen primarily for the quality and quantity of natural resources nearby – good soil, rivers for irrigation and transport, woods or forests for building houses and fires for cooking, the presence of berries, nuts and fruits, and wildlife to supplement a domesticated diet. With natural advantages, and with good weather and growing conditions, such sites would have been good places for settlement. In such circumstances, as Brody (2002) and Scott (2018) point out, whilst the women of many hunter-gatherer communities might need to consciously delay childbirth until they remained in one place long enough for the birth and support of a child in its early months, agricultural communities would have had much less need for such birth control. Pregnancies would then have been more frequent than with hunter-gatherer groups, resulting in greater increases in population, and therefore the greater ability to take possession and control of territories and their resources, gradually marginalizing most hunter-gatherer groups.

This may seem a very positive development for agricultural communities, but the impact of expanding numbers can have a sting in its tail: an increased number of mouths to feed would place extra demands on available resources, with crops needing to be planted, and more animals domesticated. Such expansion might be sustainable over time in some contexts, but in other instances there might come a point where not only land quality would decline through over-usage, but the demand for more resources could be realized only by exploiting poorer-quality land. This could lead to community collapse or to members of a community moving away to find new land. In many cases, though, populations expanded and agricultural communities became towns, and then small cities surrounded by expanding agricultural land. Yet at some stage the same problem would likely present itself once more: more land would be needed to support further expansion. Then, as Leick (2001) points out, such cities, in utilizing more land to support their populations, would sooner or later bump up against the land required and requisitioned by neighbouring towns and cities to support their own increasing numbers. In such circumstances, relationships might well become fractious, and, as Scott (2018) suggests, the need might then be felt to defend the city by building walls around it, and its leaders would begin to recruit or compel inhabitants to be armed in preparation either to defend their land against the predations of neighbouring city states or to annex the land and cities of other communities.

Of course, war was not the inescapable consequence of difficult relations between states. The first known international treaty, between the Egyptians and the Hittites at Kadesh in 1259 BC, was signed precisely to avoid such conflict. Indeed, Cline (2014) shows that diplomatic correspondence at the time sounded remarkably similar to the language and objectives of diplomacy today. Yet, the victories and defeats resulting from struggles between Middle Eastern city states like Ur, Uruk and Lagash, and then by empires like Babylon, Assyria and Egypt, have become the standard, if highly simplistic, way of describing the 'evolution' of states, accompanied by accounts of individuals who won or lost armed encounters. Yet this remains a covert narrative, one which describes the imperative need for resource security which sounds remarkably familiar to such attempts today: Klare's (2012) *The Race for What's Left* then describes how the long history and causation of this scramble for resources has altered remarkably little, with nation-states today jostling with each other for the remaining fossil fuel resources, as well as for food and water security.

Yet whilst trade relations, political marriages, diplomacy and a growing interdependence were all attempted in the ancient world to avoid armed conflict, Cline's (2014) work on the simultaneous collapse of a large number of Middle Eastern civilizations around 1177 BC suggests that such complex interdependence might actually increase, rather than mitigate against, state collapse, particularly if invasions by the as-yet-unidentified 'sea peoples' (Middleton, 2017) acted to bring about a situation rather like a row of dominos, where the collapse of one state had knock-on effects on their neighbours. This ancient problem of complex interdependency then exists today, particularly with respect to economic relations, as modern states rely on global networks to interact seamlessly in the production of goods, but where the breakdown of one element of a network – such as the blockage of transport routes – can cause damaging breakdowns elsewhere, with unpredictable 'wicked' repercussions.

What then emerges in discussions on the collapse of ancient communities is a fundamental concern about the acquisition of adequate resources to sustain increasing populations. Now such collapse of ancient civilizations has over the last few decades been subject to major revisions, with research suggesting that a critical factor in many cases of collapse might well have been climate change. Thus, writers like Fagan (2005), Homer-Dixon (2006), and Diamond (2006) have all argued that early societal collapses may have been caused by different combinations of the factors described earlier, but where in many cases the crucial tipping point was that of climate change. Civilizations like the Akkadians in the Middle East, the Anasazi of Southwestern United States, the Maya of Mexico and the Moche of Peru then all seem to have come to an end because climate change accelerated crop failure, leading to widespread starvation and finally full societal collapse.

More recent reviews here (e.g. Butzer et al., 2012) and Middleton, 2017) now argue that whilst overpopulation, unsustainable land usage and climate change may all have been possible contributory factors, each example of 'societal collapse' needs examining within its own particular context to see whether and to what extent macro-, regional and local factors played significant parts. This is the kind of approach that Fagan (2005) took when examining the collapse of the Mayan civilization, suggesting that climate change was but one of a number of contributory ecological, political and sociological factors. This need for such contextualization applies strongly to sustainability issues today, as lack of access to sufficient resources by expanding populations remains a constant threat to their sustainability, and damaging climate events might well exacerbate such problems. Other contextual factors, such as the degree of resilience within a society (Scheffler, 2016; Downey et al., 2016), might, however, prevent such collapse. Once more, then, historic and prehistoric events remind us that if we fail to recognize the re-occurrence of the same dangers in the present, problems of sustainability now and in the future may well result, even as it needs remembering that the severity of the problem may vary from context to context.

Conclusion: Implications from the deep past and from covert interpretations of the deep past

This chapter has described a number of macro-threats in the deep past in order to examine their relevance today and has then argued that because humanity is the only species on the planet capable of addressing these current threats, educational leaders need to see planetary stewardship as a new and critical part of their role. A strong appreciation of the causation of such past events could then provide educational leaders with a much greater awareness of potential future threats. The history of the human race, and particularly the development of its civilizations, so often presented as a series of beneficial advances, then needs painting in more nuanced – perhaps darker – tones. Historical perspectives which depict an inevitable and upward growth of societies do future generations few favours if they fail to point out the problems that accompanied such developments and which still threaten societies today. The problems stemming from demands for increased growth, reduced resilience and the interdependencies and complexities which grow with the expansion of social, political and economic structures suggest that educational leaders need to equip their students with understandings of the near future which incorporate the recurring problems of humanity's past, as well as the values, structures and actions which sustain their societies. After only about 300,000 years of existence, we are already beginning to discuss the possibility of our own extinction. It is often said that those who cannot remember the past are condemned to repeat it. Whilst exact repetition is unlikely, for temporal and geographical contexts can make huge differences to actual outcomes, nevertheless the causes and the threats still exist, and need to be intelligently applied to present situations. But if one requires a reason for looking into humanity's deep past, this is a most pressing and important one for re-framing the leadership role.

However, the steward leadership role is not only about preparing future generations for the forthcoming challenges of climate change. It is also essential in providing students with a critical awareness of the assumptions that others use when making claims, for within such claims can be embedded dangerous values and feelings which, if then swallowed uncritically by the unaware, may lead to highly damaging outcomes. I then want to finish this chapter with a final example of issues from the deep past, but this instance is concerned not with what has been discovered about the deep past, but about how such discoveries have been interpreted. Thus, over the last decade, explorations for early *Homo sapiens* remains – from well before 40,000 years ago – have led to some astonishing discoveries not only about such primitive *Homo sapiens* but about other hominids as well. Indeed, as researchers like Higham (2021) and Wragg Sykes (2021) have shown, we not only inhabited this world for many tens of thousands of years with other hominids – Neanderthals, Denisovans, *Homo Naledi*, *Homo Luzonensis* and *Homo Floriensis* – but we also evolved from the same ancestors as Neanderthals and Denisovans. Most spectacularly, though there is now very solid evidence that *Homo sapiens* not only mated with these other two streams of hominid but also produced offspring which survived. We then need to begin to think of these and ourselves as belonging to the same species, for as Wragg Sykes (2021, p. 356) argues,

> Biologically speaking, individuals who can mate and create viable offspring are the same species.

This explains why it is now realized that most modern human beings contain small percentages of either Neanderthal or Denisovan DNA in their genes, and the accumulating evidence on their intelligence, resilience and adaptability is now comparable to the attributes of early *Homo sapiens*. This calls for a radical re-evaluation of what 'being human' amounts to. As Higham (2021, p. 233) says,

> We humans have always thought of ourselves as unique: it turns out that in evolutionary time this uniqueness did not exist until yesterday.

Feelings of loss of kindred may then begin to replace a very different picture of how we have viewed prehistoric others, and particularly Neanderthals, who since the first discovery of their remains in Germany in 1856 have been described and used as detailing a hierarchy in which present white Western males came top. As Wragg Sykes (2021, p. 368) points out, 'Right from the start' the interpretation of the accumulated data on Neanderthal remains has been one where 'Neanderthals were embedded in justifications for white racial supremacy.'

Early depictions of the limited intelligence of past and present hunter-gatherers have already been described in the chapter, and interpretations of Neanderthals follow much the same line in assigning to them the same savage, stupid and animalistic behaviours, in so doing justifying both slavery and colonialism. A final point in this supremacist argument was very simple: these other evolutionary strands had died out, whilst *Homo sapiens* had survived, and one particular race, white and Western in nature, now dominated the globe. Interpretations of such early palaeo-anthropological findings were then co-opted into much more recent justifications of racial superiority. The use of such covert assumptions has not disappeared: in the next chapter, we shall see how the same kind of currents run through many present-day populist themes in the political arena, themes which also attempt to undermine critical rationality by foisting unexamined and hidden assumptions upon populations. The critical recognition of how this has happened many times before in the interpretation of the past and the deep past is then another essential quality which educational leaders urgently need to cultivate in their role.

6

Educational Leadership in an Uncertain Political Future

Introduction

This chapter examines the most likely political settlements over the next two to three decades to see not only how these might impact on education and educational leadership but what kinds of responses are needed to them. This analysis travels back a number of decades in order to explain how the expansion of a globalized politics and a dominance of economic narratives – particularly that of neoliberalism – have come about in many democracies, and argues that the neoliberal approach to governance and the general dominance of economic thinking have been damaging in both economically developed and developing nations. Job *in*security has become a reality in many nations, even as their political elites either have seemed unaware of such impacts on their fellow citizens or have simply declared that there is no alternative to such movement. Disgruntled populations have then found that global market forces, underpinned by an economic ideology, have removed their work, and they therefore have become open to the siren calls of populist politicians promising to rebuild job markets at home through greater economic protectionism and to reassert workers' self-respect in making the country great again. Populist leaderships have then presented new challenges in many countries, for whilst some of these have identified real democratic deficits in the neglect of some sections of the electorate, such movements have also begun to threaten the bases of democratic processes and institutions. This chapter then argues that if a first narrative contributing to a political future has been that of a dominant economic view of society, a second has been that of populism as a response to its failures. There is, however, a third narrative which needs adding to this list, a social communitarian response, and whilst part of its genesis, like populism, stems from the failings of dominant economic viewpoints, it has also been prominent in responses to Covid-19, as different sectors of society have contributed to combatting this virus by their personal sacrifices.

However, these three political narratives need placing within a complex and fast-changing global context, where both uncertainty and unpredictability have increased, as have the number of 'wicked' problems arising. In unstable contexts many people have sought for greater certainty and reliability, even as others have become concerned that we may be moving into a 'post-truth' age (Snyder, 2017), where the use of democratic processes of critique, evidence and rational argument is neglected, and foundations are being laid for a non-questioning authoritarian fascism. This chapter then discusses these three possible types of future governance – the neoliberal and economically dominant, the populist, and the social communitarian, within contexts wishing for greater certainty in an uncertain world, which impacts not only upon economic and political agendas but upon the nature of education and educational leadership as well, and to which, this chapter argues, educational leaders need to proactively respond by creating a thinking space which nurtures both democracy and environmental sustainability.

Power groupings in an emerging macro-terrain

Nation-states are but one form of macro-power grouping, the other principal ones being global-level and regional-level institutions, and multinational corporations. Now at the turn of this century the political world seemed to be changing from one of nation-state dominance to one where forces both above and beneath the level of the nation-state were challenging its pre-eminence whilst also changing the demands placed upon educational leaders (Bottery, 2003a, 2006). One change was the expansion of supranational institutional power, which was drawing power upwards to bodies like the UN and to internationally competitive groupings like the EU or NAFTA. At the same time, there was a leaking of power outwards to multinational corporations, who had the advantage of not being bound by any geographical location. Finally, power was also moving downwards to subnational levels, as people sought greater personal meaning from smaller bodies. This, it was argued, was leading to a decline in the nation-state's ability to retain the undivided loyalty of its citizens (Bottery, 2003b), as Heater (2004) suggested that this was leading towards a 'nesting' of citizenship loyalties at subnational, national, regional and global levels. Finally, and also weakening nation-state power, was the neoliberal idea that nation-state citizenship was in reality a business strategy, offered by countries to individuals, in a variety of forms, in exchange for their loyalty to the nation-state. Advocates like Davidson and Rees-Mogg (1999) then argued that citizenship was only a market relationship, and so individuals should 'shop around' for the best citizenship 'deal'. The influence of such trends was so strong at the time that writers like Ohmae (2006) could argue that 'The End of the Nation State' was not far away.

Nearly twenty years on, the same global players remain, but with some surprising changes in status. Nation-states remain firmly on this macro-terrain, though individual differences are now much clearer: those with imperialist ambitions, like the United States, China and Russia, exercise power beyond their geographic location, and not only dominate countries and cultures geographically proximate but also generate influence well beyond their borders through political, military, financial and 'soft' cultural power (Nye, 2002). Less powerful nation-states, experiencing a reduction in their power, have ceded some of their sovereignty to larger international groupings like the EU or NAFTA. The UK's withdrawal from the EU in late 2020 then raises interesting questions about the future of greater national self-determination versus potentially reduced international influence, and whether nations asserting such independence will be sufficiently powerful to thrive against larger groupings of nation-states.

A second macro-grouping, that of global-level institutions, was created in the twentieth and twenty-first centuries in attempts by more powerful nation-states to jointly manage international and global problems. A significant weakness in these institutions has lain in that most of their funding has come from nation-state payments, with the United States usually paying the lion's share. Currently, for example, the United States pays 22 per cent of the cost of running the UN, whilst China, the next highest contributor, pays just 12 per cent. Some of these institutions are primarily political, like the United Nations; some economic, like the World Bank, the International Monetary Fund and the World Trade Organization; and some humanitarian, like the World Health Organization and the United Nations Children's Fund. Such institutions, in part designed to help nation-states take collaborative action on problems, have in reality often been relatively ineffective as their funders have refused to cooperate on many issues. In the UN, for instance, many resolutions condemning atrocities by nation-state regimes on cultural minorities have been rendered impotent by vetoes from their superpower backers. There have also been international groupings, like the EU and NATO, created to compete with other economic, political or military groupings, like NAFTA and the now-defunct Warsaw Pact, which have also resulted in the ceding of national power, as larger nation-states have steered the actions of smaller ones, or as noted nation-states have located themselves within larger bodies in order to be part of a grouping at the top table in global power and trading disputes.

The third macro-grouping, multinational corporations, have existed for hundreds of years, and have influenced nation-state policy for all that time. Present-day members sometimes have higher annual revenues than mid-sized nation-states (Walmart, for instance, had higher revenues in 2016 than either Spain or Australia), but the nine largest annual revenues in 2021 currently remain those of nation-states. Nevertheless, such corporations have much greater flexibility than nation-states, and relocate their activities to suit their business interests, thus putting pressure on nation-states to retain their involvement. Multinational corporations have expanded their influence and profits, for two main reasons. One is that in an 'Age of Access' (Rifkin, 2000), huge profits can be made by facilitating better person-to-person communication, and access to online consumer experiences, and companies like Apple (in 2021, having a net worth $2 trillion), Microsoft ($1 trillion) and Amazon ($1.7 trillion) have been extremely successful here. Second, these companies have benefitted hugely from the Covid-19 outbreak, as more business, social communication and consumerism have needed conducting online. In then becoming trillion-dollar companies, they have often been able to dictate to nation-states the types of production and worker skills they want if they are to continue to locate workplaces within a country, as well as avoiding taxation by locating their bases in tax havens like the Cayman Islands, Luxembourg and Gibraltar. However, in June 2021, the powerful G7 nation-states, in a clear move to exercise greater control over such corporations, have agreed on joint action for a global tax on such companies, currently suggested at 15 per cent. This still has some considerable way to go to full realization but fits well with the argument that the nation-state has not died and indeed has been rejuvenated over the last two decades. With this power play in mind, it will be very interesting to watch such developments.

New challenges in changing times

So these macro-groupings still exist, but, as already noted, times have changed. The promises of globalization, following the collapse of the Soviet Union in 1989, led the US commentator Fukuyama (1991) to argue that history had ended and that a particular kind of political governance – unsurprisingly perhaps closely resembling American liberal capitalist democracy – would now be the only viable form of governance globally. All nations, he hubristically argued, would reject authoritarian regimes and instead embrace a citizenship celebrating individual freedom and consumerism, as global free markets furthered international competition and economic growth. However, the events of 9/11 scotched the idea of a lack of oppositional ideologies, whilst the global financial crisis of 2007–8 demonstrated that neoliberal capitalism, largely unrestrained by nation-states, might further the interests of international banking corporations and wealthier members of nation-states, but it was the taxes of the average citizen in these nation-states which would be needed to bail out their failures. 'Too big to fail' – a situation accepted by many traditional political parties – angered the many who had had to pay for this debacle and led to short-lived movements like 'Occupy Wall Street', but left deeper and longer-lasting sources of grievance for populist leaders to exploit.

Moreover, as societies – and their educational institutions – were infused with neoliberal practices and assumptions of individual, institutional and national competition, so a politics was neglected which supported communities caring as much for the less gifted as for the best equipped in a race for life. Public sector educational leaders were increasingly selected for their entrepreneurial abilities, to run their institutions like businesses, employing marketing strategies to sell their schools to parent consumers in competition with similar institutions, their failure and success being calculated by examination, test results and the rising or declining numbers of children at their schools. In the process, primary social values like trust and care were eroded, or were reduced to second-order values: Fukuyama (1996), for instance, argued that economic growth was aided by strong trusting relationships in society, implying that this was the principal reason for the cultivation of such trust.

Now whilst neoliberal governments steered institutions into competing in educational marketplaces, centre-right parties and political leaders like Clinton and Blair accommodated to such ideological dominance, only adjusting their educational policies to promise that all candidates would begin the race for life at the same start line – and hence Blair's trumpeting of 'Education, Education, Education' as the principal means by which this would be achieved. Yet such promises very largely failed to change the economic, social and political reality: those lucky enough to be born with the right attributes, and into the right families, would continue to have the best chances of success, and those from impoverished contexts, with lesser abilities, or poor parenting, would very likely remain the losers. Moreover, as Young (1956) argued over half a century ago, and as developed more recently by Sandel (2020), such a meritocratic approach attributed success to an individual's personal effort and not to the luck provided by genetic endowment, parentage and its income or general context. The result, as Piff et al. (2018) demonstrate, is that many individuals who succeed come to believe that they are personally entitled to such rewards, disregarding not only the large slice of luck given to them but also the plight – and the resentment – of the losers. Market and meritocratic arguments then combined to suggest that those who lost their jobs, or failed to climb the social mobility ladder, had only themselves to blame: it was then their fault that they were society's losers.

One extra piece of this societal jigsaw now needs adding. This is the hugely impactful work of Piketty (2017) who argued that the negative consequences of much neoliberal policy is in actual fact mostly the consequence of the current workings of capitalism, as societies in this century have entered a period in time when those with wealth are able to generate more return from the interest on their capital than those with lower incomes can gain from any economic growth in their country. When this happens, the income and wealth of the rich inevitably grow faster than the income of poorer sections of society, and the gap between them keeps on increasing. As importantly, Kaufman and Stutzle (2017) point out that meritocratic education may cease to have the intended effect of convincing those less well-off that they can join the ranks of the wealthy by talent and hard work, as this ceases to be plausible the more that the wealth gap increases through inheritance rather than work. Real antagonism may then be created between these social classes and Piketty (2017) urges for greater taxation of the wealthy to reduce this gap, not because of moral outrage at such inequity but rather because of the need to bolster capitalism's sustainability. As Kaufman and Stutzle (2017, p. 58) suggest, 'he wants to protect capitalism from the poor – not the other way around.'

In many societies, then, a political time bomb has been set running. Globalized neoliberal economics has led to traditional jobs in richer countries being moved elsewhere; capital accumulation through inheritance has led to an increasing gap between the rich and the poor, and the argument for meritocracy may no longer convince if however hard you work, you are never going to reach the top. So, as the more fortunate enjoy capital accumulation and a globe-trotting existence but fail to see that others' lack of success has a great deal to do with their own good fortune, then bitterness rises. At the same time, traditional political parties which had historically drawn on the support of both blue-collar and white-collar bases have now begun to lose sizeable chunks of these previously loyal electorates.

Instead, the grievances of the dispossessed, the resentful and the dangerously angry were noted and exploited by politicians more in tune with – or adept at exploiting – such resentment.

Enter Covid-19

This was the complex, uncertain and worrying global political background that existed when Covid-19 arrived in 2020. It was a shock to many then when almost immediately, nation-states took on the financial and political responsibility for dealing with the virus, borrowing hugely, bailing out businesses with grants or loans, and underwriting the furloughing of large numbers of workers. Such policies continued well into 2021, at the same time as new waves and variants of the disease appeared in places like the UK, South Africa, India and Brazil. Such state actions were remarkable in that they were diametrically opposed to much dominant economic wisdom, which argued that that nation-states needed 'hollowing-out' (Rhodes, 1994), their only function being to oversee the proper workings of internal markets. Perhaps then *the* political consequence of Covid-19 was to demonstrate that nation-states as forces on the global stage not only were very much alive but were the undisputed level of governance for dealing with this global crisis – and potentially for dealing with many others as well.

However, the domestic reaction within many nation-states to this emergency was just as surprising and important. Neoliberal thought and practice had long argued that public sector institutions were not only inefficient, and threats to individual freedom (Hayek, 1944; Friedman, 1962), but also sinecures for public sector professionals exercising 'occupational closure' in their practice (Collins, 1990). Remarkably, then, the response to Covid-19 was the reassertion in many countries of the need for a strong public sector and of genuine public admiration for the many healthcare and education workers, who gave of their time, effort and sometimes their lives, in caring for victims.

Yet whilst these actions renewed appreciation for public sector practice, considerable gratitude was also expressed for workers in the private sector, as the efforts of delivery drivers, cleaners and supermarket staff were also recognized and highly praised. Societal appreciation of those most exposed to the disease then transcended any public/private sector debate and began to focus instead on the contribution of the most poorly paid in both. As public/private concerns were replaced as a political debate by rich/poor issues, questions were raised about national income distribution, and what Sandel (2020) described as an occupation's 'contributory good' – the degree to which different kinds of work contribute to public welfare. The Covid-19 outbreak then highlighted the fact that those who were paid the least on many occasions contributed the most to their society's welfare, which then raised the question: should societies, proclaiming belief in fairness and justice, consider a redistribution of monetary rewards, judged by what an occupation contributes to that society's sustainability?

The experience of the virus then produced some unexpected responses. One was a movement away from a more globalized world, and towards the recognition that nation-states were the principal actors dealing with the pandemic. It also fore-fronted a much greater appreciation of how belief in social cooperation and the notion of shared public goods were key elements in sustaining societies in combatting the virus, once more demonstrating how limited were neoliberal beliefs in the pre-eminence of self-interest and competition as drivers of social action.

However, another response was more covert and more discordant, for in dealing with Covid-19, governments needed to balance a number of demands. The most difficult was probably that of keeping people socially distanced or isolated whilst also maintaining economic functioning and keeping people working, which often reduced or abolished such distancing. This, it quickly became clear, was not a 'tame' problem easily resolved but a constantly changing wicked one. The result in many countries then was often a series of difficult, and sometimes confused, political decisions. Covid-19 then was a strong example of a 'wicked' problem in that:

1. There were no definitive set of rules for governments to use in combatting the disease when it first appeared.
2. There was a number of ways of understanding its threat – including denying that there was a threat.
3. There was considerable uncertainty as to whether actions taken would actually solve the threat addressed.
4. Attempted solutions of one part of the threat could create problems in another part: for instance, as social isolation began to cause mental health problems, actions to allow greater social mixing to reduce this problem could lead to a resurgence of the virus.

At the outset then governments were unable to provide 'silver bullet' solutions to eliminate the threat, the best responses often being 'silver buckshot' solutions – ones in which a combination of actions was attempted, in the hope that the threat would at least be slowed down or ameliorated. However, whilst 'silver buckshot' is often the best response, politicians, the media and the general public tended to possess a rather 'tame' belief in what needed doing. Sometimes this was betrayed in the language used, as, for example, when political leaders talked of 'roadmaps' as the way out of the crisis, then suggesting that they knew how events would develop, even though the progress of the virus was highly unpredictable. The development of vaccines was seen by many in similarly tame terms, but this was still no silver bullet solution, as the virus mutated, and a number of variants of Covid-19 appeared in 2020 and 2021, some increasing the speed of spread, others more resistant to existing vaccines. Few outside of expert circles understood that the relationship between virus and vaccine is a lethal dance, where the vaccine is designed to suppress the virus, even as new strains of the virus are selected to avoid the vaccine's actions. There is then no gold-plated guarantees of solution here, even if progress can be made in better understanding and responding to the threat.

So whilst much of the experience of Covid-19 has consisted of wicked problems, a fair amount of global political behaviour consisted of presenting tame conceptions of the problem and therefore of similarly tame solutions. In a 24/7 sound-bite world, attempts to fully explain the complexities of the problem were being provided to audiences conditioned to quick and snappy answers. The appeal of simpler, more confident and more certain approaches to frightened electorates should not then be underestimated, as the cultural belief that most problems and solutions are essentially tame in nature creates the very real danger that the depth and complexity of a problem are not fully appreciated or addressed, and when tame solutions are then used but fail to deliver, the opportunity arises for new political players to promise more certainty.

In addition to the problem of tame beliefs, there were also significant minorities in many countries which refused to believe in the disease's existence and therefore of the need to take precautions against it. This was one more symptom of a growing loss of trust in many governments and other major societal institutions, as a particular breed of political commentators branded much mainstream news as 'fake news', with the consequent generation of a relativism of facts and falsities. Rush Limbaugh, a right-wing US broadcaster, for example, described the government, academia, science and the media as 'the four corners of deceit' (Stanley, 2020, p. 52). By 2020–1 such a poisonous atmosphere had been created in some countries that a significant minority of these populations were no longer searching for evidence and critiquing arguments to distinguish between different claims. Instead, a largely unrestrained and unpoliced internet and social media facilitated the broadcasting of large numbers of conspiracy theories, endorsed by populist leaders who derided traditional political parties, experts and mainstream media, and spoke of their aspirations for a nation free from such malign influences. Such claims can be alluring to the confused, and dangerous to democracies when they dismiss the idea that complex explanations are often needed to properly understand wicked problems and solutions, and try to replace these with the false certainties of populism. This background needs keeping in mind as we move to examine the principal forms of political response to current – and potentially many future problems. The responses examined are then (i) the economically dominant neoliberal state; (ii) the siren calls of the populist state; (iii) a reinvigorated social communitarian state. We can then better see what each position implies for societal and educational futures.

The neoliberal state

Some of the major elements of neoliberal theory and practice, the dominant narrative of most governments over the last fifty years, have already been addressed. However before examining neoliberalism specifically, it is important to note that it is the prime example of an ideological approach which prioritizes economic issues over all others. This is important because in so doing, it de-emphasizes other concerns that should have much greater priority. If one considers three areas for possible priority – economic theory and practice, social functioning and environmental health – it could be argued (Bottery, 2016) not only that economic theory and practice are much narrower in scope than social functioning, but that such practice also depends upon the resilience of societal values like promise-keeping and trust if it is to remain sustainable. Moreover, if social values and functioning are themselves to be maintained, then they will ultimately depend on a healthy natural environment. In other words, there is very good reason to argue that current priority of economic activity over social and environmental maintenance needs radical reversal. Undue emphasis upon economic activity can lead to the use of heavily criticized measures of societal well-being like that of GDP, rather than wider and more inclusive terms (Hamilton, 2004). It can also lead to extensive environmental destruction for short-term economic growth and consumption, producing many of the problems encountered today. Neoliberalism then is an example of an economically dominant ideology leading to highly damaging myopic views of human, societal and environmental functioning.

The dominance of neoliberal thought has been aided by the influence of international bodies like the International Monetary Fund, the World Bank and the World Trade Organization. These, predominantly funded by the United States, have normally made the adoption of neoliberal economic policies and practices the condition for the granting of loans to countries in financial difficulties and thereby have made this ideology a truly global influence. Now whilst there are different versions of neoliberal governance, they very largely hold to policies of free trade at national and global levels, and therefore to greater privatization, government deregulation and reductions in government spending. Newly elected neoliberal governments have sometimes then exercised a surprising degree of state power in order to enforce compliance to marketizing legislation. Educational institutions, for instance, have been steered into competition with one another, their success or failure determined by performance in this market. In so doing, their curriculum and management, as well as the mentality of both pupils and staff, are steered to embrace new competitive ways of thinking, and to employ charismatic individuals, acting as both director and entrepreneur, in leading others in competing against other such 'businesses'.

In reality, few nation-states have come close to being fully transformed by this vision: many of their citizens have stubbornly held onto the values of previous practice, such as cooperation, concern for others' welfare and the belief that many prized items and activities, such as the value of a life, and of feelings of well-being, cannot – and should not – be thought of and expressed primarily in monetary terms. Whilst an entrepreneurial model of leadership is sought under neoliberal governance, many principals do not uncritically embrace such change, and resist seeing traditional educational values as subservient to overarching corporate goals in a competitive environment. Instead, a whole spectrum of defensive attitudes may be employed, which, as one headteacher described to the current author (Bottery, 1998, p. 24), ranged all the way from 'defy' through 'subvert' to 'ignore', on to 'ridicule', then to 'wait and see', to 'test' and, in some very exceptional cases, to 'embrace'. So whilst 'professionalism' has had a very critical literature over the last few decades, at bottom it incorporates not only notions of an expertise others do not share but also a commitment to a set of ethics to be held to and practised, regardless of social or political pressures. With education, these almost invariably include notions of care, personal development and critique – notions which do not always sit comfortably in heavily neoliberal contexts.

Indeed, whilst the hollowing-out of state power may be a principal neoliberal objective, there have often been occasions when such state powers have been used to enforce policies emanating from this ideology. Moreover, global markets can not only lead to the destruction of nationally located workplaces, as jobs are outsourced to cheaper locations, but they can also increase, rather than reduce, societal inequalities. Global-wide competition, allied to multinational strategies, has then led to major winners and losers within and between nation-states. Moreover, as Picketty (2017) argues, when the rate of return on capital is greater than that for economic growth, then wealth can become so concentrated in the hands of the few that not only will inequality increase but so very likely will social and economic instability. Finally, the work of Wilkinson and Pickett (2009, 2019) demonstrates that such inequality affects the well-being of both the poor *and* the rich in highly unequal societies much more than it does in more equal ones.

The result of these growing reservations about the underpinning assumptions of this ideology, when allied to a lack of respect and trust in traditional political elites, has generated strong resentment by those suffering under such political and economic regimes, which becomes all the more understandable if mainstream political parties then struggle to find policies to address the consequences of such inequality and diminished well-being. In such circumstances it is not that surprising that there has been a rise in the attractiveness of a very different political and economic agenda, as populist leaders have recognized the existence of large numbers of an electorate whose complaints have fallen on deaf ears, whose wishes have not been responded to.

The populist state

'Populism' is an increasingly used and discussed term, but there tends to be a significant lack of clarity in defining what it means. There are a number of reasons for this. One is that 'populism' is a 'thin' word (Mudde and Kaltwasser, 2017), which basically suggests a popular response to social, economic and political conditions. However, 'responses' need attaching to particular concerns, and these can be very different in kind (e.g. left- or right-leaning, green or cultural). The word can then be attributed to a variety of different political positions. A second reason is the fine dividing line between 'popular' and 'populist', with the former simply describing a position held by many in a population, whilst the latter has become attached to a movement probably less numerous, but more organized, and probably more dangerous. So a final reason is that the term is often conflated with extreme positions, where populist responses to policies or ruling parties develop into a series of violent and threatening actions. When this happens, populism may then be attached to anti-democratic movements, and some mainstream parties may encourage the conflation of populism with violence, in order to 'fix' this attribute in the minds of their electorate, in an attempt to discredit populist critiques of their party's policies and actions.

So it is important to be clear: forms of populism which energize the critique of existing policies and vocalize new issues can be a vital part of democratic functioning. This can clearly be uncomfortable for many traditional parties, if populist critiques focus on issues they have neglected. Indeed, whilst some parties may come into existence in order to protect an elite's wealth and power, many others begin as movements which begin as external critics of traditional parties, but then gain representation within the electoral system, and find that their concerns begin to be accommodated within the policies of other parties, and ultimately they may gain sufficient electoral support to have a direct say in the nation's governance.

Eatwell and Goodwin (2018) suggest that the majority of current populist movements in Western democracies then reflect some or all of following four concerns:

1. An increasing belief by many citizens that the political elite in their society do not respect or take into account their concerns and grievances.
2. An accentuation of such distrust when nation-based jobs disappear through globalized economics; this results in a decline in many workers' income, not only compared to wages in previous decades but also compared to the current wealth of the more affluent in their society.
3. The fear that their traditional national culture and identity are being eroded as immigration increases the influence of other cultures within that society.
4. That because traditional parties no longer reflect their concerns, political culture fragments, voters rapidly change allegiances and new parties suddenly rise to prominence, creating, for some at least, a highly uncertain and threatening political climate.

Now politicians of traditional parties may not welcome or even respect the basis for some of these protests: to be told that they don't care for or understand the problems of the 'ordinary' worker may not be something they want to hear. Many may also believe that there is no alternative to job loss through globalization. In addition, fears over loss of national and cultural identity have been noted by some (e.g. Huntingdon, 2004, in the United States), but often such concerns are dismissed as racist in nature and therefore worth condemning, but not worth debating. Finally, in more extreme cases, populist movements may be described by mainstream parties as anti-intellectual, irrational and emotional, and there is good evidence that some movements deliberately favour this direction. This is the point of Stanley's (2020) analysis of the rise of extreme right-wing parties in Europe, and particularly of Nazism, in the first half of the twentieth century. In addition, Snyder's (2017) work on Fascism in the modern world and Temulkuran's (2019) description of Erdogan's transformation of democracy in Turkey to authoritarian rule make much the same point. Stanley (2020) argues that the rise of the Nazis was caused by a combination of national economic problems, political instability and the widespread belief that former national greatness had been stolen by both internal and external enemies. This kind of narrative is very much alive today, as populist leaders like Trump have claimed that the economically comfortable have embraced and profited from global change, but have paid little attention to the plight of those losing their jobs and their self-respect because of such changes. Certainly, giving voice to such discontent does not of itself constitute a major threat to democracies, particularly if traditional parties then pay greater attention to the problems of disgruntled voters. However, if they fail to address the bases of such problems, they leave the gate open to movements with more extreme policies, and then democratic processes and institutions may be used to gain power, only then being abolished. As Goebbels said almost a century ago, 'one of the best jokes of democracy [is] that it gave its deadly enemies the means by which it was destroyed' (in Stanley, 2020, p. 32).

When populist movements develop down non-rationalist lines, they tend to invoke conspiracy theories about the intentions, morals and actions of those 'others' who they blame for the nation's problems. Such attacks may be based on unsubstantiated claims or bald lies, but such accusations can be highly attractive to an audience wanting to find people to blame for their current predicament. Some of the tactics of fascist parties in the 1930s are now echoed in the tactics of populist leaders like Trump in the United States, Putin in Russia, Erdogan in Turkey, Duda in Poland, Bolsonaro in Brazil and Modi in India, and are normally contextualized variations of the following strategies:

First, a narrative is created in which the nation is described as formerly being a great power, and by selecting supporting narratives, and misrepresenting others, they produce what is essentially a mythic history of the nation, which they claim can only be restored by rejecting and then excluding from power those responsible for such decline. Such 'others' may be immigrants, people of different colour or culture, or liberal plurally minded politicians; but whoever they are, they are described as needing to be separated from the 'real people', that is, those who support the leader (them) and the party. Donald Trump use of the phrase 'America First' at his inaugural address, then recalled the name and intentions of the America First Movement of the 1920s and 1930s which celebrated the past 'glories' of a White Supremacist slave-owning America, of which he and others would have been strongly aware.

Such leaders also tend to describe their core base – normally those who have lost out or have been dispossessed – as law-abiding and hardworking, in contrast to the 'others' who are described as undermining traditional values and so weakening the nation. Core supporters then are supported in being 'righteously' angry with these 'others' and so legitimate the leader in taking the aggressive steps necessary to prevent these others from subverting the nation's greatness.

The leader's core support will then engage in what Uslaner (2002) called a 'thick trust', which binds together the like-minded, but which doesn't extend to a 'thin trust' which reaches out to other groups in an attempt to create a set of shared values. 'Thick trust' is then seen as the basis for the claim of holding the kind of values that will make the nation strong once more. These usually include a respect for 'natural' hierarchies in society, particularly with respect to hierarchical differences between male and female, old and young, leader and followers, and white and others – or whatever is the majority skin colour. These 'others' will then be excluded from the nation's governance, as followers become emotionally committed to the will and policies of their leader, rather than indulging in weak liberal negotiations. The leader's aim then is not to appeal to the intellect of the core base, but rather to sway its will, and, as Snyder (2017, p. 18) argues, for this base to ultimately develop an 'anticipatory obedience' to him (and it is normally a 'him'), who therefore sets the course, direction and aims of national policy, which followers are to embrace and implement without questioning the message.

Under such populist leadership, education systems are then steered into celebrating this mythic national past, and students are indoctrinated into its recreation, in much the same manner as happened in Nazi Germany (see Sunker and Otto, 1997, on this). The educator's role is based on conforming to the hierarchical implementation of this vision, primarily via repetition and emotion rather than rationality and criticality, whilst any teachers who refuse this role are branded as disloyal and are very likely to be dismissed, as has already happened in contemporary Poland and Hungary.

Educational leaders in democratic states should then have a number of other reasons, apart from losing their jobs, for being concerned about such populist directions. First, because populist approaches are based more often on raising emotions than on cultivating a respect for rationality and evidence, contentious issues and questionable claims are likely to remain unexamined, with notions of 'truth' and 'falsity' being based on political authority rather than through discussion, critique and argument. Under extreme variations of populism, educational purposes will be focused on moulding students into acquiescing to the will of the leader, and 'knowledge' will come to mean that which is approved by this leader, and couched in absolutist and indisputable terms, rather than being critiqued on the basis of the best evidence available, and thus permitting the possibility of change if new evidence and argument are produced.

At the same time, problems and issues will very likely be described in tame, propagandist language rather than in more nuanced and informed terms; for ultimately, if critical education, expertise and the use of sophisticated language can be devalued and despised, intelligent debate becomes much more difficult. Leaders are then able to tell populations whether there is a problem and what the problem is, and threats like Covid-19 can be derisively dismissed until such time as its effects become so serious that other explanations need to be rolled out. Ultimately, citizens are then reduced to compliant followers, and in so doing, Snyder (2017, p. 66) argues, 'you submit to tyranny when you renounce the difference between what you want to hear and what is actually the case' – between, then, the reality of current uncertainties and the false certainties of populism.

Such movement may not gain dominance in resilient democracies, for many populist critiques are likely to be debated within a resiliently critical culture, and elements of a populist discourse may then be incorporated into normal political – and educational – thought and practice (Gutmann and Thompson, 1996). But two further issues of concern may arise. A first is that a minority, who only listen to what they want to hear, continue to protest and try to convert others. The second is that some leaders do push further, and, as Snyder (2017) argues, they often test how far they can go, and what they can get away with, and if sufficient resistance does not result, they are likely to push further still, and history demonstrates how quickly such actions can change the nature of a nation-state. No country or its citizens should then assume that 'it couldn't happen here', and no democracy is guaranteed sustainability just because it possesses democratic institutions and practices. Instead, democracy gains its sustainability through upholding fundamental values and practices, and educational institutions need to be key elements in any such defence, providing the intellectual tools to combat extremist narratives. Fascism then is not a new threat, and can appear covertly under other names; but it is a danger inherent in many populist approaches. In democracies, then, education systems and their leaders should see it as a core obligation for them to not only be aware of this potential threat but how they can build resilience and criticality to it.

The social communitarian state

The third and final form of potential governance, the 'social communitarian state', is proposed as a possible political future, on the basis of developments in a number of liberal democracies. It proposes a more cooperative version of society than an economically individualist one, and a more pluralist and inclusive version than a populist one. If neoliberalism is premised on the necessity of economic competition by self-interested individuals, and populism is based on the concerns of a neglected set of interests, the social communitarian state is based on the notions of greater cooperation, the reality of a public good and a fuller appreciation of how people's work can contribute to societal sustainability. Social communitarian responses therefore in part look back to a period before and following the Second World War when government intervention into economic and social affairs was seen as essential to social progress. However, whilst such Keynesian economics and strongly interventionist governments were largely sidelined from the early 1970s, a number of recent events suggest the possibility of a reframing of such aspirations. This belief is based on four different arguments.

1. **The 'thinness' of current economic policies:** As noted earlier, such 'thinness' led to major criticisms of measures of what constitutes the 'wealth' of a nation-state, which for some considerable time has been based on a formulation of GDP (gross domestic product) which essentially measures the total value of all goods and services which a society produces. Yet as far back as 1968, Robert Kennedy argued that GDP

    > measures neither our wit nor our courage, neither our wisdom nor our learning, neither our compassion nor our devotion to our country. . . . It measures everything in short, except that which makes life worthwhile.

Kennedy's speech was later lifted virtually word for word by David Cameron, the English prime minister (2006), demonstrating how widespread was the interest in national wealth being based on more expansive notions of personal and societal well-being (and see Hamilton, 2004; Jackson, 2021). Such sentiments may have begun with individual and pressure group criticism, but they have now moved much closer to the mainstream of political thought, being expressed by the Sarkozy commission of 2009 and most recently in 2019 by the New Zealand government. The argument that a more sustainable society is not only more egalitarian but also one in which a fulfilling life differs from and greatly exceeds 'thin' economic wealth is now a mainstream political argument.

2. **The return of the interventionist state:** This resulted, against neoliberal wisdom, from the financial crisis of 2007–8 being largely resolved by nation-states bailing out financial institutions; and when Covid-19 appeared early in 2020, it was once again the nation-state which moved to slow down the progress of the disease and provide businesses with financial support to keep them viable. If some had argued that there was no alternative to neoliberal 'hollowed-out state' economics, it was in fact the interventionist nation-state which confronted this crisis.

3. **A resurgence of communal values like cooperation and trust:** Other elements of the responses to Covid-19 suggested a resurgence of the communal and cooperative values central to earlier welfare states. One example was the remarkable display of solidarity and togetherness within communities, and the palpable public appreciation of those who risked their lives in dealing with Covid-19. Another was not only the strengthening of 'thick trust' mentioned earlier, between the many likeminded: societies were also reaching out beyond particular social and cultural groups to create large elements of the 'thin trust' which linked different communities and viewpoints together, and which directly opposed the 'us' and 'them' rhetoric of populist leaders. These kind of responses then suggest the possibility of a return to more communitarian societies and their governance, as communal attachments cease to be viewed – as neoliberal thought does – as

   > cannonballs chained to inmates legs . . . [but rather as] . . . the social fabric [which] sustains, nourishes, and enables individuality rather than diminishes it. (Etzioni, 1997, p. 27)

   The values of trust, cooperation and an equality of respect are then seen as central to a nation-state's sustainability and resilience, and education would play a key role in imparting such values and practice to future generations. As Grace (1994, p. 214) has argued, education could then be seen as an institutional form of public good which engaged in 'developing a moral sense, a sense of social and fraternal responsibility for others'.

4. **Support for a greater degree of income equalization.** Finally, the response to Covid-19 and its effects has not been an equal burden. Those in poorer households have suffered more than the wealthy, not only from the disease spreading more readily in cramped accommodation, but also from the stress caused by needing to continue working in order to pay their bills, whilst many of the more affluent have been able to save money during the crisis (Blundell et al., 2020). If one adds the inequalities exposed by Covid-19 to those inequalities generated through neoliberal policies, this could create added pressure on governments to consider a greater equalization of incomes. This is further strengthened by Sandal's (2019) argument that societies which support the values of fairness and justice should rethink the financial rewards that different societal occupations receive, in part judged by what they contribute to the public good of that society. One might also add that Picketty's (2017) arguments to sustain capitalism, if rather paradoxically, also support greater wealth redistribution.

So, if the calculating and self-interested values of neoliberalism were to be better balanced by values of cooperation, care and trust, this could facilitate the creation of social communitarian states which became the basis for political settlements drawing on greater communal effort in dealing with new and emerging challenges.

Nurturing a democratic space in a complex and uncertain world

Over the last couple of decades, global forces have profoundly affected nation-state policies, which in turn have affected the life and work of educational leaders, as their roles not only have become more fragmented by market pressures but are also increasingly controlled by nation-states co-opting their work into the state's response to such global competition. However, it seems highly unlikely that any of these narratives will dominate global or nation-state agendas in the near to middle future to the extent they have done. The future is likely to be more fragmented, and governance in democracies may well be a mixture of capitalist, populist and social communitarian narratives. This chapter then concludes by examining the contribution education and educational leaders in particular can make to this future.

The neoliberal capitalist narrative and belief in the fundamentally competitive nature of human beings are unlikely to disappear, and within education systems, variations on the economic curricular code described in Chapter 1 will continue. As important as this domestic picture is the international picture, which could be more concerning, because the continuation of a heavy emphasis on competitive economics would likely increase nation-state competition, rather than bringing them together to cooperate in solving global problems. As noted, Klare's (2012) *The Race for What's Left* international resource exploitation is aggressively alive and is beginning to focus on environmentally fragile polar regions. Moreover, in the roll-out of the Covid-19 vaccine in early 2021, the head of the World Health Organization warned of 'a catastrophic moral failure' if wealthier countries monopolized first use of vaccines at the expense of poorer countries in what has been called a 'vaccine nationalism'. The potential tragedy here is that most emerging global problems require international cooperation to resolve them. The replacement in 2021 of Trump by Biden as US president might contribute to a more positive picture, but much remains to be done.

Under governments reflecting or responding to strong populist narratives, the role of education would probably be strongly influenced by what a particular populist narrative focused upon. When such populism translates into more authoritarian forms of government, educators might find that an increasingly thin line may be drawn between education and indoctrination. Moreover, populist state policies on the environment are likely to be determined by the causes that gained them electoral attention. On the positive side, there does seem to be greater governmental attention to an increasingly concerned public of this need (Guardian, 28 January 2021), so perhaps such a beneficial populist agenda may grow.

Finally, whilst social communitarian narratives might reinvigorate the state in rebuilding a more resilient pluralist democracy, and may attempt to reduce the growing gap between the rich and the poor, they will likely be subjected to well-rehearsed criticisms from neoliberal populists of the dangers of the intrusive state, the abrogation of personal freedoms and the inefficiencies of non-market mechanisms. Yet on the positive side, the reassertion of social values like care, trust and cooperation within nation-states might also suggest that, at a time of global environmental threats, the practice of such values domestically needs reflecting beyond nation-state borders. This fits well with a social communitarian narrative arguing that economic systems depend upon sustainable social values, and these in their turn depend upon a sustainable global environment. The neoliberal narrative is then turned on its head, and an unusually optimistic, but still credible, future scenario for environmental sustainability could then be created.

Conclusions

Whatever future democratic governance scenarios look like, educational leadership can help preserve the kind of space necessary for ideas to be discussed critically and openly. Educational institutions then need to be framed and led as vital democratic spaces, nurturing five particular qualities: a *debating* space which focuses on better understanding current threats and issues; a *safe* space where different opinions are not only tolerated but also encouraged, as long as they permit the voicing of other opinions; a *critical* space in which the full use of evidence, logic and argument is deployed in examining each proposal to assess its validity; a space in which a *public good perspective* is developed, which looks beyond individual self-interest and seeks to develop strategies and systems which benefit the community as a whole. Finally, a *developmental* space for the education of future citizens and environmental stewards.

In so doing educational leaders can help nurture an essential regard for the wider environment but also educate minds and voices in sustaining a democratic spirit in that society. In an age of uncertainty, educational leaders need to demonstrate how individuals and societies can learn to live with this condition, rather than being seduced by the dangers of a false certainty.

7

Understanding and Preparing for Tipping Points

Introduction

Previous chapters have examined four influential, but under-recognized, covert processes: wicked issues, positive feedback, exponential growth and connectivity issues. The ultimate threat of all four derives from the probability that the systems within which they occur might be changed substantially by their impacts and then have such damaging effects upon human and wider system sustainability that a new irreversible state is created which is highly unsuitable for many existing life forms – including our own (Gunderson and Holling, 2002). The moment when this happens is usually described as a 'tipping point'. However, this term is used in many different ways and therefore we begin by discussing the term's origins and usage, before examining its potential effects with Covid-19, with the natural environment and with educational sustainability.

As already noted, tipping points can be the result of instances of both positive feedback and exponential growth, and because these processes are often under-recognized or underestimated in their influence, tipping points may then appear unexpectedly, only being identified when it is too late to avoid them. Some of the difficulty may be because they can also be the result of 'wicked' problems, where an understanding of what is happening is hindered by the complexity and interactions of the processes taking place. The development of a macro-stewardship element in an educational leader's role then needs to include an understanding, not only of the processes leading to tipping points but of the nature of tipping points themselves, which occur not only in the natural environment but also in many areas of social functioning, including education. This makes the stewardship element of an educational leadership role even more important.

'Tipping points': Origins, meanings and implications

The term 'tipping point' probably originated in the physical sciences, where it refers to that moment when extra weights are added to a balanced object until that object topples over. This core meaning – the addition of an extra element causing a sudden and major change in an existing state of affairs – prompted Grodzins (1957) to use the phrase in a sociological context, to suggest that an increase in the number of Black families in predominantly white neighbourhoods in the United States, upon the addition of extra numbers of such families, would, at a certain moment in time – the 'tipping point' – cause many white families to move out of the neighbourhood. Another variation has developed in environmental studies with respect to the growing awareness of climate change and global warming. Here, the use of the term has come to refer to particular thresholds, which, if exceeded, lead to large changes in a system, or even to the creation of an entirely new system. Lenton et al. (2008, p. 1786) then suggest that climate change tipping points are critical thresholds 'at which a tiny perturbation can qualitatively alter the state or development of a system'. Finally, whilst there is no agreed meaning on the term in the educational literature, it is often seen in negative terms as 'the straw that broke the camel's back' – where, for example, a fairly minor blow to a leader's morale causes the tipping point which firms up thoughts of early retirement.

However, and importantly, tipping points can be benign as well as malign: in educational terms, these might be little more than small acts of kindness or thoughtfulness that a leader makes to others (that's a lovely painting, Jenny ... thank you for sorting out the hall after the parents meeting, Lawrence. . .) which may be critical at that moment in changing someone's self-concept, or in encouraging future actions in unexpectedly significant ways. Educational leaders then need to remember to cultivate the small positive things, as well as the big ones in their relationships with others. Whether tipping points are viewed as malign or benign often depends, as with wicked issues, upon how such an event is viewed. So the physical tipping point of adding small extra weights to a balanced object until the object topples over is a description of a physical tipping point, but it is the perception of the implications of that event which determines whether the effect is viewed as malign or benign – or neither, if nothing significant happens because of it. Tipping points are then not only physical, chemical or biological events, but oftentimes have human judgements attached to them. As with the wicked example of the growth of dandelions in a garden, this is a biological event, but may be viewed as malign if it is seen as an undesirable weed. Similarly, Grodzin's (1957) example of 'white flight' could be viewed positively or negatively, depending on the views by an individual held about racial segregation. Finally, the notion of environmental tipping points seems so obviously negative – particularly when adjectives like 'catastrophic' are so often attached to them, that we can forget that human judgement is involved here: these are judged to be negative events because of their damaging impact upon *Homo sapiens*. Many other current species are adapted to present conditions and so may also suffer as badly as ourselves, but other kinds of creatures may flourish under such changed conditions; 'malign' and 'benign' are then not neutral terms.

The individuality and contextualization of tipping points

Now, with respect to the kinds of forces creating tipping points, Lenton and Williams (2013) argue that two of the most important tipping points in the earth's history occurred in the very deep past, 2.4 billion and 640 million years ago. The first of these was what we would view as a 'benign' tipping point, as it created stable atmospheric oxygen, and in so doing laid the foundations for the evolution of the diversity of life seen today. The other tipping point – that of 'Snowball Earth' glaciation – was initially much more damaging, nearly extinguished all life on the planet, which makes it sound extremely malign, though as noted earlier it is now believed that after the retreat of such extreme conditions, there was a massive expansion in the variety of life, and so some would argue that its effect was ultimately very benign. Moreover, the five great species extinctions in the earth's history all seem to have been caused by tipping points (Brannen, 2018) and can be viewed as either malign (in all cases extinguishing the dominant species of the time) or benign (allowing the flourishing of new dominant species). Without the asteroid strike and the extinction of the dinosaurs, we almost certainly would not be the dominant species today.

Such extinctions suggest a second issue – the speed of such tipping points. Writers like Brook et al. (2018) argue that tipping points are so dangerous because of their rapidity, to which human beings may be insufficiently prepared to react. Indeed, other species seem to have died out relatively quickly, the dinosaurs being the prime example, but 'quickly' is a relative term, and such extinctions didn't happen overnight, but more likely over several thousand years. This is a blink of an eye in geological time but a very extended period in human time. This places in context Hughes et al.'s (2013) comment that the feared rapidity of current tipping point threats largely reflects the timescales human beings use to measure events. Other tipping points – such as the extinction of the dinosaurs, or planetary glaciation events – can then take considerably longer. So we need to recognize that some important tipping points may occur over only a matter of hours or days, but they can also take decades, centuries or even millennia. Much of human focus is on tipping points that are sudden and just a little way off in terms of our timescale, so part of a macro-stewardship attitude then needs to include awareness of how humanity may contribute to much longer-term impacts.

A further issue comes from asking whether a particular tipping point is global or local. Like a tipping point's speed of impact, global effects from tipping points usually create greater concern than more local events in an audience, probably because global tipping points sound like much larger threats to human existence. However, dangerous tipping points may be local or regional, particularly if you live in the area where the impact occurs. Many animal and plant species usually occupy geographically limited eco-zones, but the extinctions of the Tasmanian tiger, the American passenger pigeon and the Mauritian dodo were not global events, yet for many all three can provoke feelings of profound loss, and the destruction of species from which humanity might have learnt a great deal. Further, Lenton and Williams (2013) point out that the local and the global are rather more interconnected than is often assumed: the global dominance of angiosperms (plants that have protected seeds) over gymnosperms (plants with unprotected seeds) took millions of years to occur, and seems more likely to have been a series of local tipping points in different locations at different times, rather than one simultaneous global occurrence.

Barnovsky and Hadley (2015) also argue that another essential difference between tipping points is their reversibility or irreversibility. Thus, when heat is applied to water as a liquid, at some point a tipping point occurs and the water turns to the gaseous state of steam. However, if the steam is allowed to cool, it returns to its liquid state. The tipping point of boiling water is then a reversible tipping point – and we may be less concerned about such events if the possibility of a return to a previous state is possible. However, many tipping points exhibit an irreversibility, or 'hysterisis', largely because of the complexity and interactions of the processes involved in producing the tipping point. You may easily burn a book to charred leaves of paper, but returning it to its original condition is beyond present human capabilities. Societies may collapse due to such a wide range of interacting factors, of which many may be unknown, as may their relative contributions to such collapse (Fagan, 2009). Once more, we are in 'wicked' territory: not being gods, human beings lack the ability to fully comprehend, to control and then to reverse many factors in complex events. As Barnovsky and Hadley argue (2015, p. 15):

> The more parts to a system, and the more interdependencies between them, the harder it is to get all the pieces back in the same order if it happens to fall apart.

This Humpty Dumpty example once again suggests that there may be complex links between tipping points and 'wicked' problems – which in themselves are highly complex, and may be poorly understood and are less amenable to control and reversal than 'tamer' examples.

The varying rapidity, the contextualization, the reversibility or irreversibility of individual tipping points, and the addition of human judgements as to their benign or malign natures all demonstrate that tipping points are likely to be more complex and more singular than is often assumed. The development of a stewardship role is then aided by a more nuanced understanding of the individual nature and complexity of different tipping points, and in so doing a more subtle awareness can be applied to micro-, meso- and macro-systems and events.

Tipping points in practice

Given this background, how do tipping points work in practice? It has already been suggested that the covert processes already discussed can in particular contexts contribute or directly produce tipping points. So in this section, these covert processes are applied to different areas of potential tipping points, in order to demonstrate such interactions, and particularly how tipping points are likely to be highly individual in occurrence and impact. The three different tipping point areas chosen are:

1. Covid-19 tipping points, as these have been a recent and threatening concern.
2. Environmental tipping points, as the concept of tipping points has entered educational thought largely through growing awareness of their contribution to different areas of potential environmental collapse.
3. Educational tipping points, as these demonstrate their existence and impact in many readers' occupational backyards.

A summary of the ways in which covert processes can produce tipping points in particular contexts is then provided in Table 7.1.

Table 7.1 Covert Processes and Tipping Points in Three Areas

Tipping point characteristics Processes	Covid-19 tipping points can occur when	Environmental tipping points can occur when	Educational tipping points can occur when
Positive feedback	The more staff infected, the less staff remain to combat Covid-19, the harder it is to prevent its spread	The less ice coverage there is, the less heat is reflected back, and the more ice melts, leading to its absorption, and the more the ice melts	The more that teachers believe ability is linked to personal traits, the more some students are likely to conform, the more such beliefs are reinforced
Exponential growth	Growth in Covid-19 patient numbers expands beyond existing health system capacity	Resource demands by expanding populations exceed natural system capacity	Population expansion leaves systems without sufficient flexibility to cope with new challenges
Hyper- and under-connectedness	Health service crash impairs connected services (e.g. care homes)	Human/environmental 'cowboy' under-connectedness leads to overuse of natural resources	Standardization of practice leaves systems without sufficient flexibility to cope with new challenges
Tame and wicked problems	Disease expansion reaches a stage where too many events occur to track and resolve such increase	Highly complex environmental systems may be extensively damaged by tame assumptions about their functioning and exploitation	The more that people assume that most problems are tame rather than wicked, the less likely they are to find the right solutions to wicked problems

Covid-9 tipping points

A strongly feared Covid-19 tipping point by most governments has been the possibility of health system collapse, first through an inability to cope with increased numbers of patients, and second through inadequate supplies of personal protective equipment (PPE) for critical staff. Here the tipping points are when – perhaps realized over a few days – a health system cannot meet the rising demand for treatment, PPE and staff. This tipping point has in some cases been made more likely by the increased infection of health-related staff. In addition, a number of governments were underprepared for the initial appearance of Covid-19, either because they did not have the resources to adequately react to a pandemic, because they had prepared for a different, flu-like virus, had been preoccupied by other concerns, or their leaders had summarily dismissed the threat. Many governments then needed to perform acts of policy triage, deciding which groups were to be prioritized for protection and treatment. Health workers and health-related workers, as well as those performing other designated vital services were usually given priority by being provided with limited PPE and testing. Others who were vulnerable through being elderly or possessing underlying health conditions were told to fully isolate for extended periods. However, in some countries the elderly in care homes were not initially given the level of attention and protection needed, nor were those who were caring for them. A little later down the line, vaccinations were similarly triaged, with the most vital workers and the most vulnerable normally being selected first.

In terms of underlying processes, then the exponential growth in patients and health workers due to the highly infectious nature of Covid-19 led to the fear that the rate of increase in numbers would overwhelm a health system. Further, positive feedback effects meant that the more the number of infected health workers increased, the more likely that greater numbers of others would be infected, and that there would be less healthy staff to combat the disease. This reduced the efficacy of prevention and treatment, and led to the greater likelihood of more being infected. Conversely, the more people that were tested, the more that infected people and their contacts could be identified and isolated. In addition, the more people that could be vaccinated, the less it was believed the disease could spread. Finally, in modern complex hyper-connected societies, there was always the danger of disruption to systems which made social distancing highly problematic, or the dislocation of such hyper-connection resulted in heavily pressured health systems being unable to provide adequate help to other services like care homes.

Now one of the major challenges of Covid-19 in most countries has been its novelty. Some East Asian countries like South Korea and Hong Kong had experienced SARs, a similar coronavirus, in 2003, and were initially able to successfully apply lessons learnt there to the Covid threat. Many other countries, however, had not been so directly affected, and had not learnt much from this experience. In many parts of the world, then, Covid-19 infection was not anticipated or understood, and even in 2022 (as this is being written), there was still a great deal about the disease and its impact which was not mastered – including concern about the lack of global distribution of vaccines, and whether existing vaccines could deal with new variants of the disease. Covid-19 then seems a strong example of a 'wicked' problem, as it is not a problem responsive to single 'silver-bullet' solutions. The best policies so far have then been national 'messy' responses (Rayner, 2006; Grint, 2008) in the form of trial and error experiments.

Thus, as Ackoff (1979) argued in another context, we are not faced

> with problems that are independent of each other, but with dynamic situations that consist of complex systems of changing problems that interact with each other. I call such situations 'messes'.

Significantly for the role of the educational leader, Ackoff went on to suggest that 'Managers do not solve problems, they manage messes.' The result, oftentimes, as with most responses to wicked problems, has been only partial success and other 'different or additional' strategies have needed introducing. There has been much criticism of governments which misunderstood or did not recognize the wicked nature of the problem; but even when they did, public responses could be highly critical, assuming that such responses were U-turns as governments backtracked on previous mistakes – and sometimes this is what they *were* doing. All of this strongly suggests that educational leaders could and perhaps should have a major role to play in terms of societal understanding of wicked and tame problems, of their application to real-world problems and of educating colleagues, students and communities into such complex but necessary understandings.

Environmental tipping points

Ice melt and the release of methane hydrates from Arctic sea beds through the rise in sea temperatures have already been described as examples of environmental change through positive feedback processes. Whilst the threat from ice melt has been recognized for some considerable time, the threat of methane hydrates has only recently been recognized as a potential factor in any near-future tipping point in this area, largely because the majority of methane hydrates deposits have lain frozen under high pressure in deep oceans. Earlier predictions (e.g. Flannery, 2005) suggested that major releases were unlikely to happen for many decades. However, recent reports (e.g. *Guardian*, October 2020) suggest that Arctic temperatures – where methane hydrates are much closer to the surface and therefore more exposed to warming – are now increasing methane release much faster than predicted. This then raises the possibility that this positive feedback process could lead to a methane hydrate tipping point sooner than previously expected.

Exponential growth is also a highly important process involved in other environmental concerns – particularly the way in which an expanding human population places demands on resources that exceed the growth rate of a natural system's reproductive capacity. The human consumption of resources is compounded by the manner in which many societies now lack a feeling of 'connectedness' with the natural environment, which has contributed to the limited appreciation of natural environmental limits, then leading to the overuse of its resources. Moreover, the fact that interactions in most environmental systems are highly complex and interdependent make them extremely difficult to fully understand, which then has major implications for creatures living in such systems. As Wilson (2003) pointed out, it is often well beyond human ability to know which of the following are central to a particular species' extinction: the destruction of its habitat, the invasion of this habit by new species, increased pollution, increased human intrusion into the species' territory and the overharvesting of resources by human being. In some cases, all or only one may contribute, in others only some may be involved, Once again, the tame assumptions that human beings often bring to their understanding of natural systems is in itself a covert threat resulting in poor decision-making, and then potentially creating extensive damage to other species' habitats.

Educational tipping points

If 'tipping points' are often thought of as problems, potentially causing considerable destruction, it has already been noted that some tipping points may be viewed as very benign in nature. In education virtually all individuals in schools and universities have tipping points – 'lightbulb' moments' – when they suddenly grasp the nature of an issue or understand a problem in a deeper or more comprehensive way than previously, and educators can be critical facilitators of such tipping points. Many small acts of kindness can also have considerable effects upon those to whom the act is directed. As with malign tipping points, exactly what processes contribute to such benign moments may well be as varied as the moments themselves. At the larger scale, Newton talked of 'standing on giants' shoulders' when describing how he came to his paradigm-changing scientific insights, as using the findings of scientific predecessors allowed him to see a greater interconnectedness of concepts. Yet instances of scientific progress – indeed most intellectual progress – are very seldom the final word. Much scientific work fails to deliver any 'final' conclusion, even if this is thought so at the time. Often it is the best that can be achieved at that moment in time but will be superseded at some stage in the future by intellectual tipping points creating further insights. Karl Popper (1982) made this point, arguing that any breakthroughs or tipping points may well help to see the world in a different way, but they will not be the final insight, because

> The empirical base of objective science has . . . nothing absolute about it. Science does not rest upon solid bedrock. The bold structure of its theories rises, as it were, above a swamp. It is like a building erected on piles. The piles are driven down into the swamp, but not down to any natural base . . .if we stop driving the piles deeper, it is not because we have reached firm ground. We simply stop when we are satisfied that the piles are firm enough to carry the structure, at least for the time being. (Popper, 1982, p. 111)

Tipping points are also implicit in the work of Thomas Kuhn (1970), in his descriptions of the principal means by which science makes progress. Most researchers, he suggests, practice 'normal science', working without questioning on the kinds of problems generated by the assumptions of the particular paradigm they are working within. Behavioural psychology, for example, has clearly defined assumptions and acceptable terms, and the definition of what is a 'problem', the methods used and the assessment of 'correct answers' will all be based upon assumptions underpinning this paradigm. Thus, recommendations for improving child behaviour will be defined in terms of operant-conditioning techniques, and will not use the assumptions underpinning cognitive-developmental or humanist psychologies in attempting to solve such problems. Nevertheless, in the history of science there are numerous occasions when some individuals – and Newton was one – see the issue in an entirely different – and often cognitively more satisfactory – way. This 'tipping point' moment often leads to the development of an entirely new paradigm, with new questions and new answers. Such challenges to the 'normal' approach, as Kuhn (1970) recognized, is often greeted by strong and sometimes angry resistance, as such insights might invalidate much previous thought, practice and achievement. Once again, an intellectual tipping point may be viewed as benign or malign, depending on your assumptions about the nature of the field in which you practice. Nevertheless such 'tipping points' often come to be seen as essential growth points in an intellectual discipline, and also in an individual's intellectual and affective development.

Finally, and as noted in Chapter 3, the dynamics of trust relationships can be strong examples of positive and negative feedback, and of how malign and benign tipping points can be created through their actions. When trust relationships are being built it may be through the use of a benign positive feedback, where one act of trust inspires a return of such trust by the other. Moreover, when one of these parties acts in such a way as to suggest that they are reducing their level of trust, the other may react with anger, and the first party may then move to employ a different tactic, and use negative feedback, as they attempt by various means to return to the trust equilibrium that formerly existed in the relationship, and sometimes this can produce a similar response by the other party, and the balance of trust may then be restored. However, the reverse is also true: when one party (for instance a government) for a variety of reasons decides to reduce this level of trust (as happens when high-stakes accountability systems are introduced into schools) (and see Chapter 11 on this), this apparent reduced level of trust may induce a similar reaction from the other in that relationship, which then provides proof to the first party that their reduced trust was justified. When this happens a downward spiral is very likely to occur which may arrive at a tipping point where both parties believe the relationship cannot be returned to its previous state.

Understanding the nature of particular tipping points

So far, then, a number of possible meanings of 'tipping point' have been discussed, as well as the role that covert processes can have in their emergence. The individual natures of tipping points are now examined by focusing on a number of salient aspects. We then begin by selecting a potential tipping point, and each of the following six aspects is considered in turn and then combined to ask a final question on the likelihood of finding responses to prevent this particular tipping point from occurring. Whilst such an exercise is highly unlikely to provide details of precisely when a tipping point would occur, nor its exact impact, this cumulative assessment helps determine the degree of confidence to be had in understanding the nature of the tipping point chosen, and whether the proposed solutions are appropriate. Each of the six aspects will then be examined in turn.

Aspect 1: The degree of complexity of the system within which the tipping point occurs. Questions about the degree of system complexity are important because discussion so far suggests that the less complex the system, the easier it is to understand its functioning, and therefore the greater likelihood of being able to exert a degree of control over that system, which then increases the possibility of preventing the emergence of a tipping point. Conversely, the more complex a system is, the less confidence one should have in being able to achieve such objectives. For example, global climate change is highly complex, and knowledge of underpinning processes and particular factors in individual contexts suggests the need for continued research and modelling, and considerable time and effort in understanding the generation of tipping points, at the same time as creating multinational agreements on greenhouse gas reductions. Covid-19 similarly interacts with and impacts in many different and unpredictable ways upon individuals, institutions and societies, and such interactions can produce surprising and problematic impacts, even as the development of effective vaccines against Covid-19 has been remarkably swift. Tipping points can also occur within educational systems at micro-, meso- and macro-levels, and educational leaders should probably have more confidence in dealing with any emerging at the level at which their work predominates. Whilst much less confidence will likely be displayed in judgements and actions when impacts take place beyond levels of experience, the acceptance of a macro-stewardship role can be an inducement to better understand processes at this level.

Aspect 2: The degree of research consensus on how a particular system functions. Whilst certainty cannot be guaranteed on such functioning, if a diverse group of leaders and stakeholders, and robust evidence is brought to bear, the more likely judgements will have greater accuracy than those where strong disagreement continues to exist, or when agreement is only possible between similar members of a group, and only limited evidence is available. The development of a consensus then is not the result of groups conceding or abandoning views, but where ways are found of integrating disparate arguments. This will be an essential function for any group leader. With climate change, the greater the scientific consensus on such functioning, the more valid will likely be agreed hypotheses on tipping points. The work of the IPCC over the last couple of decades then seems to be the critical foundation for agreement and then action in this area. The same kinds of discussion have been applied to the understanding of Covid-19, even if comprehensive understanding has been hampered by a lack of evidence, by its effect in different contexts, by the emergence of variants of the virus and by the necessity of balancing health and economic concerns. With educational issues, because functioning is often a dialectic between factual evidence and educational values, and because greater confidence is usually felt by institutional leaders about issues situated at micro- and meso- rather than at macro-levels, more accurate hypotheses are likely to be held about issues located in familiar contexts. This strongly argues for a cross-level consensus where those with greater macro-level expertise and experience take on board the views, knowledge and expertise of those functioning at other levels.

Aspect 3: The degree of random or unanticipated fluctuation within a system. In searching for the degree of random or unanticipated fluctuation within a system, a major assumption is that the *less* the degree of such variation, the greater can be the confidence in prediction and intervention; and conversely, that the greater the degree of variation, the less confidence there should be in detailed prediction and control, because of the lack of understanding about such fluctuation within the system. These assumptions reflected the movement in the Western business world in the twentieth century of a general endorsement of transactional leadership to a more transformational model, one which attempted to move leaders and therefore their organizations from working within 'tame' assumptions of control and predictability to one where it was accepted that companies needed to be more responsive to the unpredictability of a rapidly changing business world. Yet such transformational leadership still contains within it a strong assumption of certainty, in that it assumes that institutional direction can be largely led by charismatic individual leaders, when in fact what was needed was rather more caution, more widespread consultation and more of what the poet John Keats called 'negative capability' – the need in a highly complex world to not commit too quickly to one course of action (and see Clarke, 2015 on this). In a world where politicians are expected to deliver quick answers, and accustomed as they are to a politics of evasion, it takes courage to step outside of accepted rules, and instead argue that many problems will not be solved quickly, for uncertainty and complexity will be features of everyday life for the foreseeable future. Indeed, in all three systems examined so far, the degree of unanticipated variation is high, because of the complexity of each, and because of the limited understanding of their functioning. If then there will be a significant degree of random variation within each of these systems, then one needs to be careful in ensuring that any claims to strong understanding of system functioning don't descend from confidence into personal hubris.

Aspect 4: The degree of research consensus on the likely nature of tipping points within a particular system. Underlying this statement is another assumption that the greater the consensus on understanding a problem in a varied group of contributors, the more confidence one can have in a suggested intervention. Such confidence should, however, not be assumed if contributors all or mostly have similar experiences, knowledge and values. An initial diversity of views is very important, just as it is with attempts at defining and resolving wicked problems. With climate change, the research published by the IPCC from a range of academic disciplines suggests a growing consensus and confidence on the nature of the major environmental tipping points, particularly with respect to global temperature increases, sea-level rise, weather volatility and species extinctions. With Covid-19, there seems strong international agreement that the most dangerous initial tipping point would be the collapse of a nation's health system, which might then induce collapse in other areas of societal functioning. Finally, whilst there is much discussion about educational leaders' sustainability, there is little consensus about the possible tipping points ending such sustainability. Literature searches suggest that these might well include: damage to government–educator relationships; differences in perceptions of leadership purposes; increased accountability and surveillance; increased use of power rather than persuasion to effect educational changes; increased complexity of the leadership role; the effect of the growth of blame and guilt cultures upon individual leaders; their increasing and often excessive workload; and an insufficient preparation for the role (see Bottery et al., 2018, on this). It is an area ripe for research.

Aspect 5: The degree of research consensus on the timing of tipping point within a particular system. Searching for evidence on this issue once again assumes that the greater the degree of consensus in a diverse group of stakeholders, the greater the confidence can be had in determining the timing of tipping points. With climate change, the considerable research over the last couple of decades strongly indicates continued increases in things like greenhouse gas emissions, global temperature and sea-level rises, even if there remains considerable uncertainty in the speed of such processes and therefore of potential tipping points. With Covid-19, increasing amounts of new information, and clarity about what a tipping point here would amount to, give greater confidence than with climate change in estimating the timing of such an occurrence, but Covid-19 still produces surprises (such as the potential danger of re-infection, and the re-emergence of new variants triggering new waves of infection). With educational systems, an additional factor is that different parties may differ on whether a tipping point would amount to something malign or something benign. Whilst the early retirement of leaders created by institutional, systemic or legislative change might be viewed by many educators as a malign tipping point, for some the moment when such leaders feel they can no longer carry on may be viewed as a benign tipping point, for it may be seen as creating room for the promotion of new policies and of individuals more suited to such new policies. Yet with little discussion on the meaning of the term in such contexts, and what would be the impacts, questions on the timing of 'malign' tipping points are seldom addressed, and such apparent lack of interest may seem to some as a covert threat in itself.

Aspect 6: The degree of consensus on the reversibility of tipping points within a system. So far then reflection has concerned the complexity, the functioning, the fluctuation, the nature of and the timing of particular tipping points. This list is completed by considering the degree of consensus on the likely reversibility or irreversibility of the tipping point being considered. Considering each aspect in turn, and then reflecting on what confidence can be gained by reflecting on all six aspects, then allows one to ask a final summative question:

> What is the likelihood of being able to prevent a particular tipping point from occurring?

This process can then be used to assess the probability/possibility of the emergence of three potential tipping points: those with respect to climate change, Covid-19 and educational systems.

Applying the process

Such an exercise can then help to firm up conclusions on the likelihood of a tipping point occurrence. However, given the complexities and the wicked nature of many issues surrounding tipping points, including the limitations of human understanding, answers to such questions are unlikely to provide any great degree of certainty, and similarly recommendations as to their prevention will likely be messy, incomplete and probably consist of a lot of 'silver buckshot' in nature. Nevertheless, given the speed, unpredictability and covert nature of many tipping points, this process may still be the most appropriate form of response.

With respect to the issue of climate change, the systems within which climate change takes place are highly complex, and therefore extremely difficult to understand, predict or control. Nevertheless, considerable progress has been made over the last two decades in research and understanding in this area, and there is increasing scientific consensus on system functioning (IPCC, 2019), and on the identification of the environmental boundaries it would be dangerous to cross (Rockstrom and Klum, 2015), which then generates an improved understanding of the nature and emergence of tipping points in this area. Adding to the complexity of such prediction, however, is how political change can affect this process. Currently, there is the possibility of a political sea change in the United States as President Biden seems to be taking the issue much more seriously both domestically and internationally than his predecessor. Such discussion also seems increasingly supported globally, which, in isolating the previous positions of countries like China, Russia, Brazil and Australia, may force their rethink and prompt the emergence of a more coordinated global policy towards this issue. However, despite such optimism about political progress, research is still needed for systems which are possibly changing faster than the research on them, such as ice melt at the poles, and particularly the Larsen-B ice shelf in Antarctica, as well as the release of methane hydrates in the Arctic. Strategies for the prevention of tipping points then seem heavily dependent on continued monitoring and research, with greater global cooperation preventing global temperatures from rising by no more than 1.5°C.

With respect to Covid-19 tipping points, it is important to note that the social systems within which outbreaks have their effects are also highly complex, and tipping points here may also be difficult to predict and control. Nevertheless, there is a strong research history on virus genetic structures, virus behaviour and the nature of previous pandemics, and current research for Covid-19 is global and very well financed. Moreover, new vaccines utilizing genetic fragments of viruses (Corum et al., 2020) may yet prove to be a major breakthrough. Moreover, the strong consensus that the first major Covid-19 tipping point in a country would be the failure to sustain a country's health system, has meant that prevention of such an event, as in India in April–May of 2021, has been understood, targeted and the subject of international aid. Predictions of tipping point timing are also strengthened by the better recognition by policymakers of the exponential growth in the spread of the disease. However, such work to prevent a Covid-19 tipping point is hampered in many countries by (i) the undoubted need to maintain a country's economic sustainability (which many times requires more social interaction), (ii) increasing fatigue at social distancing measures and (iii) the arrival of autumn/winter when the virus seems to be more stable, and at a time of annual flu outbreaks. Covid-19 tipping points are then very possible, particularly as countries have entered successive waves of the virus, and perhaps most importantly in poorer countries where vaccine roll-out needs the financial support of those more wealthy.

Finally, with respect to educational leadership and system sustainability, there is also considerable complexity and an interdependency of factors in their functioning at micro-, meso-, and macro-levels, and whilst leaders working in educational institutions may feel some confidence in their ability to manage issues at these more familiar levels, their necessarily more limited understanding of the impact of macro-level events on lower levels makes the prevention of threats leading to tipping points more difficult, even as consensus on the nature and progress of a tipping point is not just divided by evidence interpretation, but probably more importantly by a general failure to frame educational problems within tipping point frameworks. Finally, and very importantly, the value-based nature of much educational debate affects perceptions of whether a tipping point is a benign or malign occurrence, and whether the collapse following one is a highly damaging event or one which opens up new possibilities – echoing the kind of 'creative destruction' which Schumpeter (1942) described in functioning capitalism, a view which has been repeated in work on system change (Gunderson and Holling, 2002). Thus radical policies which were intended to undermine traditional educational models – and in the process the sustainability of individual leaders with particular value-sets – might lead to tipping points creating high unsustainability, which could be seen by policy creators as benign rather than malign tipping points. Whilst there seems strong overall agreement of some pressures on leadership sustainability – such as that of overwork and lack of preparation for the role – there may be less agreement on the reduction of other factors, such as the stress caused by increased inspection. There is also relatively little thought or agreement on how contextual and personal factors might feed into an understanding of the nature and timing of tipping points. So prevention or reversal of tipping points may, in their own ways, be as problematic as with the other two examples.

Conclusion

In so examining the origins and meanings of the term 'tipping point', this chapter has suggested that an acceptable overview definition of the process would be one describing incremental changes which at some stage exceed particular thresholds and so critically affect the system involved. Nevertheless, it would be dangerous to assume that tipping points closely resemble one another: they are often highly individual and contextualized in their nature. Moreover, it would also be dangerous to assume that tipping points are essentially malign: rather like sustainability, whether they are thought of as having a malign or benign nature may depend not only on the amount of damage they do but also on what they damage. This doesn't seem to be a major issue with either climate change or Covid-19: it would be hard to find too many people currently who believe that soaring temperatures, turbulent weather, habitat destruction and species extinctions were 'good' things. Similarly, few would believe that the death of over three million people from Covid-19 globally was a benign event. Education, however, is rather different, for benign or malign views of tipping points seem much more heavily dependent on what are valued as a system's ultimate objectives. The destruction of one system (e.g. a welfare state) and the creation of another in its place (e.g. a Neo-Liberal state) may generate tipping points of leadership unsustainability which to those holding 'traditional' values may be seen as malign, but to others desiring such change, might well seem positively benign. Whichever is the case, prior discussion on this in many cases may be essential for their greater understanding, prediction and decisions on what actions are necessary. This takes this tipping point analysis to a position where it can be argued that if the nature and the contextualization of tipping points are better understood, there can be greater confidence in devising means of increasing or preventing their occurrence. This is the subject of the next chapter.

Part III

Leadership Responses

8

The Prevention of Tipping Points
The Educational Leader's Role

Introduction

In the previous chapter, the origins, meanings and functioning of tipping points were considered in three different contexts, and it became apparent that tipping points could be both malign and benign. This chapter focuses specifically on malign tipping points and considers different non-specialist ways in which the emergence of these might be prevented. A first way consists of prioritizing tipping points in order to make preliminary estimates of the damage they might cause, as well as the time and effort needed for any intervention. A second way is to identify the early warning signals which are often seen prior to the emergence of tipping points and to then use these signals, along with assessments of probable tipping point damage, to begin to estimate the magnitude of their impact. A third move is to identify and utilize a number of 'leverage points' (Meadows, 2008) – actions which can impede or prevent the processes facilitating tipping points. A fourth and final way is to apply these three steps to potential tipping points to see what differences in application are produced. The three contexts discussed in the previous chapter will again be used here – those of Covid-19, of global temperature rises and of leadership sustainability. These help demonstrate how tipping points emerge in different ways due to their different natures, the different contributions of covert processes and their different contexts. The conclusions align with much else in this book – that understandings of this phenomenon need to utilize macro-, meso- and micro-perspectives and remediations.

Triaging tipping points

Even though the nature, causes and speed of many tipping points may not be fully understood, it is still important to try and understand their functioning and impact, as time, effort and resources need to be spent wisely. So a number of criteria are used here to create initial pictures of particular tipping points, in order to decide whether interventions are necessary. Discussions in the previous chapter have already suggested two of these criteria.

A first criterion is whether a tipping point is reversible or irreversible. The notion of reversibility is often viewed positively, as it can suggest the possibility of lessening or completely reversing a threat. Irreversibility, on the other hand, tends to have darker hues, as it tends to suggest that the best possible response can only be one of developing greater adaptation and resilience to its actions, and so having to live with a 'new normal'. However, whilst such reversibility – and hence the possible elimination of the threat – may seem a good reason for making this threat a priority, caution is needed because irreversibility can signal a change so serious that priority needs to be given to actions promoting resilience and adaptation to inevitable change rather than trying to maintain present levels of sustainability. Reversibility/irreversibility is then a choice to consider, but a choice which needs a fully contextualized understanding of the threat before any final decision is made.

A second criterion, which will impact on the reversibility criterion, is whether a tipping point is likely to cause major or minor damage. So as just noted, an irreversible tipping point might cause much greater damage than a reversible one, and hence priority might then be given to it, with action on a reversible tipping point delayed until later. Once more, however, it is important to examine and understand the context of each case, rather than simply assuming that criteria can be given priority universally. Furthermore, when two tipping points seem equally damaging, other criteria may well be the decisive factor in determining priority

A third criterion concerns whether a tipping point is likely to occur in the near or later future. Tipping points likely to impact sooner may well be given priority, but one can imagine instances where more distant occurrences are assigned priority because of the damage they are likely to cause. Whilst this rule of thumb certainly applies to work in educational leadership, the strongest examples currently are those related to the effects of global warming, such as the effects of ice melt, and progressively higher annual temperatures. Both have often been seen as distant or insufficiently intrusive to raise great concern, but the increased evidence of their effects and the scale of their damage not only to future generations, but to present ones, now seems to be giving them much greater prioritization.

A fourth and final criterion for measuring the importance of tipping points lies in comparing their ease of avoidance. Now it might be thought that events which are difficult to avoid should, almost by necessity, be given priority:

avoidance may involve much time and effort, and if they are products of complex situations, avoidance may be very limited. However, difficulty of avoidance does not of itself mean that the threat has highly damaging consequences: some issues which are relatively easy to avoid may be much more dangerous, and so may require prioritization. Once again, the context and interactions involved need careful examination before any decision is made in terms of prioritization.

To take an educational example of the use of these four criteria, imagine a new 'troubleshooting' principal brought into a school because long-term problems have resulted in the resignation of the former principal (see Bottery et al., 2018, chapter 7, for examples of such an event). This new principal may begin by considering whether the likely damage from the situation is major or minor, and may come to the decision that unless action is taken quickly, it will be major, both to the school and to its external reputation. The principal may also reflect on whether a tipping point is likely to happen very soon, and what it would look like. They may decide that the tipping point in this context is not a sudden collapse of the system, but rather a decline over weeks and months as staff become more depressed or aggressive, as student behaviour and academic progress decline. They may then decide that this is an issue which cannot be avoided – in part because they have been appointed to deal with the situation, but possibly because their initial information and assessment agree with this notion. They may then decide that any full collapse is not immediate, but it remains difficult to tell whether any tipping point will emerge later. They will take into consideration two other conclusions: first, that the deterioration in morale and behaviour cannot be allowed to continue, and they must act to reverse the situation. However, they also have a little while to devise remedial measures, as the summer holidays are only a couple of weeks away, and one major source of disruption will be retiring. They may then conclude that radical and immediate action is not needed, and instead will likely focus on what holding actions need performing in the short term, before major interventions are taken at the start of the autumn term. In the cases studied (Bottery et al., 2018) the priority of most troubleshooting principals interviewed was to focus upon 'healing' the school, through working on better relationships within it and beyond it, rather than to concentrate on a results-driven agenda.

Identifying and understanding early warning signals

These four criteria – *reversibility/irreversibility; major/minor damage; near in time/further in the future; difficulty/ease of avoidance* – can be used to estimate the danger of particular tipping points by identifying any early warning signals before a tipping point occurs. Investigating the context to identify any such signals is highly important, in order to prevent the *unexpected* emergence of tipping points, as a lack of preparedness can cause considerable long-term damage.

This combination of making criteria decisions and identifying early warning signals can be demonstrated through a number of examples. A first, the potential collapse of a national health system due to the effects of Covid-19 would be a highly dangerous tipping point for any society, and from the experiences globally in 2020-2, the early warning signs seem to be (i) the percentage of a population infected by the disease and needing hospitalization (ii) the percentage of a population dying from the disease and (iii) the levels of PPE equipment, beds and resources like oxygen and breathing apparatus available (iv) the percentage of hospital staff either ill or having to self-isolate. Other warning signals may emerge as experience increases. One other that emerged from early UK experience was that whilst many experts, politicians, civil servants and private businesses were involved, there was a lack of clear communication both upwards and down, and many people talked but didn't feel that they could act. As already noted, countries in the Far East, having experienced SARS two decades previously, had better systems and communication in place when Covid-19 arrived.

A second example is that of global temperature rises which may create substantial flooding of major coastline cities and an increased severity of weather events (Ward, 2010). Some early warning signs are now appearing earlier than previously expected, which include substantial ice melt at both poles, more and larger forest and bush fires, and the release of the methane hydrates from under tundra and in the Arctic Ocean (New Scientist, 2018).

Finally, with respect to educational leadership, some early warning signals for tipping points signalling a lack of sustainability can comprise a significant decline in the numbers applying for the role; negative feelings from leaders about the demands of the role; a decline in the number of those wanting to remain in the role; increasing numbers leaving early, and increasing numbers of institutional vacancies.

Again, whilst broad early warning signals like these are global in character, the actual impact is likely to be different in different contexts, in different institutions and with different individuals. To take an example, 'overwork' as a major cause of a tipping point needs assessing not only with respect to the damage it does to individuals but also whether all individuals react in the same way. The dangers of long hours and 'function creep' (Starr, 2015) on the general health and sustainability of educational leaders are well documented, but there *are* exceptions which buck this trend. Thus, research in England and Hong Kong did find that many individuals were highly – and worryingly – aware of the pressure they faced:

> Pat: '...we haven't even got time to think about the fact that we haven't got time...'
>
> Bill: '...countless, countless, countless initiatives...'
>
> Angela: '... comes in great big piles. I take home boxes of the stuff...' (Bottery, et al. 2018, p. 156)

However, there were some significant individual exceptions. One of these was John, a Hong Kong principal, who told us that he was working '14 hours a day . . . and loving it' (p. 212), because he found the challenge of keeping his school open enormously fulfilling. However, when he eventually succeeded in preventing closure by merging his school with another, he became increasingly frustrated at the amount of bureaucracy he now had to deal with, and it was this that ultimately led to him leaving the position. The point to note here is that macro-causes of tipping points – such as the increased legislative control of institutions and leadership functions in Hong Kong – do not necessarily impact in a standardized way to lower levels, and may instead impact there in different and unexpected ways.

It is also important to note that many tipping points may be the result of essentially wicked problems. This is in part because many situations are so systemically complex that any assessment is unlikely to produce a full understanding of the situation. The sustainability of individual principals can only be fully explained – and remediated – by having access to information which examines causations at micro-, meso- and macro-levels, but most understandings and possible resolutions do not reflect this degree of complexity nor the different strength of the contributions to such pressure from each level. The seriousness of a problem is also likely to be assessed differently by different individuals and groups in different contexts, so *any* standardization of proposed resolutions, instead of making a situation better, may only make them worse. Leadership sustainability, for example, may be seen by governments as essentially an issue of inadequate preparation and overwork, whilst many in a leadership role may instead see it as a consequence of their holding values which conflict with those of their government, as they then encounter legislation for which they have a fundamental antipathy. Finally, and because of the wicked nature of such issues, there can be little certainty of complete success in any solution adopted.

The use of language like 'best guesses', 'silver buckshot' or 'messy solutions' very often reflects the reality faced, rather than a rhetoric being used which suggests full understanding of a problem and a conviction in the certainty of success. Many approaches to problems characterized by such certainty may add to the damage rather than reduce it, and so attitudes of humility, caution and negative capability then need to be key leadership attributes.

Assessing the danger of individual tipping points

So far, then, different criteria have been used to assess the potential seriousness of a tipping point, and ways of identifying early warning signals prior to their emergence have been proposed. The identification of the nature and danger of individual tipping points can now be made using these and the influence of the covert processes discussed in Chapter 4. In reality, assessments made will need to be dated, because as circumstances change, so probably will the level and timing of a threat.

Covid-19

The first example is of Covid-19, and the suggested macro-picture is shown in Table 8.1, though to gain a more contextualized sense of the threat, the exercise would need performing at the level in which most interest is expressed.

Humanity has reacted to Covid-19 rather like frogs placed in rapidly heating water: there was a small period before its appearance in Wuhan, China, was globally appreciated, and then, apart from a few political leaders denying its importance or existence, there was worldwide recognition that this disease was not only life-threatening but also likely to cause major threats to national health and social and economic functioning. The level of concern rose quickly, particularly as it was soon viewed as an invisible killer which could infect people asymptomatically, whilst its exponential growth caused a rapid increase not only in infections but also in the number of deaths. The length of time during which this level of threat continued varied with a country's level of infection, its death rate and its access to effective vaccines. Indeed, in terms of tame and wicked solutions, the creation of effective vaccines seemed to many like a 'tame' silver bullet answer and was heralded by some as eradicating the virus threat. However, emerging variants may reduce vaccines efficacy, with new vaccines or booster doses needed, and so the effects of the virus – and of 'long-Covid' – on employment, mental health and nation-state relations remain highly

Table 8.1 Covid-19 and Potential Health Service Collapse

Nature of tipping point criteria	Covid-19 threat to UK health service collapse	Early 2022: Assessment of tipping point threat
First criterion: Degree of reversibility	Possibly reversible but heavily dependent on vaccines being produced and remaining effective	Early 2022: vaccines now in gradual global deployment, though many poor countries remain without
Second criterion: Degree of damage	Highly damaging to staff, infrastructure and other societal functioning	Individual death still high in some countries, but tipping point much less likely in countries with widespread vaccine access
Third criterion: Near or distant occurrence in time	Distant now in countries with vaccines, but if not addressed properly still very high	Unlikely in countries with vaccines, but still high if not addressed properly in other countries
Fourth criterion: Ease of avoidance	More now known about disease, but isolation fatigue setting in	Easier to avoid with less cases, but new variants seem more infectious
Signals of tipping point emergence	Four well-recognized: (i) number infected; (ii) number hospitalized and having died; (iii) level of PPE, other equipment and beds available; (iv) number of hospital staff ill or self-isolating	Informed actions now being taken to address such signals, but vaccine supply still very variable
Influence of covert processes	Exponential growth least grasped; wicked complexity of effects still surprising many	Lack of understanding of exponential growth still adversely affecting public behaviours
Overall current assessment	Still life-threatening for many, but vaccine production now making major difference	Tipping point much lower in countries with vaccine supplies; still dangerous where supplies are limited

complex. Other unanticipated wicked questions have then been raised: what, for instance, is the proper balance between measures to prevent the spread of the disease and those aimed at opening up a nation's economy and social life? There is no tame or simple answer here, and nation-based experimentation at developing a viable health/economic balance has taken place, but in some cases has resulted in further waves of the disease. As there is currently little agreement or uniformity between nations on the correct balance of preventive measures, or on the level of dissemination of the vaccine to poorer countries, it remains highly possible that variants could return to countries which had thought the problem solved. At the moment, this is a problem which seems to be creating a number of different and unexpected concerns: at the G7 summit of June 2021, the international response to supplying vaccines to poorer countries seemed to descend into one of political rivalry, as G7 democratic countries competed with authoritarian China in promising to be the main providers to poorer countries.

Despite the time-limited nature of any assessment, Table 8.1 still makes clear two important points. The first is that some of the unhelpful reaction – by policymakers and the general public alike – to measures intended to reduce the incidence of the disease, stemmed at least in part from a lack of understanding of the nature of its exponential growth, which not only facilitated its early expansion but later was probably one of the reasons for unhelpful and uninformed demands for early relaxation of rules and measures. This has considerable implications for an education in understanding exponential growth when combatting other problems caused by the process, particularly with respect to population growth, and resource and energy consumption. Moreover, it seems increasingly clear that denial by some of the danger of Covid-19, as well as rejection of the vaccines for it by others, is based on a number of factors. One is an uncontrolled and uncritical social media spreading both unfounded rumours and outright lies about the disease and the vaccine, which returns one to questions about the dangers of irrational versions of populist politics and the need for a greater educational focus on this problem. Another factor is the impact of the social history of a number of marginalized groups, deeply suspicious of the countries creating vaccines because of their previous colonial abuse. This then is another important area for educators to raise greater awareness of how past injustices can shape present reactions.

Global temperature rise tipping points

If reactions to Covid-19 have largely been like frogs introduced into rapidly heating water, global temperature rise is more like the frog introduced into tepid water which now seems to be moving from gradually heating up, to a quickening of pace. Whilst Covid-19 was seen at first as an acute threat, the threat capability of global temperature rises has been seen for the past few decades as more of a chronic, rather than an acute, problem. However, there now seems growing public and political awareness that its effects are threatening sustainability on a global scale, and a growing belief that unless action is taken quickly, it may be too late to prevent catastrophic worldwide damage. Individual instances of its effects, such as Australians watching from beaches as their houses were destroyed by bush fires in 2019–20, and Americans and Canadians on the West Coast experiencing unheard of high temperatures in 2021, have fed a growing awareness of the dangerous potential of such temperature increases. Nor is the fact that such events are now happening in the wealthiest countries unimportant, because this greatly increases the promotion of the problem.

Table 8.2 then demonstrates recent significant changes in attitude to this threat. The year 2020 was the third warmest year on record for the planet, and the

Table 8.2 Global Temperature Rise Tipping Points

Nature of tipping point Criteria	Global temperature rises	Assessment of tipping point threat in early 2022
Degree of reversibility	Possible, but figures over last two decades all point in the wrong direction	Global temperatures still rising; 2020 third warmest year on record
Degree of damage	The most damaging of all three examples for the future	Urgency seems now being recognized: though COP 2021 was a disappointment to many
Near or distant occurrence in time	Many countries now reporting this damage, worse to come	Many effects are already with us, and worse is to come
Ease of avoidance	Still possible to avoid, but impact now evident to many	Rising global consciousness of potential tipping points but little actual action
Signals of tipping point emergence	High temperatures, deaths of older people, forest fires, increased severity of weather events	Some signals not entirely global but becoming so; statistics on global temperatures still rising
Influence of selected covert processes	Positive feedback very evident, exponential growth in resource extraction leading to environmental degradation; hyper-complex interaction of many factors	Approaching a highly worrying combination of major covert processes
Overall current score	Temperatures still rising as underlying processes not brought under control, creating a highly threatening global situation	The most dangerous tipping point currently and still moving towards it rather than reversing away. Reverse seems still possible, but with every year, increasingly difficult

last decade has been the warmest on record (World Meteorological Organisation, 2021). These are now figures remarked on not just by climate scientists but also by the general media, by governments and their publics. In 2021 Sky News in the UK began a nightly updating programme on climate change – something unimaginable only a short time previously. There seems much less resistance than formerly to the idea that international and national measures now need instituting to combat and reverse global climate trends, even if this involves major lifestyle changes. Increasing numbers of people then seem to recognize the signals preceding such a dangerous tipping point: recurrent droughts, forest and bush fires, crop failures, excessively high temperatures, increasing numbers of elderly deaths, as well as the now probable flooding of major cities consequent upon ice melt and extreme weather events sometime in the next few decades. However, given the resources needed for dealing with Covid-19, governments might be hesitant in committing to the dramatic levels of investments required for this threat; and whilst many remain ignorant of the role that positive feedback and exponential growth processes play in warming trends, a lack of understanding of the deeply wicked nature of climate change processes still remains. These issues are then fundamental tasks for educators to take on in order to educate and equip their students and communities for a now rapidly emerging future.

However, there seems to be an unexpected link between Covid-19 and climate change which may help this situation, due to the astonishing speed in the development of vaccines for Covid-19. Vaccine development has normally taken a decade or so from first recognition to the roll-out of injections, but for Covid-19 it took less than a year. This remarkable achievement has then bolstered belief that humanity may be capable of not only of responding to global problems, but in a much shorter period of time than normally assumed, and in consequence there does seem to be significant movement away from the fear, guilt and powerlessness by individuals about global trends described in Chapter 2. The climate change frog then seems to be appreciating how warm is the water in which it is sitting. Perhaps then the same urgency adopted for Covid-19 could now be applied to climate change.

Leadership sustainability

The final tipping point is a collapse in the number of those wishing to take on or continue in the role of educational leader, with major ramifications for the functioning of their educational system. Its recognition as a problem has both similarities and differences from the other two examples (Table 8.3). Whilst the

Table 8.3 The Threats to Educational Leadership Sustainability

Nature of tipping point criteria	Declining leadership sustainability	Assessment of tipping point threat in early 2022
Degree of reversibility	Currently, little sign of positive change	Continuing and constant pressure on leaders
Degree of damage	Dependent on individual personality and context	A continuing but little changing concern
Near or distant occurrence	Little or no indication of major change to current levels of pressure	Unlikely to get better, though it may worsen (reduced finance, populist movements, pressures from Covid-19)
Ease of avoidance	Avoidance of pressure difficult and likely to be possible only through personal strategies rather than substantial culture change	Little positive culture change, added pressures
Signals of tipping point emergence	Negative feelings about the role, numbers leaving early, numbers not applying, large number of institutional vacancies	Little movement currently
Influence of selected covert processes	Positive feedback generates poor levels of government/professional trust; wicked nature of pressure generation	Neoliberal influences still strong; increased distrust by many populist political leaders
Overall current score	Little to suggest present reduction in pressures, though some evidence of political change favouring traditionally held leader values	Most static of the three issues: more challenges, more solutions, could come into play; this remains an issue still to show real movement

threat of a tipping point caused by Covid-19 was recognized and responded to relatively quickly, and the threats ensuing from global temperature rises are only just being fully recognized, declining leadership sustainability has been researched, recognized and reported on internationally for over three decades (Fullan, 1988; Starr, 2015; Bottery et al., 2018). It is then not a frog placed in either boiling or lukewarm water, for the water temperature has been uncomfortably warm for many during most of this period: the similar experiences of principals in many countries suggest an international experience over the last few decades, as the values and practices of markets, competition and managerialism have challenged traditional educational values of care, cooperation and social cohesion. Whilst many governments have attempted to ameliorate some of the threats to leadership sustainability by endorsing more distributed forms of leadership to lighten the load on individuals, or by creating leadership colleges and thus providing greater preparation for those moving into the role, such moves probably address only a fraction of the causes for the problems, and then probably only the most presenting ones. Current pressures then not only seem unlikely to decline but may actually increase with the demands placed on the role with the emergence of the kind of threats discussed in this book, and other pressures such as low-level government–educator relationships, major differences in perceptions of the purposes of the role, continued high-level accountability and surveillance, the use of power rather than discussion and persuasion in determining the nature and scope of the role; an increasing complexity of the role, and the continuation of blame and guilt cultures.

However, it seems highly unlikely that in the foreseeable future educational systems will collapse due to a decline in the number and quality of individuals taking on a leadership role. Nevertheless, long-term problems with leadership sustainability will now probably be increased by the kinds of challenges outlined so far. This then is an area which needs continued careful monitoring.

Identifying levels and types of leverage points

Through using the criteria for evaluating major threats, by being aware of early warning signals of tipping point emergence, and by estimating the degree of threat posed by tipping points in different contexts, a degree of confidence in understanding these threats may be had. A further measure can now be added – the use of 'leverage points' as suggested by Meadows (1999, 2008).

One way of understanding the nature of leverage points is by imagining a timeline flowing from left to right which ends with the emergence of a tipping point. Prior to this point on the timeline a whole series of other lines feed into it. These are lines of causation – contributory causes to the production of the tipping point. So if some of these can be preventing from feeding into the main timeline, the tipping point may be prevented from emerging. Examination of this timeline prior to a tipping point is then highly important, and needs examining in order for such lines of causation to be identified, and then leverage points need selecting in order to weaken or prevent their contribution to the tipping point. Now in what are highly likely to be complex areas of causation, there may be many contributory lines of causation, with different degrees of influence, and some of these may not be identified because in many cases it will simply not be possible to be aware of all the processes and causes involved in such complex events. However, if a number can be identified which previous experience suggests can significantly influence the process, then leverage actions can be selected which impact upon these, and which may then help to prevent tipping point emergence. Moreover, when such actions are performed a number of times, and added to those of previous experience, then patterns of effect from the application of such leverage actions can be learned, which can then be applied later to similar cases. If, however, these leverage actions have little or no effect, or the context in the second case is realized as insufficiently similar to the first, then other causes for the symptoms need seeking, and other leverage actions will need selecting in line with the new 'diagnosis'.

However, it needs repeating that the generation of many tipping points is often highly complex, and many elements leading to the creation of a tipping point may not be recognized. In such circumstances, many diagnoses will inevitably take the form of 'best guesses'. Even in what appears to be the occurrence of relatively simple and 'tame' symptoms, there may still be much that remains unknown: the resignation of an educational leader may be thought due to personal reasons, but the origins of these personal reasons may stem from unrecognized meso- and macro-level influences. Indeed, when large numbers of leaders, internationally, want to leave their role, there may be similar macro-level causations producing this reaction. However, the nature of the actual impact will depend upon the personal and contextual circumstances of each individual case.

Whilst then 'silver bullet solutions' are unlikely to work, this does not mean that the emergence of tipping points is not preventable. As most are the outcome of a series of complex events, slowing down some of these events, hindering or eliminating others, and introducing 'benign' processes running counter to those causing the tipping point might well have important beneficial effects. Indeed, the lessons learned from such 'experiments' or past history can provide information to be used later when similar tipping points occur. This was an important lesson from Chapter 5 on lessons from the deep past. However, one also needs to keep in mind Bassey's (1999) argument that most scientific generalizations cannot be applied to the complex and wickedly contextualized nature of most human encounters, and therefore that most generalizations in such circumstances can be no more than 'fuzzy' ones, where comparison between the similarities of events needs to be applied in a cautious and considered manner. One may then generate helpful actions and interventions, which could change important elements so that a tipping point is delayed or prevented, even as it is recognized that such actions may not resolve the problem completely.

Now Meadows (2008) suggests that such leverage points are situated at three different levels, each level having different degrees of influence on tipping point formation. The first level, she suggests, consists of the 'mental models' which we use when trying to understand the world around us. These are probably the most important leverage points, because such mental models frame and direct our perceptions, attitudes and actions. Indeed, the use of the term 'mental models' seems interchangeable with that of the 'frames' which leaders need to adopt to better position themselves in dealing with emerging problems. So, a person who holds a mental model or a frame which assumes that people are basically untrustworthy, or that leadership is essentially about achieving better test results, will interpret situations, and choose actions in line with such assumptions, which will likely differ significantly from those more inclined to trust others, or who believe that developing strong relationships is fundamental to an effective leadership role. Indeed, holding some mental models or frames may actually *contribute* to the creation of particular tipping points, whilst the adoption of other models or frames may act to prevent them. From now on, to avoid confusion, the term 'frames' will be used to encompass the meaning of 'mental models'.

This first level then suggests that a major way of preventing tipping points may lie in a radical rethink of existing frames, and whether more appropriate ones could be adopted. These level one frames will then have profound implications on level two leverage points, which are mostly concerned with the choice of organizational rules which reflect level one assumptions. These in turn can determine the nature of third-level leverage points, which consist of things like the physical elements of an institution, or its normal working parameters. Each level then suggests the use of different kinds of leverage actions in preventing tipping points, with higher levels largely dictating the nature of decision and choice at lower levels.

Identifying leverage points

The different levels of leverage points can then be very useful in helping prevent processes like positive feedback, exponential growth, hyper- or under-connectedness, and wicked issues from facilitating tipping points. Examples are then provided in Table 8.4.

With many covert threats, the most effective leverage points are probably going to be the adoption of frames which help raise awareness of both the threat and the reasons for its covert nature. This can be a very effective educational

Table 8.4 Using Levels of Leverage Points to Prevent Covert Threats and Their Tipping Points

Tipping points and levels of prevention of covert threats	Principal tipping points	Level 1 of prevention: changing frames	Level 2 of prevention: changing information and feedback elements	Level 3 of prevention: changing physical elements and normal parameters
Positive feedback	Runaway effects with ice melt, methane hydrate gas emissions, soil exhaustion and forest fires	Ensure people are more aware of how positive feedback works; emphasize the value of negative feedback	Slow/decrease positive feedback loops; increase strength of negative feedback loops	Disable or reduce elements which facilitate positive growth problems; introduce elements which facilitate negative feedback
Exponential growth	Runaway growth in human populations, resource consumption, and in much disease spread	Recognize issues which exhibit this kind of growth and the dangers therein, especially economic growth; provide alternate visions of well-being	Slow/decrease such growth in problematic areas; increase possibilities of slower forms of growth	Disable or reduce elements which facilitate exponential growth problems, enable elements which facilitate other kinds
Connectedness	Damage from a lack of social and environmental connectedness; hyper-connectedness of social and media links	Identify and emphasize a more optimum level of connectedness	Increase activities which are better aimed at optimal connectedness	Introduce elements which encourage increase in desired degree of connectedness
Wicked issues	Incorrectly identifying wicked issues as tame, thereby generating other covert threats	Critique tame models and embrace a greater understanding of wicked models	Increase the number and variety of inputs for framing problems and solutions	Change aspects which facilitate tame identification and interpretation of problems and their resolution

strategy, and without it and the awareness it brings, individuals may continue to think that diseases like Covid-19 spread in an arithmetic manner rather than in an exponential one. This then is one important educational leverage point – the raising to higher levels of such awareness in students, teachers and community, and particularly of the link between the R-rate and exponential growth.

Similarly, wider understanding of the nature and effects of positive feedback on threats like global warming enables greater appreciation of how the generation of greenhouse gases, the cutting down of rainforests and ice melt can generate more of the same threat. In like manner, a better understanding of the nature and effects of hyper-connectivity in areas like digital communication can help an appreciation of how positive feedback can reduce headteacher sustainability, whilst developing a frame which better understands and communicates the nature and effects of human under-connectivity with the environment can help create a more focused stance on natural world sustainability. An education in the highly complex nature and functioning of these processes would highlight how difficult they are to predict or control, and so help develop a frame of intellectual humility which develops attitudes of greater caution and care.

Finally, as the strategies for preventing or reversing covert processes are examined, a further major leverage point lies in conducting a complete organizational audit, using information gained at higher levels of leverage to develop information and practice at lower levels facilitating the creation of organizational rules, physical structures and working parameters which make the organization more resistant and resilient to such covert processes.

Applying leverage points to three macro-tipping points

If then the discussions of this chapter are now applied to the three macro-tipping points discussed earlier, it is possible to suggest leverage points which might hinder or prevent each one. These analyses then add to those of Tables. 8.1–8.3, as they not only identify leverage points which could be applied to these tipping points, but can also be used in making an assessment of each tipping point at a particular period in time.

So with respect to the *Covid-19 threat to a national health service*, key leverage points are probably:

- Rolling out vaccine immunization as quickly as possible to as many as possible;

- Continuing to prioritize key staff and those most at risk;
- Ensuring that PPE equipment is available and widely distributed;
- Preparing booster doses for new variants when necessary.

For educational leaders in particular

- Using institutional and teaching time to counter rumours and false claims about Covid-19 and the purposes of the vaccines;
- Educating pupils and communities to better understand the contribution of underlying covert processes to this and other potential tipping points;
- Educating pupils and communities about the historical reasons for the distrust of authorities and expert advice by some groups over vaccinations and other policies.

There will almost certainly be additions to these, as circumstances change, and each context is examined.

With respect to *the global warming threat*, key leverage points are likely to be:

- International agreements on policies reducing and then eliminating fossil fuel use;
- International policies on heavily and quickly reducing greenhouse gas emissions;
- Reducing resource extraction and redirecting consumption;
- International agreements on differing national financial contributions to such policies;
- Discussions on the contributions of population growth to this problem.

For educational leaders in particular

- Using institutional and teaching time to develop critical faculties which can critique rumours and claims about Covid-19 and the purposes of the vaccines;
- Educating towards greater environmental concern through developing macro-stewardship roles and responsibilities;
- Educating against the paralysing inaction caused by fear, guilt and powerlessness often associated with such macro-concerns by demonstrating the efficacy of micro- and meso-actions.

Once again, there are very likely to be amendments to these lists, as new events occur, and as individual contexts are examined.

As regards the threats to educational systems through decreased *leadership sustainability*, key leverage points are likely to be:

- A more nuanced understanding by governments of the causes of threats to such sustainability, and the reasons for such causes;
- Policies which address these more nuanced understandings;
- A wider policy embrace of macro-stewardship values by governments seeing the need for these at micro-, meso- and macro-educational levels;
- The realization of the need for the greater contextualization of problems and their responses.
- *For educational leaders in particular*
- The development of greater trust in the integrity and expertise of those working through solutions in micro- and meso-contexts;
- The development of social communitarian values at micro- and meso-levels;
- The greater embrace of stewardship values at the community level;
- The replacement of punitive and conformist inspection policies by ones fostering greater social community and stewardship attitudes.

Unlike the first two examples, there is little sign internationally that the sustainability of educational leadership is viewed as a dangerous tipping point with respect to educational systems. Pressures on school leaders are unlikely to decrease, and may indeed ramp up as governments ask them to put a great deal of effort into post-Covid student academic recovery. The length, intensity and content of such an exercise may be very impactful on the implementation of the kind of changes suggested in this book.

Conclusions

This chapter has then suggested a number of ways in which tipping points may be impeded or prevented. One could begin by using a variety of criteria to prioritize different tipping points and then try to identify the early warning signals often seen prior to the emergence of tipping points. These could then be used to estimate the impact of particular tipping points. A number of leverage actions could then be identified to impede or prevent those processes facilitating tipping points. Applied to different examples of tipping points, these methods demonstrate that tipping points are highly likely to emerge in different ways because of their different natures, the different contributions of covert processes and their different contexts. A major conclusion from such an examination fits well with an ongoing argument in this book – that whilst such strategies provide a degree of clarity in understanding and preventing such phenomena, this is no simple task: these threats need to be recognized as highly complex in nature, and responses to them need to be similarly complex. One will then need to utilize macro-, meso- and micro-perspectives and remedies, and apply these to a detailed contextualization of the problems encountered.

The prevention of tipping points does not, however, exhaust the strategies which might be drawn upon by educational leaders in responding to the kind of covert threats and tipping points described in this book. Perhaps surprisingly, one other highly useful approach would be to take lessons from the impact of the Covid-19 outbreak and apply these to many of the other threats currently faced. This is the subject of the next chapter.

Future Threats

Covid-19 as an Aid to an Educational Leadership Response

Introduction

It may seem a little strange, at this relatively late stage, to return to the Covid-19 experience. However, there remain significant issues raised by this pandemic and particularly for educational leaders dealing with the uncertainty that comes from such new challenges. A first issue is that there are signs that humanity is in a process of transition with respect to the recognition of such events. As argued in Chapter 2, there seems to be real movement from a prolonged period of doubt and denial about environmental issues to one of growing awareness of such threats and of the need to take action on them. Klein in 2014 argued that, for her, the threat of climate change now dwarfed the influences and excesses that global capitalism had exercised over economic, social and political life for the past four or five decades. Yet there is more than a touch of hyperbole here, for it seems more accurate to say that whilst the threat hasn't changed, the awareness of it isn't in the same league. Whilst increasing numbers of political leaders now talk about the threat of climate change and make promises of achieving targets over the next couple of decades, there still seems a reluctance to do a significant amount to enable such targets to be reached. Moreover, the extremely limited coverage of this topic in educational leadership literature suggests that it is not yet part of many leadership agendas either. So, examination of a continuing reluctance remains highly necessary, and this chapter argues that the reaction to Covid-19 can suggest ways in which educational leaders may be able to help move such awareness towards a greater action-orientation.

A second issue lies in the sudden and game-changing nature of the appearance of Covid-19 in 2020. For many months in 2020–1, it was centre stage on many government agendas, diverting attention away from other threats, as actions to combat it took time and effort away from issues like transitioning to a low-carbon economy, at a time when experts had been arguing (IPCC, 2019/20) that this was precisely the time when they were most needed. Yet the seriousness of the threat was not reflected in the fractious nature of nation-centred debate demonstrated when COP 26 met in November of 2021.

A third issue is that Covid-19 has not been a totally catastrophic experience. Whilst millions have died from it, and others have found prolonged social isolation extremely challenging, the lack of travel has meant lower vehicle emissions, the presence of wildlife near and in villages and towns, and a significantly lower industrial output in most countries, which has reduced fossil fuel usage and its emissions, and has then created smog-free major cities not seen in decades. In addition, the social isolation measures needed to combat Covid-19 have unexpectedly given many individuals the time to reflect upon the nature of their personal relationships, their own work–life balance and their society in ways which have been surprisingly beneficial.

Perhaps, however, the most important things that educational leaders could learn from the Covid experience would be those things which suggest new and different ways of understanding and reacting to other global threats. Five elements of the Covid-19 experience are then singled out for discussion in this chapter as ways of raising awareness of other threats. These are:

1. The manner in which Covid-19 has undermined much certainty and normal feelings of control; to some this might seem a very negative lesson, but it fits well with previous discussions about the effects of different kinds of complexity and other covert threats upon individual and societal mindsets. From an educational leadership point of view, it strengthens the call for a role which helps others to live with such uncertainty and lack of control.
2. The way in which despite such a threat many people have risked their lives in caring for others, which suggests a very different picture of societal relationships from that of competitive individualism. It then opens up the possibility of educational systems – and an educational leadership role – which is more concerned with nurturing a common good, with developing a compassion for others, and for cooperative support for and with others which transcends individual and national competitive interests.
3. The way in which the Covid-19 experience suggests a reinvigoration of not only a concern for the public good but also for the need to nurture

the notion of civil society to balance the market and the state, and of how educational institutions could play a vital role in this.
4. The role that exponential growth has played in generating unexpectedly large and sudden increases in Covid-19 is now, if not globally appreciated, still better understood by many; a greater focus on this process – in government, the media and educational institutions – could help develop a better understanding of its potential role in other threat contexts, and so could better prepare populations for such developments.
5. The manner in which Covid-19 has generated not only deep-seated fear and concern but perhaps more importantly innumerable examples of caring and brave responses, which might be used to help develop more effective responses to other kinds of threats, a role that educational institutions are ideally placed to take on.

This chapter then will discuss these elements of the Covid-19 experience, using them to show how reactions to this challenge can be developed to help advance awareness, understanding and remedial actions with respect to other threats.

The undermining of certainty and control

A first issue then is the extent to which Covid-19 destabilized many people's beliefs in a world supposedly governed by certainty, predictability and human control. Much of this, as argued in Chapter 5, probably stems from humanity's experience in its deep history of a relatively benign interglacial period, though it was also probably driven by a deep primordial need by early *Homo sapiens* to intimately understand their environment for survival purposes. More recently, as societies have become more ordered and more hierarchical, so greater means of control have been developed by dominant groups not only to control other members of their society but also to subordinate other groups to their own wants and needs. Then, as humanity moved into an industrial age and new forms of control management were created, so individuals were increasingly treated as cogs in huge industrial machines, as the occupants of tightly defined and controlled role-boxes in bureaucracies (Merton et al., 1952). Even the purpose of science has been viewed as the establishment of eternal facts and truths to gradually lead to a complete understanding of how the universe works – and therefore of its greater control (Chalmers, 1999). Whilst there have been plenty of other – and opposing – models of humanity (Morgan, 2004) this machine metaphor has probably been the dominant one, and through social rules, workplace control and educational processes, people have been conditioned into seeing themselves as part of this larger machine (F. W. Taylor, 1911; Toffler, 1970). Yet this machine model has major flaws, particularly by a seduction into a limiting consciousness which poorly equips the individual to deal with a reality which is much more changeable, unpredictable and much more difficult to control than is suggested by this metaphor. The arrival of Covid-19 also undermined many people's view of social normality as they isolated themselves from friends and community, and life for many suddenly became a challenge of extended quarantine. For those isolated with close family, this could become an opportunity to strengthen personal bonds, but for others it had the potential to intensify simmering conflict. Moreover, when individuals first ventured out, they often awkwardly and apologetically kept physical distance from friends and strangers alike, worrying that any quick trip outside of their safe space might be their death sentence. Finally, the regularity of contact and purpose provided by the workplace was removed as most businesses had to close, and in the process financial insecurity became a further uncertainty, particularly for those on low wages, even as the surreal act by governments of paying part or all of the wages of many private and public sector workers heightened the difference from a normally functioning society. Almost overnight, then, many of life's regularities, predictabilities and certainties vanished.

Such destabilizing events were accompanied by abnormal behaviour in many political arenas. Government ministers were equally unsure of what was emerging, and how to act, and for a significant period of time at the start of the outbreak, many dropped stock-in-trade behaviours of avoidance or deflection to media questioning, and instead acknowledged the complexity, speed and changeability of the virus, and admitted to an ignorance of what the right answer might be to critical questions. They instead deferred to expert advice, which was probably a sensible, even intelligent, thing to do, but which failed to realize on most occasions that even these 'experts' didn't have 'the truth' either, and, whilst better informed than most, were still making judgements and recommendations from the data which could – and were – challenged by others with similar expertise. Such expert advice permitted unusual moments of political honesty, which only began to disappear as questions about governmental lack of preparedness for the pandemic were raised in many countries. For a brief time, though, profound uncertainty helped politicians to behave more honestly, more openly and more flexibly, and suggested a different way of viewing challenges and behaviours. Phrases like 'it's terribly complicated' and 'we can't be certain' were then often not meant – nor taken – as examples of evasive manoeuvres, but more often as accurate descriptions of highly complex events.

Politicians and the general public then came to see that Covid-19 was of a different order of problem from just about any they had previously experienced. Uncertainty about the threat was often not an indicator of personal incompetence but rather a recognition of the need for 'negative capability' – of refusing to rush into action. In a world of quick answers and a politics of evasion, it takes courage to step outside of such habits, and instead to recognize that these were problems which were not going to be solved quickly, but would form part of an uncertainty and complexity that would constitute everyday life for the foreseeable future. This then has the potential to be the beginning of a worldview of a 'new normal', where a lack of certainty and control needed incorporating into daily life. A key area for such induction could then be educational institutions and an essential part of a new educational leadership role.

Bravery, personal care and professional commitment

If some politicians had the bravery to admit that their previous worldviews and political behaviours had been unsuited to coping with Covid, a different order of bravery was exhibited by those having to care for the casualties. A major and widely acknowledged indication of societal collapse was the feared inability of national and local health systems to cope with Covid-19 numbers, and to prevent this, in many countries the medical staff, nurses, social workers and a vast array of others essential to keeping hospitals open discounted or ignored the danger to themselves, and kept on turning up for work, even as some of their colleagues succumbed to the disease. In many cases they suspected or knew that governmental policies were not fully thought through, and could see that much essential protective equipment was not always available. Yet the vast majority resolved to staunchly maintain an ethic of care for those with the infection and in so doing disregarded thoughts for their own personal safety. It was an astonishingly brave and courageous thing to do, reminiscent in many respects to the decision made in 1665 in Eyam in Derbyshire, England, where all of those in that village agreed to remain within a constructed perimeter until the bubonic plague had done its worst. Both in 1665 and 2020, people could not see the disease, and could not detect it, and yet remained to care for the sick and dying. Those in 1665 did so to protect their families and friends, but also those in neighbouring villages; in 2020 many were caring for people they did not know, but saw it as essential to the maintenance of their hospitals and as a personal compassionate response. It is important to note that whilst governments applauded these individuals in 2020-1, and many encouraged others to applaud them, the actions taken by such 'volunteers' had little to do with official exhortations, and even less to do with market demands. The commitment to the care of others was in part an instinctual personal response to others' plight, and in part by a professional ethic of care, much derided in the late-twentieth-century critical literature on professionals. Both were demonstrated in the most important way by individuals being prepared to risk their lives for others. They also provide a very different affective base for educational activity, in caring for others' well-being and sustainability, and are essential underpinnings of a stewardship orientation.

Reinvigorating notions of civil society

Such acts of bravery were then in large part a product of personal commitment, separate from those of the state and the market, which sought to develop within their communities a more caring, cooperative and just ethos. Such discourse – part ethical, part social, part political – has over the last few decades been squeezed between the globalization of neoliberal economics and national enforcement of market rules. Yet many of the positive actions and reactions to Covid-19 have been responses to the cries for help from others in the community, once more demonstrating that societies are not necessarily composed just of individuals steered by state directives and market activities. Societies can also develop a broader civic culture underpinned by deep ethics of care and justice (Etzioni, 1993, 1997). The experience of Covid-19 then provides the opportunity for the reinvigoration of such ethics, and the re-injection of these values into society and its major institutions in combatting other emerging threats. The perceived importance of such discourse then explains the immensely angry reactions when government ministers and their advisors flouted communal agreements on self-isolation for their own personal benefit.

This coalescing of individual responses into group and community responses, and the notion of an emerging civil society, is one in which educational institutions can also play a critical part. Barber (1984) has argued that these organizations, as sites for civil society, could transcend both state interventionism, and the marketization and commodification of activity, in developing an independent critical role. As argued in Chapter 6, educational institutions are ideally placed to develop this notion, as educational leaders help nurture essential qualities to create a democratic space; a safe space, a debating space, a critical space and a developmental space in which to foster a public good perspective for the education of future citizens with stewardship responsibilities. In so doing educational leaders can help educate minds and voices in sustaining a democratic spirit in society, as well as nurturing an essential regard for the wider environment.

The experience of exponential growth

It is significant that exponential growth, a crucial process in the generation of fear and concern by the pandemic, had hardly appeared in public discourse before the appearance of Covid-19. Now, as noted at several places in this book, the process has been a key factor in the increasing dangers of climate change, population growth and consumption activities, and the term 'exponential growth' has been used in the media, though seldom properly explained, its relevance to such problems also often ignored or misunderstood by politicians, which has contributed to the limited action on issues in which this process is involved. Nevertheless, Covid-19 has brought the term centre stage, and a great deal of the concern about the spread of this virus still stems from the speed of its expansion, due to its exponential growth. As already noted, Covid-19 doesn't spread arithmetically but rather exponentially. With linear growth, after 8 rounds, it would only be *36* (1+2+3+4+5+6+7+8). After 8 rounds, with exponential growth, it will not be 128 people that are infected (the number in the eighth round), but *255* (1+2+4+8+16+32+64+128) – the number in all rounds combined. As the number of rounds increases, so an even larger difference appears between linear and exponential growth numbers.

This then is the essence of a disease's 'R rate' – a term which since 2020 has almost become global common currency. The R rate refers to the average number of individuals likely to be infected by someone already infected (Francis, 2020). An R rate of 1 means that those infected by the disease remains at the same number, and if it drops below 1, this signals that it is starting to die out, as less people are now being infected than those who already have the disease, and they will either become immune to the disease or die from it. This R rate varies greatly from disease to disease. Seasonal flu has an R rate of between 0.9 and 2.1, the difference between these two numbers being due to different research estimates, and the context within which the disease is found. Spanish flu had an R of about

1.8–3.00, medieval bubonic plague is now estimated to have had a larger R rate of between 5 and 7, and measles has an astonishing R rate of 12–18 (Francis, 2020). Within a matter of days, the spread could be uncontrollable – and for populations with no previous experience of the disease, absolutely calamitous.

The reason for including discussion of exponential growth here then is not as a warning about Covid-19 per se nor even about the effects that exponential growth has. Rather, the reason is that for the first time in recent history, the concept has been brought centre stage, and there remains real potential for its danger to be better appreciated. If one of the problems with respect to other current and imminent threats like population increase and resource consumption has been a *lack* of appreciation of the role of exponential growth in creating these problems, humanity (and particularly its policymakers and educators) now has a real opportunity to communicate to others the basis of the dangers of this process.

The employment of Covid-19 concern for other threats

The experience of Covid-19 is not new, but rather the latest in a long line of traumatic pandemics. The bubonic plague of 1347–9, for example, probably killed about 50 per cent of the population of Europe, with reports of bodies being left in the street and wolves roaming the outskirts of major cities (Martin, 2015). People were traumatized by such terrible events, in part because at that time the existence of both bacteria or viruses was unknown, there was also no proper understanding of the vectors of the infection and no knowledge of effective treatment, and such profound ignorance was often couched within a worldview of a supreme being who was causing such outbreaks in order to punish a sinful mankind. With so little known but the effects so dreadful, these must have been truly awful times.

The more recent global pandemic of Spanish flu in 1918–19 killed over fifty million people worldwide (Spinney, 2017), and probably began in the United States, before being transported by troops to Europe. It entered a world exhausted and still fighting the First World War, where secrecy was a prime objective, and where troop movements facilitated its worldwide spread. Yet again, lack of knowledge was a major contributor to its spread: wartime secrecy was part of this, but knowledge of viruses was still very limited whilst a great deal was known about bacteria, and perhaps unsurprisingly then the medical diagnosis was that Spanish flu was a strain of bacteria. Unfortunately, it was a virus which remained untouched and unchecked by most treatments, and terrifyingly took out the youngest and healthiest of populations.

Medical and epidemiological sciences have developed considerably since then. When the Covid-19 outbreak began in 2020, it was quickly identified as a virus, as was its genetic structure, its zoonotic nature and its initial location, possibly spread by animals to man at a wet market in Wuhan, China, though little is certain about this at present. Yet despite swift and informed action, it still produced reactions similar to earlier viral outbreaks: there was considerable fear of this invisible killer, and a lack of understanding of personal avoidance; moreover, a largely unrestrained 24/7 media coverage kept such concerns front and centre, some reports based on the latest events and research, but others based on rumours and half-truths, which created even more panic and disorientation.

If one compares levels of concern for Covid-19 with those for other present forms of threat – like climate change and environmental destruction – it is clear that over the last few decades these other threats have failed to attract the same level of high and immediate attention that Covid-19 did. This is perhaps understandable: Covid-19 has been an immediately presenting concern, and globally people have seen body bags, people struggling to breathe, hospitals built in days rather than months or years and health workers in tears from sheer exhaustion. As already suggested, the reaction to Covid-19 was not unlike a frog dropped into boiling water: the frog almost immediately realizes that it needs to get out very quickly if it is to survive. The covert danger from other recent threats, however, is more often like frogs being dropped into lukewarm water, where they run the different danger of acclimatizing to the water's rising temperature. One of the key lessons which might be learnt from Covid-19 then is that the experience of the virus might be used to help raise greater awareness of these other threats. It is to this educational objective – changing understanding and experience of other threats from a lukewarm to a much warmer response – that the chapter now turns.

From lukewarm to warmer responses

Covid-19 has then been a sudden, unexpected and, for too many, a deadly experience, and governments have scrambled towards containment, to create testing and remediation strategies, to producing effective vaccines for a rapidly moving and invisible killer. Such a 'boiling water' level of awareness would then likely be very helpful in focusing more attention – and then more action – upon 'lukewarm water' perceptions of issues like climate change, rather than waiting for them to become boiling water events – even as events in Australia and the Western United States and Canada in 2020–1 suggest that the water is beginning to feel much warmer. One way to do this would be to use the different experiences which Covid-19 has generated and apply them to issues so far greeted with only 'lukewarm' responses.

Many of these experiences have been negative ones – fear and concern probably being outstanding, and it may be thought rather problematic to utilize such feelings as stimuli for greater awareness and action. However, such feelings can be part of exercises asking people to understand and share the feelings of those who have gone through a similar experience in order to develop a greater empathy for them. Furthermore, whilst fear is an emotional component of many experiences, it can be used positively as a component of concern, where individuals attempt to understand and find ways of resolving such concern. Perhaps most importantly, such reactions are very often accompanied by positive feelings of care, compassion and cooperation, thereby demonstrating the bravery of individuals in such situations.

With such considerations in mind, we begin by examining how both positive and negative concerns generated by Covid-19 might be applied to issues given more 'lukewarm' attention. Such concerns are derived from a number of sources: a personal analysis of negative and positive media reactions to Covid-19; negative and positive reports on consequences; genetically inherited responses to threats (Marshall, 2015; Gardner, 2009), and finally from the qualities used in analysing the risk of an event (Slovic, 2000). The four major forms of concern are then suggested as:

1. Concerns about the unknown;
2. Concerns about uncertainty;
3. Concerns about harm to oneself;
4. Wider concerns about the consequences.

The following are not intended as exhaustive summaries of the possibilities but rather as providing starting points from which more detailed examples can be developed.

Concern about the unknown

Concern about the unknown may stem from when there is so much that is not known about a particular threat that the parameters of the threat cannot be identified. So, a first example of such 'concern of the unknown' would be:

a. A lack of knowledge or understanding about the nature of a threat.
This deficit can be underpinned by other examples:

b. A lack of understanding of how the impact of this threat will occur.
c. The realization that if a threat is initially invisible, then the impact is unlikely to be detected until it actually occurs.
d. A lack of understanding of how to prevent such an impact.

Concern about uncertainty

Concern about the unknown is then highly likely to produce feelings of general uncertainty and once more there may be different kinds of examples, which could include:

a. Uncertainty from a feeling of lack of personal control.
b. An uncertainty stemming from the fact that the threat seems to spread more rapidly than it can be tracked.
c. Uncertainty about how to prevent the impact.
d. An uncertainty stemming from the feeling that a society, or key institutions within it, are no longer coping with the threat.

Concern about personal harm

Understandably, concern for one's own safety is usually high on most people's agendas and may contain examples of:

a. The degree of perceived personal risk.
b. Those parts of the threat which cause most individual concern (perhaps the ease and unseen nature of its transmission).
c. The immediacy of the risk to oneself.
d. How personal knowledge and/or experience of similar episodes can exacerbate this fear and concern.

Wider concerns about the consequences

Concern doesn't just relate to the effects upon oneself. They can also relate to:

a. Effects on identifiable others – family, friends, community and individuals highlighted in the media.
b. Concern about the personal financial cost of its occurrence.
c. Increased concern for oneself and others as death tolls rise.
d. Concern raised by extensive and overhyped media coverage.

However, wider consequences can also refer to positive responses and much can then be made of such concerns as will be seen in Table 9.2.

These forms and their different examples suggest that the concern, and more positive feelings and thoughts about a particular threat, are unlikely to be caused by just one example of a threat, but more likely by a combination of different feelings, thoughts and events, each of which may vary in importance depending on the context and the individual. So, by examining different forms and finer-grained examples, it may be possible to make comparisons between responses to Covid-19 and those of other threats which as yet are not fully developed. This can then help generate greater focus – and concern – about these other threats before they become really damaging.

However, if this is to work, then the comparative level of the threat needs taking into account. Climate change, for example, is not one threat, but an 'umbrella threat': a combination of several. Even though it has one central cause – the increase in greenhouse gases through humanity's overuse of fossil fuels – 'climate change' is still a shorthand for a number of threats, most noticeably (i) increases in global temperatures, (ii) significant rises in sea levels and (iii) increases in weather volatility and severity. From these can come even finer-grained threats. Thus, rises in global temperatures will likely result in new health concerns amongst which are likely to be: the spread of 'tropical' diseases; more and larger forest and bush fires; crop failures, species' extinctions and damaging weather changes. Sea-level rises will likely result in greater ecosystem damage; the flooding of previously productive land and increased soil salinity; significant declines in food production in such areas and the probable future evacuation of coastal cities. Finally, increased weather volatility and severity will create major threats to personal and community safety, extensive damage to property and crops, and also to ecosystem sustainability (Henson, 2011).

Covid-19, however, is not an umbrella threat, but rather a single threat caused by the impact of a particular virus on human beings, even as a number of unexpected impacts from it have affected the functioning of different parts of human societies. 'Climate change' is then of a different order from Covid-19, and the threat from this virus then needs comparing with a similar level of threat. The threat of global temperature rise will then be used, and different examples of the two threats are compared in Table 9.1.

Now if one compares issues of concern for Covid-19 and global temperature rises, it can be seen that the examples in the first three areas – 'fear of the unknown', 'fear from uncertainty' and 'fear of personal harm' – have generated stronger reactions to Covid-19 than they have so far for global temperature

Table 9.1 Threat Qualities and Concerns – Comparing Covid-19 and Global Temperature Rise

Category	Quality	Covid-19	Global temperature rise
Concerns about the unknown	1. Unfamiliarity with the nature of the threat	Initial high concern – last global pandemic 100 years ago	Low-medium concern: 'weather' events are thought to be understood
	2. Lack of understanding of how the impact will occur	Medium/high concern – some knowledge, but much still not understood by the general public	Low-medium concern – this is thought to be largely understood contextually
	3. Invisibility: impact cannot be detected until it occurs	High – and likely to continue high as virus variants appear	Low-medium concern – threat understood, if actual events still relatively unpredictable
Concerns of uncertainty	1. Lack of personal control	High – due to the large number of 'unknown' qualities	Low-medium concern: only perceived as a fear-inducing event when extremes are experienced
	2. Threat can spread very rapidly	High concern, due to rapid incidence of infections	Seen as low-medium – concern can be raised by tracking changes over many years
	3. Uncertainty over how to prevent impact	High – due to highly infectious nature even when a carrier displays no symptoms	Medium, but not high concern due to lack of immediacy of impact and long-term impact on many occasions
Concerns about personal harm	1. Perceived personal risk	High at peak of outbreak – and appearance of new variants	Low concern most of the time, though strong contextual examples are increasing in number
	2. Nature of threat causing most individual concern	High due to categories 1 and 2.	Low concern, though strong contextual element
	3. Immediacy of risk to oneself	High but context-dependent	Low concern, though again with strong contextual examples are increasing
Wider effects	1. Effects on identifiable others – family, friends and community	High concern declining to medium as vaccines are produced	Low-medium concern, contextual
	2. Concerns about financial costs	Initially low, moving to high, and only slow decline	Low-medium concern currently, but contextually variable

3. Increased concern as death toll rises	Higher as death rate rises, lower as it falls	Low-medium concern, but an increase in contextual examples
4. Media coverage accentuates concern	Very high; not reduced to medium due to introduction of second and third waves of infection by new variants and clash between health and economic concerns	Initially low-medium concern, moving to medium-high as climate change issues become globally concerning

rises. This is unsurprising: Covid-19 was completely unknown, and it infected populations rapidly and invisibly, hospitalizing and killing significant numbers in the process. In contrast, people may still think that they understand the consequences of large temperature rises because of previous experiences of localized high temperatures, and therefore greater confidence is felt in preparing for instances of this threat. Moreover, some may still feel that there is no real proof to suggest that such warming events are symptomatic of a long-term dangerous trend. In so doing, they ignore decades of data drawn from many different sites which support longer-term higher temperature projections (Henson, 2011; IPCC, 2018). However it remains the case that many fail to take sufficient interest to incorporate such understanding into their worldview of potential threats. The large proportion of areas of 'high concern' with Covid-19, as opposed to the 'lows' and 'mediums' of global temperature increases, is perhaps then not that surprising, even as the high responses to Covid-19 may be reduced somewhat by greater understanding of the nature of the disease, by effective vaccines becoming globally available and then by local and national mortality rates declining.

In contrast, ratings of rising global temperatures for all areas will probably increase, not in the medium to long term as previously thought, but in the short-medium term, as this threat is now becoming more noticeable and more worrying, and accompanied by increased feelings of personal threat. Indeed, as global temperatures rise, and there are more frequent occurrences of extreme weather, this threat will become much more comparable to the present threat of Covid-19; there is also likely to come a point in the short-medium term when the overall perceived danger from rising global temperatures overtakes that of the perceived danger of Covid-19. The more seriously the threat is taken, and the more quickly action is adopted, the less damage it is likely to cause in the future. Comparisons between perceptions of the Covid-19 threat and that of global temperature rises could then help develop greater awareness in educational institutions and in education generally of rising global temperatures. This will be addressed in the next section

Heightening perceptions

Table. 9.2 then summarizes the manner in which the reasons for the generally higher levels of concern for Covid-19 might currently be used to increase awareness of global temperature changes and of the potential for positive responses to such concerns.

Table 9.2 Increasing Awareness of Global Temperature Rises

Category	Quality	Covid-19 concern level	Increasing the awareness of global temperature rises
Concern about the unknown	a. Unfamiliarity with the nature of the threat	High concern because last global pandemic with high death rates was a century ago	Highlight examples of unrecognized consequences of temperature increases – and actions that can be taken
	b. Lack of understanding of how the impact will occur	Medium-high concern: lack of clarity why some groups are most likely to become casualties, e.g. the elderly	Point out how some groups are more likely to become casualties, e.g. the elderly (as with Covid) – and how this needs preventing
	c. Invisibility: the impact cannot be detected until it occurs	High concern because virus is undetectable to the average person	Highlight how some temperature increase impacts may be unrecognized, e.g. heat stroke, but what actions can be taken to reduce such risk
	d. Lack of understanding on how to prevent the impact	High concern moving to medium as/if effective vaccines become available	Low concern over short-term impact – so highlight impact of long-term trends, with examples of remedies for this problem
Fear from uncertainty	a. Lack of personal control	High concern: often, only possible personal control seen as avoiding contact with others	Show how impacts in the long term can be countered by present-day actions under personal control
	b. Threat can spread very rapidly	High concern through much recent experience	Show how distress from extreme temperatures can occur quickly, and detail possible preventive actions
	c. Uncertainty concerning how to prevent impact	High concern reducing to medium as vaccines come on stream and numbers of casualties decline	Demonstrate how current small personal actions can moderate longer-term consequences
	d. Concern that society is no longer coping	Context-dependent, but has occasionally reached high-medium	Use past and near-future stories to contextualize threat, to highlight dangers and remediation

(Continued)

Table 9.2 Continued

Concern over personal harm	a. Perceived personal risk	High concern at peak of outbreak, now national and local variations in casualty numbers, and appearance of new disease variants	Describe, contextualize and personalize near-future personal risks and the means of their avoidance
	b. Nature of threat which causes most individual concern	High due to unknown and unpredictable nature of threat	Which consequences of temperature rise cause most individual concern, and what remediation can be applied?
	c. Immediacy of risk to oneself	High concern declining as number of casualties decline, rises as new variants arrive	Contextualize and personalize near-future immediacy of risks and potential remedies
	d. Personal knowledge and/or experience of similar things	Low-medium cause at first, increasing to high/medium as more infections take place, reducing as casualty numbers reduce	Draw on personal memories and extrapolate to near future contextualized instances with potential remedies
Wider negative and positive impacts	a. Effects on identifiable others – family, friends, community	High concern, but also uplifting events, concern declining as casualty figures decline	Personalize and contextualize past negative and positive examples, using data, and near-future stories
	b. Concern about personal financial costs	Initially low concern, increasingly moving to high	Personalize costs now and in the future, with negative and positive events
	c. Increased concern as death toll rises	High concern as death rate rises, declining as vaccines come on stream	Use longitudinal data to personalize and contextualize both negative and positive long-term impacts
	d. Media coverage	High effect on concern at first, but many positive stories possible of bravery, resilience, etc.	Prioritize media coverage which ensures both positive and negative issues are brought centre stage

Issues of pedagogy

As important as are the actions suggested in Table 9.2 to make current threats of global temperature rise more immediate and important, and to highlight positive aspects of this experience, it is equally important to consider the best means of communicating these. Following are suggestions of a number of ways in which interest can be stimulated (and see Gardner, 2009 on this as well).

So whilst the use of rising and declining numbers of casualties can be impactful, use of figures and statistics tends not to 'stick' in the mind as much as personalized stories. This being the case, positive and negative news and events are often better remembered when they are communicated as stories. Moreover, the use of stories as means of communication can normally be made more memorable if they are personalized. In other words, it is usually a good idea to place recognizably unique individuals (both fictional and non-fictional) within stories of particular threats, with variations on how resolutions were devised, as well as variations on how successful these were.

In addition, both negative and positive events are also made more memorable if a real person's memories of such events are used. With Covid-19 the content of such memories changed as the pandemic was responded to. With rising temperatures, there is a much longer history here, one which can draw on examples from the level of the personal experience, through to those at the level of communities and beyond to national and global levels.

However, an important caveat here is that stories are almost always more convincing if they are contextualized to places, times and events that readers can recognize. Many will then resonate to stories of health workers, care home workers, delivery drivers and teachers all coping with new and unexpected situations. However, other more historic examples of bravery – such as that of Eyam described earlier – can broaden the picture and stimulate thoughts and feelings of empathy for individuals hundreds of years distant.

Moreover, stories are also made more interesting if novel or unrecognized angles or impacts are utilized, and again all the more so if they are true. The example of Captain Tom Moore and his 100 walks around his garden in 2020 to raise money for the UK National Health Service was an amazing and heart-warming story, an effort which raised over £30 million. Such stories can then be used in any number of ways – of how even the oldest in society can contribute to the communal, of how often and quickly people pick up and celebrate the efforts of such individuals, and as examples of how societies are not necessarily based on individual self-interest, but often on unstinting attempts to contribute to the greater good. Once again, such examples are not meant to constitute an exhaustive list. The huge well of creativity that exists in virtually all teaching professions would ensure that this list is easily expanded, contextualized and personalized, in ways that make positive and negative experiences of threats more relevant to particular audiences. The manner of the communication is as important as the nature of the communication.

Finally, educators can make significant contributions here by identifying critical 'leverage point' actions which mitigate the effects of a threat before it has become substantial. This could be a strong curricular innovation, as stories of future threats – both positive and negative – can be made more relevant by explaining how small current actions can act as important leverage points to impact in significant ways on existing situations, thereby reducing the impact of future threats. In so doing, educational institutions would also be making early contributions to needed changes in a social and political culture.

Concluding thoughts

Utilizing experiences from the Covid-19 threat, this chapter has attempted to make more relevant the danger of threats which, if not focused upon now, may become more dangerous in the future. It has looked at personal and political reactions to the appearance of Covid-19, and how different kinds of emotions and actions – including bravery and care – have been demonstrated by individuals facing this threat, reactions which might be used to help raise awareness of other kinds of threats.

Covid-19 has also demonstrated once more how complex and unpredictable many events in this world are, which in itself further questions a worldview of certainty and control. Yet in trying to design systems which *guarantee* greater certainty and control, societies may be adopting models of reality which do not map onto the way in which the world actually works. Reflection on the Covid-19 experience then also helps better appreciation of the uncertainty created in a world which is considerably more complex and unpredictable than is often thought.

The pandemic also showed how people are very often not driven by self-interest, but more often by care and concern for others which could help create more just and cooperative societies. Larger political questions may then also be raised by the input that educational institutions could have in developing more robust conceptions of a civil society underpinned by conceptions of national and global public goods. In thinking of the politics of society as having only two dimensions – the state and the market – this important element is omitted.

In sum, if events like Covid-19 and other future threats are to be better dealt with, then ways need to be found of accepting and working with greater compassion and consideration for the needs of others, with much greater degrees of uncertainty and complexity, and with a wider conception of citizenship participation in societal politics. These could then be foundational to the development of assumptions of what a future 'new normal' might look like, ones which could form the basis not only of future societies but of future school communities as well.

10

The Ethical Commitments of Steward Leaders

Introduction: Developing an ethical stewardship framework

In Chapter 8, leverage points were suggested which, through reducing the impact of covert threats, could help prevent the emergence of tipping points. Meadows (2008) suggested that these leverage points had three different levels, the most influential being level 1 'mental models,' or 'frames', which human beings use when trying to structure their understanding of the world around them. Because these frames focus and direct our perceptions, attitudes and actions, they are normally the most important leverage points. In this chapter I want to describe fundamentally important level 1 leverage points for developing a stewardship framework, which consist of the kinds of ethical commitments which steward leaders need to embrace, the practice of which could make a major difference to societal and educational attitudes.

The steward leadership advocated in this book is in part a leadership directed at helping other human beings, and particularly their students, in living fulfilling and sustainable lives. However, it transcends such foci through the recognition that human sustainability is dependent not only upon the social and economic values and practices of human societies but, even more importantly, upon the preservation and sustainability of the natural environment and of those things living within it. Without a sustainable natural environment, there can be no sustainable humanity. Steward leaders therefore need to embrace a new and critical part of their role: communicating these concerns and understandings to their students, colleagues and their communities. In so doing, they can raise their students' awareness of their own developing responsibilities and help them to use such recognition in critiquing personal plans and ambitions, not only in the present but also in their adult futures and to then pass this on to the generations after them.

A number of ethical commitments are then proposed to inform the nature of such stewardship. Such adoption in reality has both ethical and practical components, and whilst this chapter focuses particularly on the ethical reasons, very often practical reasons for such commitment often intertwine and support ethical positions. Such interactions between the ethical and the practical have already been raised in this book, and these will be pulled together in this chapter in order to provide a full picture of the nature of the ethical underpinnings of a steward leadership role.

The need for different ethical approaches

The commitment by educational leaders to develop their role beyond its traditional underpinnings into one which not only recognizes the kinds of threats described in this book but which also develops personal and institutional responses to them will require an approach based on different kinds of ethical theories. One kind of ethical theory is *consequentialist* in nature, arguing that ethical judgements about right and wrong are made by examining the effects of actions on other living beings. If this is the case, then clearly actions which negatively affect the well-being of human beings and of all other living things as well, need to be the subject of ethical judgements. With respect to stewardship, this kind of ethical theory is impelled by the fact that humanity has been largely responsible for the current damage to the environment and its species, and, if not careful, is liable to pass on such consequences to future generations. We therefore need to provide reparation for present damage and ensure the sustainability of the environment, other species and future human generations. A second, *deontological* form of ethical theory argues that judgements of right or wrong should be made on the basis of whether an action is right or wrong when judged by reference to a particular series of rules or laws (e.g. the Universal Declaration of Human Rights, the Ten Commandments). Legal and religious systems at least in part function through judgements on the transgressions of such rules and laws. In terms of its application to notions of stewardship, humanity is the dominant species on this planet, and the only one which understands not only the damage it has done but also the only one which is capable of repairing this, and many moral codes argue that it therefore has a duty to repair this damage and take measures to improve the planet's present sustainability.

The first of these two theories then focuses on the consequences of human actions and the second on the nature of human actions with respect to the natural world judged within particular sets of rules and the duties that emanate from such judgements. Both of these theories are then based on notions of rationality, moving from accepted standards and applying these to specific instances which then produce what many would regard as impartial judgements. However, both lack reference to the affective part of the human psyche, and the need for an underpinning *ethic of care* about the plight of others. Focusing on such impartiality and abstractness then runs the danger of neglecting that side of human beings concerned with emotional functioning. Such theories may then fail to dwell upon the uniqueness of individuals and the contexts within which they find themselves. This is why writers like Gilligan (1989), Noddings (1995) and Engster (2007) argue for the need for a third form of moral theory, based upon an ethic of care. Engster (2007) then points out that 'caring is at the heart of human existence . . . in a world without care, human life would be truly *poor, solitary, nasty, brutish, and short.*' Yet, despite such acknowledged importance, Western thought has generally not paid the role of care the attention it deserves in moral and political philosophy. So whilst Gilligan (1989), for instance, agrees that notions of justice and duty are important, she argues that one should not forget to examine the contexts and personalities within situations, and that whilst it is often asked, 'what is just?' it is just as important if not more so in real life to ask, 'how should we respond?' At bottom, the crucial impulse, Noddings (1995, p. 14) suggests, should be 'the maintenance of the caring relation'. This third kind of ethical approach is woven into higher-level cooperative and collaborative approaches to politics and society, and, in terms of a stewardship role, can and should be applied to human beings and other species who are vulnerable, dependent and unable to respond to situations threatening their existence, as it translates beyond the needs of individuals and groups within a single-species orientation, and towards support for a multi-species sustainability. Finally, it is also an ethic which, it will be argued in the final chapter, is fundamental to the creation of leadership teams best equipped to deal with the kind of wicked problems discussed in this book.

Despite the fact that these three ethical approaches often conflict theoretically, decisions in real life are very often practical attempts at assessing the claims produced by all three theories and then coming to judgements which provide a degree of recognition of all their claims. In this way, the contributions of the different perspectives and persuasions of consequences, responsibilities and care can all help to arrive at suitably 'wicked' judgements, and in so doing avoid the 'tame' application of abstract rules to particular situations. Instead, they ask that individuals and groups wrestle with the messy contextualized nature of most situations occurring in real life.

Educational stewardship is then not a tame description of a particular aspect of the leadership role, nor is it the tame application of an ethical theory. It is the wicked application of all three theories described; first, the need for individuals, their colleagues and community to consider the consequences of their actions, and particularly the recognition of the damage done by their species to this planet and to other species living upon it; second, the need to recognize the responsibility that human beings have for ensuring global sustainability, and particularly because *Homo sapiens* is the only species currently able to remedy the situation which it has created; and finally, to acknowledge and practice the calling and commitment to help others, to find solutions to problems through cooperation, and to relieve the difficulties and sufferings that many kinds of groups, individuals and members of this and other species experience, and are incapable of resolving themselves.

The ethical commitments of the steward leader

Whilst all three ethical approaches are essential, this stewardship approach is ultimately realized through the embrace and practice of six values which focus upon particular areas of stewardship concern. Now these, it is argued, are ethical commitments essential to an educational approach to stewardship, and in further developing this position, they are therefore central to those leading such enhancement. They are also all commitments which embody the three ethical positions described earlier. This chapter then explores each of the ethical commitments of a steward leader.

Conservation as an essential commitment

This ethic advocates the protection of and where necessary, the restoration of the natural environment and those living within it – in other words a commitment to preserving the biosphere. It also rejects the view that the biosphere is primarily a human resource, created for our exploitation. Instead, it argues that the biosphere contains living creatures that not only possess an intrinsic right to existence (a deontological position) but that much of the motivation for such an ethic derives from a deep care for other living creatures (a care position) and finally a recognition of the consequences not only for ourselves but for all other living creatures if we fail to do this (a consequentialist position). This ethic then argues that each human generation has a responsibility to protect the existence of other living beings and to hold these in trust for the stewardship of future generations, so that what is passed on should never knowingly be exhausted, ruined or made extinct. Transgression of this ethic would occur when this biosphere is viewed as existing primarily for man's benefit, and its exploitation leads to lasting damage, with little care or thought being given to its preservation other than as a valuable human asset.

One powerful way of understanding the range of such responsibilities is to refer to the work of Rockstrom and colleagues (Rockstrom et al., 2009; Rockstrom and Klum, 2015), who suggest that nine planetary boundaries must be maintained if conditions are to continue within which the biosphere is sustainable, and which therefore provide both ethical and practical conservation boundaries which should not be transgressed. The areas suggested by Rockstrom and Klum (2015) then concern:

- The amount of freshwater utilized;
- The amount of land converted to food production for human beings;
- The loss of species and biodiversity in general;
- The degree of air pollution;
- The depletion of the ozone layer;
- The speed and degree of climate change;
- The extent of ocean acidification;
- The degree of pollution of land, sea and air by man-made chemicals;
- The extent of the use of fertilizers.

Raworth (2017), in reviewing the level of transgression of these boundaries, suggests that most are worsening, with only one (ozone depletion) actually improving – though, as Benedick (1998) points out, the reasons for this area of improvement may be due to the conjoining of particular social, political and engineering factors which do not apply to other areas. Attenborough (2020), using a slightly different list, claims that humanity is currently transgressing at least four boundaries – the overuse of fertilizers, the unsustainable conversion of natural habitats into farmland, the excessive warming of the planet through greenhouse gas emissions and finally a biodiversity loss so severe as to suggest that a sixth great species extinction is probably in progress.

The content of any such list is clearly contestable, as is the precise specification of any boundary transgression, as transgression in one context may not be as damaging as in another, as with, for instance, the accepted boundary level for air pollution. Such estimations are more wicked than tame estimations, even as the appreciation of the complexity of such judgements is often underestimated. Such complex judgements are based on the gathering of appropriate evidence (which is a contestable and wicked issue in itself), and which then needs subjecting to both practical and ethical debate and discussion. One would also expect that when environmental conditions change, or when new factors are discovered and need including in such calculations, decisions on what are acceptable environmental boundaries, or on what other boundaries need including, will change as well. We are then in a very wicked territory – practically and ethically.

There are, however, further considerations which raise difficult ethical and political questions. There is now little doubt that human beings have over the last few centuries been the principal contributors to the vast majority of such boundary transgressions. In the last 100 years, for instance, there has been an exponential rise in human population growth with an accompanying exponential rise in the consumption of global resources, and similar rises in pollution and loss of diversity (Dasgupta, 2021). However, only a small portion of humanity has historically enjoyed the benefits of such resource extraction and resultant consumption. Moreover, it is the same minority of wealthy countries, and wealthy people in wealthy and poor countries, which have been predominantly responsible for such boundary transgressions. If such problems are to be remedied, a critical part of any discussion will need to focus upon arriving at a more equitable distribution of current resources, and the apportioning of the cost of remedial actions, which many will feel need to be laid primarily at the feet of those who historically have principally enjoyed such benefits. This is another area of wicked problems not easily resolved but in which discussion and debate about responsibility for the transgression of such planetary boundaries need to be a central concern. An education into such understanding would be a new, challenging, but essential, addition to the role of an educational leader.

An ethical commitment to multi-species sustainability

The call for multi-species sustainability is closely allied to that of conservation as both are committed to the notion that other species, besides that of human beings, have a (deontological) intrinsic right to existence. However, this commitment also has caring and consequentialist ethical roots. So there is now a growing recognition of both the intelligence and the depth of feelings of other species. In Western thinking this has been a long and arduous journey. Many of its foremost thinkers have simply dismissed the rights of other creatures. Kant (1964), for instance, argued that animals are not self-conscious, but are there 'merely as a means to an end. That end is man . . . our duties towards animals are merely indirect duties towards humanity.' Marx (1971, p. 94) similarly argued that 'nature becomes simply an object for mankind, purely a matter of utility'. Finally, Freud (1930, p. 30) was probably the most hostile, arguing that we should be 'combining with the rest of the human community and taking up the attack on nature, thus forcing it to obey human will'. With such a strong intellectual pedigree it is unsurprising that it was a long time before Singer's (1981) notion of an 'expanding circle' of ethics would be given full public consideration, proposing as it did to move beyond moral obligations to those close to us, to expand these to those within our culture, then to other cultures, and then on to the rights of other species, and of our duties towards them. Some of this movement had come from Rousseau (1950, p. 224), who, arguing from an ethic of care, suggested that the very human quality of compassion was something that 'the very brutes themselves sometimes give evident proof of'. Nor should one forget that other cultural traditions, like the Indian and Japanese, have never taken up such separation between humans and non-human animals. Moreover, relatively recent findings about both intelligence and emotion have rolled back the claims of unique human qualities, as many species of animals have unexpectedly displayed similar abilities and emotions (Midgely, 1983; Mason and Macarthy, 1996; deWaal, 2017). With what looks like an ever-closing gap in abilities and emotions between the human and other species, an expanded intrinsic right to existence, and thereby the call for human beings to have a duty to commit to a multi-species sustainability, has become all the more convincing.

Another source for such an ethic is the mystical/religious ethic that all life is precious. As Schweizer (1949, p. 245) argued:

> in world and life affirmation, and in ethics I carry out the will of the universal will to live.

Schweitzer argues that we have become aware of this precious life-ethic in ways which other animals and plants of the natural world have not, and indeed that this understanding of the unity and interdependence of all life is in practice compromised by the brute fact that 'One existence makes its way at the cost of another: one destroys the other' (p. 245). This contradiction between an understanding of the unity of all life with the realization of the competition for life within and between species then impels Schweitzer to propose an ethic for human beings where they commit to preserving the life of all species. Yet, as Attenborough (2020, p. 125) points out, in the present day one of the more noticeable things about many human societies is in fact the *lack* of any such commitment, largely because of our current *under*-connectedness with much of the rest of the living world. It is why Attenborough (2020, p. 125) suggests that over the last few centuries 'we have moved from being a part of nature to being apart from nature', and for both ethical and practical reasons, the reversal of this process is essential.

This links well with the need for a more optimal connectedness which Dunbar (2010) describes. But it is also likely to come through recognizing that multi-species sustainability is far more important in the grand scheme of things than the sustainability of just one species. Humanity then needs to develop a much greater realization of the myriad ways in which it depends on other species' flourishing for its own sustainability. Human beings are but one species in the creation of a multi-species sustainability, and the consequences of ignoring the sustainability of other species by focusing only on our species is a path to our own extinction.

An ethic of individual well-being

Raworth (2017) argues that if environmental boundaries constitute an outer circle which humanity should not transgress, indicators of well-being constitute an inner circle which describes the minimum requirements for individual human well-being. Raworth's seminal contribution, *Doughnut Economics*, invites us to imagine a doughnut where, for considerations of well-being, the inner circle line constitutes an ethical boundary and crossing this line and the subsequent falling into the 'hole' in the middle then represents well-being transgression. If the outer line then constitutes the environmental boundary line, and the inner line constitutes the well-being boundary line, then the substance of the doughnut represents the sustainable space within which human activity should be practised.

Raworth (p. 296) also suggests twelve dimensions of well-being, most of them stemming from a deep sense of care for others, which also provides indicators of the consequences of falling below such minimum condition, as well as percentages and yearly estimates for such requirements. Table. 10.1 reproduces this list, with brief summaries of each indicator.

A number of points need making here. First, Table 10.1 is a strong example of how the ethical and the practical are often hard to separate. Raworth's list is a highly practical one, underpinned by the argument that it would be unethical to deprive people of such 'goods' if we care about their personal well-being. Second, however, her list cannot be definitive, as it necessarily is a choice of well-being indicators, in part based on human biological necessities, on current cultural and

Table 10.1 Minimum Requirements for Human Well-being and Indicators of Unacceptable Deficits

Dimensions	Illustrative indicators of well-being deficits
Food	Undernourished individuals and populations
Health	High child mortality and low life expectancy
Education	Widespread illiteracy, and large numbers of 12- to 15-year-olds not at school
Income and work	High proportion of populations living at international poverty levels, and high proportion of 12- to 15-year-olds unemployed and unable to find work
Water and sanitation	Limited access to drinking water and unacceptable levels of sanitation
Energy	Lack of access to electricity and clean cooking facilities
Networks	Little or no access to people who can help in times of trouble
Housing	Large numbers in slum housing
Gender equality	Significant disparities between males and females in national governance and in earnings
Social equity	Large gap between the earnings of the top 10 per cent in a population and the bottom 40 per cent
Political voice	Limited ability to express political opinions in national and local governance
Peace and justice	People living in countries with high levels of corruption and violence

value preferences, and finally on present-day needs and wants. It then invites one to consider other items which might be included – and which might be dropped. A few items listed in Table 10.1 might come to be seen as products of their time, and might be withdrawn at some time in the future if they cease being central to what is needed for such well-being. The need for electricity might then be one to disappear at some stage in the future if other forms of energy come to be discovered and preferred. For inclusion, one might choose both 'personal fulfilment' and 'sufficient leisure time', even as there would likely be considerable debate about what the terms mean in practice, and what constitutes a deficit or ethical transgression in them. 'Access to the internet' might be another item for inclusion: whilst unimaginable fifty years ago, it is probably thought by many nowadays as essential to individual well-being, particularly if education and employment were to be largely accessed through it.

Further, and following the description of the ethics of conservation and multi-species sustainability earlier, one might ask why well-being should be considered only for human beings. Even though one of the outer planetary boundaries detailed under this ethic is that of the survival of species and biodiversity in general, merely ensuring that species survive seems a very weak minimum standard of well-being and care. This then raises questions as to what or to whom the concept of well-being should be applied and, also, what the term might mean if applied to other species. It would also be unsurprising if the idea of supporting the well-being of every species was queried: whilst we may want to maintain the well-being of gorillas and dolphins, do we really want to maintain the well-being of the plague bacillus? Serious attempts should still be made to define 'minimum standards', and to who or what these should be applied, but as with questions of justice and equity in monetary contributions to greater global sustainability, questions of defining species well-being underline the fact that creating and implementing any stewardship framework will be underpinned by varied, difficult and often extremely wicked questions. Educational leaders need to be one of the primary groups appreciating this fact, and once more counselling against the siren calls of simple and tame answers

An ethical commitment to imperative sufficiency

Whilst the first ethic discussed – that of conservation – argues that the earth's resources are much more than a list of items for humanity to consume, nevertheless it is the case that much of the biosphere is and will continue for the foreseeable future to be viewed by humans as an exploitable resource. Because of such a view of the world – and the widespread adoption of neoliberal economic thinking which facilitates it – the concepts of efficiency, infinite growth and consumption have all gained dominant roles in societal thinking. However, they are seldom referenced by the effect their practice has on the natural environment, nor that this particular economic theory fails to recognize that infinite growth and consumption are not possible in a world of finite resources. Moreover, great concern should be expressed about the consequences when human beings are classified primarily as human resources, rather than being viewed as resourceful humans contributing to the good of their community and society. The acceptance of such economic assumptions would also turn individuals into eager participants in Boulding's (1968/89) 'cowboy world', where well-being is measured by how much and how quickly they can consume the earth's resources, not by how consumption needs limiting in order to maintain such resource stocks.

Now Princen (2005) examines the different ways in which humanity has exploited this environment, and suggests that this has been performed in three major ways. He argues that we need to move away completely from the first 'cowboy' world which Boulding spoke of. This he calls a *weak sufficiency* view, one in which the environment is seen as infinitely exploitable by human beings. In practical terms, there is little doubt that humanity still has some considerable way to go in rejecting this behaviour. As Vidal (2017) has argued with respect to rainforests,

> In just 40 years, possibly 1bn hectares, the equivalent of Europe, has gone. Half the world's rainforests have been razed in a century.... At current rates, they will vanish altogether in 100 years. (*The Guardian* 23/01/2017)

Princen then moves from this weak sufficiency view towards a more *moderate view of sufficiency*, where the environment needs to be seen as part of a carefully considered trade-off between its sustainability and the wants and needs of humanity. This is probably the current position for many, sometimes from basic practical needs, sometimes from more ephemeral wants, but it is a position which because of its 'trade-off' nature is open to considerable abuse and mistakes which could still end with the extinction of large numbers of plant and animal species, and the total consumption of other resources. As noted earlier, whilst there is some movement to restrain such desires, there still remains a contrary scramble in what Klare (2012) describes as the '*Race for What's Left*'.

Princen therefore contends that humanity urgently needs to adopt a much stronger '*imperative*' *view of sufficiency*, one in which the maintenance of non-replaceable living beings and environmental attributes are not 'tradable concerns', and should never knowingly be exhausted. He instead argues that societies should ensure that the environment is conserved and maintained within the safe space of a global stewardship framework composed of the environmental and well-being boundaries described earlier. However, this sufficiency ethic, even in its strongest form, still remains in tension with the ethic of conservation described earlier, for the term 'sufficiency', in all weak, moderate, and imperative versions, still views living creatures and the natural environment as 'resources' to be used and disposed of by human beings. Yet as noted, one root of an ethic of conservation instead argues that living creatures should be seen as being ends in themselves rather than as means to other ends, where their care and well-being should be a human concern regardless of their utility. Imperative sufficiency is then a necessary, but not sufficient, condition for achieving the sustainability of resources. Resolutions of such tension will likely be resolved only through the kind of wicked discussions described throughout this book. But a commitment to imperative sufficiency will create conflict with currently practised weaker versions of sufficiency, and such conflict would also probably result in the transgression of one or several environmental boundaries. Once more, the application of a stewardship ethic will not be simple and will not be tame.

An ethical commitment to intergenerational equity

Very often equity is seen as having only deontological roots, as a position drawn from various cultural, legal and religious systems. Yet equity also has roots in an ethic of care, for many would want greater equality because of the suffering inequality might impose. Yet there is also a consequentialist argument here as well: as Wilkinson (1996) and Wilkinson and Pickett (2009) have demonstrated, more equal societies do not just benefit the poor in those societies: they have beneficial consequences for the rich as well. So equity as an ethical call is strengthened by having more than one root.

However, the question still needs asking: how far should such equity extend? Attenborough (2020, p. 127–8), for instance, points out that 'we must learn not only to live within the Earth's finite resources, but also how to share them more evenly too.' This is compelling, but almost certainly needs expanding in two different ways. First, it needs to heed the 1987 Brundtland Report, where sustainability was defined (p. 8) as 'that which meets the needs of the present, without compromising the ability of future generations to meet their needs'. Second, it needs to not only include a more equitable distribution with future as well as existing human generations, but to consider how to share such resources with other species, and with future generations of other species as well. What is meant by 'more equitably' when it comes to present and future multi-species resource distribution is another highly wicked question which will not be resolved easily, but the most impactful way presently would be in preventing the present major cause of species extinctions – the appropriation of their living spaces for human use.

Another means of developing this extended notion of greater intergenerational equity could come through developing Rawls's (1970) 'veil of ignorance' argument, where people are asked to describe the minimum level of well-being for themselves if they were to be born with no knowledge of their position in society. With an expansion of this argument into an ethic of *intergenerational* equity, thought would need to be given to situations where not only had an individual no knowledge of which generation – and therefore which context – they would be born into, but the discussion would need to include what individuals would choose if they did not know into which *species* they would be born. Now Rawls himself did not consider this feasible, stating (p. 512) that such a move would be outside the scope of a theory of justice, because his theory was one part of a contract theory, bound up with human social justice and what constitutes a fair and just society. However, just because the theory was developed as part of a discussion about social justice between human beings, this does not mean that it cannot or should not be extended beyond the focus that Rawls gave it. It might then be a powerful future argument for greater inter-species equity. The transgression of an inter-species equity ethic would then be seen partly in rich and powerful human beings of one generation consuming resources for themselves and their offspring, with no consideration of the rights and the needs of others in present and future generations, and also without consideration for the needs of other species. Once more, the title of Klare's (2012) book, *The Race for What's Left*, is a striking example of current human generations' transgression of this ethic. In extending such intergenerational equity to include other species, transgression would also be seen in increases in the global human population, through the extra land and resources that will need to be taken from other species in order to sustain itself, with the consequence of a decline in other species' numbers, and utimately in their extinction. The holding of this ethic almost certainly brings it into conflict with other ethical standpoints, for it would at some stage need to advocate the limiting of global population numbers – particularly when we live in a world where many more affluent countries are now seeing rapid population decline, and so are wanting to expand their numbers for political and economic purposes. Once again, such conflicting needs will likely lead to the need for solutions to many new and unexpected wicked problems. Such conflict, however, is not an argument for the rejection of such an ethic, but rather for considering what will ultimately happen if nothing is done, and so for the need to better understand the nature of wicked problems and their likely 'messy' resolutions.

An ethical commitment to personal humility

This final commitment, inducing us to reflect upon and come to terms with our own limitations, may seem at first blush rather distant from the other ethics proposed, and having little to do with the kind of ethical commitments essential to the underpinning of a stewardship approach. Indeed, some may feel it is hardly an ethic at all, and so would be better allocated to discussions on viable epistemological positions. Yet I want to argue that it is a crucial ethical position to take. It is like Popper's (1945) argument that the adoption of rationality is a *moral* choice, because its rejection involves the acceptance of other means of resolving problems – of which leaving it to blind luck or uncritically obeying the orders of others seem the only other choices. But with the first, you cross your fingers and hope something good will happen; and with the other you open yourself up to the dangers of totalitarian rule. Reason then is not a simple choice, like choosing strawberry rather than chocolate ice cream, because its rejection has profound life-changing consequences for oneself and the society in which one lives.

In the same way, the choice of believing in the reality of a 'tame' world, and the rejection of the reality of a 'wicked' one, has similarly profound consequences for oneself and society. Choosing to believe in a 'tame' reality results in a personal – and potentially societal – blindness to many complex and threatening events, and, with such blindness, little chance of dealing adequately with them. Believing in a tame world means that you are convinced that you *know* what the root cause of most problems are, because you have the capacity to understand how a tame world functions, even as you radically underestimate what you are going to deal with. Believing in a tame world leaves you with the dangerous hubris of *knowing* that you are right, and therefore of believing that you are capable of being the sole individual who can lead others to the resolution of presenting problems. But finally, believing in a tame world also leaves you believing that those who fail to solve the problems they are given must be either unsuited to their work, lack the intelligence or expertise to deal with them or must be trying to undermine other people's efforts to solve such problems. If *you* can't solve the problems given to you, well, that has to be your fault, doesn't it?

Adopting a tame view of the world is an ethical choice because of the profound consequences that stem from its use. Instead of such belief, then, we need to recognize that the world in which we live is actually much more 'wicked', where not only are there many things we don't know, and things we don't know we don't know, but where many problems may be created external to us, whilst many others may be of our own (unrecognized) personal creation, derived from deeply held values and understandings. In such a complex and wicked world, an ethic of humility is essential if we are to appreciate the limits of our personal understanding, of the need to be provisional in most of the judgements we make, and of the necessity to draw on the opinions of others in framing the nature of many problems, and very often in having to accept that we will probably only be able to develop 'messy' responses as the best possible solutions to the kind of threats faced, not only at personal and institutional levels but at national and global levels as well. The transgression of such an ethic is created in most cases by the belief that wicked problems can be fully solved, that they can be solved by single knowledgeable individuals and that those who fail to solve them are either unsuited to their work or are culpable of undermining others' efforts. When such transgressions occur, arrogance and hubris are very often the attitudes seen, tame rather than wicked descriptions of problems are adopted, and 'silver bullet' solutions are wrongly claimed to be possible. As this happens, not only are the natural and human environments likely to become much less sustainable, but so also will be the creatures, individual humans and their communities. An ethic of humility is then an essential attitude for human beings to adopt if a sustainable stewardship framework is to be created and maintained.

Conclusions

An ethical stewardship framework, impelled by a reframed and extended leadership role, needs acceptance and support beyond educational institutions. Implementation will likely be limited or ineffective if those with macro-level influence and power do not promote the underpinning assumptions of these new frames. Without such macro-level support, these ideas will be rowing against the tide of public and political assumptions and practice. Yet if a dominant public consciousness is composed of linear expectations, tame understandings and hierarchical solutions, and that most of what we need to know is already known, then an approach underpinned by the wicked, the systemic, the collaborative and the epistemologically humble will probably have little impact. These ideas require much greater endorsement not only from within educational institutions but beyond them as well.

They will require a government approval demonstrated by appropriate advice, directives and legislation, backed by extensive explanation of the nature and need for such changes. Whilst this might seem a rather daring and unlikely initiative by governments, the experiences and responses to Covid-19 provide some hope. Whilst some talked of 'roadmaps' out of this crisis, others realized that the nature of its threat was more wicked and complex, and they curbed the temptation to respond to urgent concerns with tame promises. Instead, they realized the need to work cautiously with medical, epidemiological and public health experts on the emerging data. In adopting this kind of approach, they accepted that any 'roadmap' had to be extremely provisional, as the road might shortly need developing in a different direction. If then this more thoughtful and restrained understanding created by the effects of Covid-19 could be learnt from, and then linked to the emerging effects of other crises, then the possibility exists for such wicked understandings and policies to become more accepted means of approaching and dealing with other crises. If the nature of wicked problems were to be more greatly appreciated, policymakers might change the focus of policy levers from ones of one-way hierarchical implementation, accountability and inspection, to ones where emerging understandings of problems and solutions were seen as needing to be tackled by different kinds and levels of expertise. In such a climate, educational institutions could be pivotal in developing such long-term understanding, and, in providing the skills, knowledge and attitudes to develop approaches to such longer-term issues of sustainability.

However, whilst some within educational institutions may be ready and capable of embracing such changes, others may not. This is unsurprising: for a number of decades, educators in many countries have been doubly steered by the tame assumptions of their governments and society, with most media demanding more of the same. Many have also been pushed further down roads over the past few decades by forms of accountability and inspection which not only reinforce tame assumptions but which have been geared to punish those challenging such assumptions. Major forms of accountability and inspection have then played significant roles in depressing the use of wicked frames and stewardship values in educational institutions. It is therefore highly important to examine how current forms of accountability and inspection might be altered to support the development of a stewardship perspective in educational institutions. This then is the subject of the next chapter.

New Frames for Accountability and Inspection

Introduction

This book argues that educational leaders need to employ a stewardship code with a set of ethical values and an understanding of wicked problems in order to make a pronounced difference when confronting many threats originating beyond education. However, to be really effective, this approach also needs to be promoted and practised beyond educational boundaries. This chapter then argues that the creation of new forms of accountability frameworks and their inspection vehicles would be highly effective in developing this wider understanding, as the relationship between those asking for an account, those accessing the evidence and those who are accountable would become a more complex and collaborative relationship than is presently conceived, and also more educational, because all parties involved in such accountability would need to understand the nature of stewardship and wicked problems, and the best ways forward on promoting these and communicating them to others. This chapter then describes a policy and accountability relationship very different from most currently experienced and argues that this could be the basis for a form of collaborative leadership which best fits the radical uncertainties of the future.

Now it might be objected that using accountability and inspection procedures to promote new ways of thinking and practice is putting the cart before the horse, as it might be thought that accountability frameworks and their inspection practices should be used *after* such intentions and concepts have been embraced, and are then being practised. However, one of the more notable things about accountability and inspection frameworks over the last few decades has been how they have been used to steer practitioners into particular thought-processes, practices and values in order to ensure that such practice becomes more widespread. As noted earlier, Fergusson (1994) describes how the effects

– and intentions – of much legislation and inspection are intended to immerse practitioners so completely in the thinking and practice behind new educational legislation that they come, at least in part, to redefine themselves in terms of these changes. Indeed, in accountability systems where agreement by implementers on the ultimate purposes of such changes is not sought, high-stakes testing and punitive inspection procedures have often been used as effective instruments to generate educators' compliance, even as they have negatively impacted on many individuals' personal sustainability. Yet, as Fullan (1991) demonstrated some time ago in a review of major educational reforms in the United States and Canada, legislation is more widely and effectively implemented when practitioners have the space and thinking time to align new directives with the unique features of their particular context and practice. Moreover, accountability procedures based on punitive imposition and low-trust relationships practically guarantee that the kind of collaborative relationships required for agreeing best ways forward with difficult problems will not be created. This chapter then argues that those holding others to account, instead of using punitive inspection systems to achieve particular ends, should change direction and begin to develop approaches in which accountability intentions are developed through inspection systems which develop a greater understanding of the wicked problems likely to be encountered.

This chapter then begins by describing the nature of two forms of accountability system and their accompanying inspection vehicles, before contrasting these with the kind of accountability and inspection regime which would be needed to develop a better understanding of the kinds of wicked problems increasingly faced in educational systems and society in general.

Different political regimes, different models of accountability and inspection

Lindberg (2013) has argued that models of accountability and inspection can be highly varied in form and function, and Table 11.1 uses three different forms to point up major similarities and differences. These models are necessarily broad-brush in their description, and each will vary depending on context and time period, but the differences in purpose and practice are very clear. A first model, *a welfare state model*, was used in much of the Western world until the 1970s. Welfare states were – and some still are – essentially types of national government which are designed to play a major role in the protection and promotion of the

Table 11.1 Three Different Models of Accountability and Inspection: Aims, Structures and Consequences

Accountability questions	Welfare state accountability	Neoliberal vertical accountability	Wicked accountability
Who is accountable?	Those professionals practising in educational institutions	The producers of services (normally the teaching force)	All parties involved in creation, implementation of policy and resolution of problems
What are the purposes of accountability?	To provide an account to peers, and local and national bodies, to develop greater trust, and to develop personal and group expertise. **Key words:** expertise, autonomy, and trust	To control and steer practice down market and privatised roads as improved student scores boost national competitive advantage. **Key words:** power, control and steerage of producers	To develop better understanding of a stewardship account in dealing with wicked issues and problems. **key words:** multi-strand accountability, collaboration and education for complexity
To whom should the account go?	local advisors, regional bodies and government	To those with the power (normally governments and their inspection proxies)	All parties involved in the endeavour for reflection, comment and action
What is the relationship between those seeking an account and those providing it?	Initial disengagement, but trust between professionals and the public, and increased professional learning and expertise	Practitioners performing to government demands, and responding to market and consumer steers	Developed understanding and trust between different views for more nuanced – and educational – accounts
What is provided as evidence?	Observations, comments, students work: professional expertise usually determines the choice of evidence	Inspections, standards, high-stakes quantitative data and testing	Materials illustrating and justifying different points of view, potential linkages action on ways forward

What does the inspection vehicle for this form of accountability look for?	Improvement in all forms of student learning, professional judgement of colleagues and increased trust of public	Student achievement of government-mandated standards and success in market criteria (e.g. student enrolments, consumer satisfaction surveys)
What does this form of inspection look like	Low-stakes, collegial, with links between micro-, meso- and macro- mostly advisory, but with possible teeth by staff employers	High-stakes, hierarchical, quantitative, punitive, to central authority, perhaps through designated proxies
What are the likely consequences of such accountability and inspection?	Pros: using the advice of expert others from regional and national level, greater collaboration Con: in-house beliefs and values which may not correspond with wider societal concerns	Pros: High control of those accountable, clarity of data Cons: limited room for creativity, differing opinions, or for nuanced evaluation
	Evidence of all forms of student learning, evidence of a fusing of different accounts of problems, creating wicked questions and 'messy' best ways forward	
	Low-stakes, diverse expertise, qualitative, educative, with initial priority on education and coaching measures before any disciplinary decisions	
	Pros: Variety of opinions, greater creativity, staff education in wicked issues. Cons: Danger of lack of consensus on ways forward, staff dislike of responsibility, individual preference for tame roles	

economic and social well-being of their citizens, often with elements of such power devolved to more local levels. Varying in emphasis and practice, Esping-Anderson (1990) has suggested a tripartite division of such state involvement, from a Liberal, market-oriented variety in the United States, the United Kingdom and Australia, to an insurance-funded Conservative form in countries like Italy, France and Germany, and finally to a strongly interventionist Social Democratic variation in Sweden, Norway and Denmark. Whilst there have been criticisms of Esping-Anderson's analysis, more remarkable perhaps is the degree of similarity between it and later analyses (e.g. Powell and Barrientos, 2004; Green et al., 2006; Bambra, 2006; West and Nickolai, 2014).

This interventionist, socially supportive form of government was confronted in the 1970s by major political and economic challenges, and in many countries was superseded by more market-oriented governments, particularly in countries like the United States and the United Kingdom, with neoliberal political tendencies. The changes in their accountability models reflect this wider political movement, as many welfare state accountability models moved from a degree of central disengagement which permitted degrees of local autonomy and professional independence, to an abrupt change, particularly in the more neoliberal variants, to a paradoxical combination of market principles with a greater centralization of power to enforce such market ideals. This produced a second major accountability model, that of *neoliberal vertical accountability*. Table 11.1 then describes the principal characteristics of these two models, whilst also introducing the third potential model, a *wicked accountability model*. Aspects of this third model are present in welfare state models, but it has a very different focus and epistemological base, and is therefore, it is argued, better suited to dealing with the kinds of problems which most societies and their educational systems not only currently confront but are likely to face even more in the future. These accountability models then provide illustrations of very different aims, structures and consequences.

Table 11.1 then describes some strong threads running through the use of the term 'accountability' over the last five or six decades, as well as some recognizable changes in its meaning. The principle that a person, institution or group should provide an account of their practice to another party has then been located on a spectrum from *voluntary* to *mandated* accountability, though some 'voluntary' systems have in practice been created almost by default, as relatively disengaged governments were preoccupied with other concerns. The result was then a varied picture, oftentimes with professionals being inspected on an infrequent and irregular basis. This permitted a variability in teaching quality and of professionals enjoying a considerable amount of personal autonomy. This picture of low-stakes accountability and variable professional practice was particularly noticeable after the Second World War and for three main reasons. A first was the focus that governments needed rebuilding, funding and policy creation, and rather less on personal and institutional practice. A second reason lay in the assumptions underlying the literature on professionals, which described them as altruistically committed to their clients' welfare. As Tawney (1921, pp. 94–5) argued,

> The difference between industry as it exists today, and a profession is then simple and unmistakable. The essence of the former is that its only criterion is the financial return which if offers its shareholders. The essence of the latter is that though men [*sic.*] enter it for the sake of livelihood, the measure of their success is the service which they perform, not the gains they amass.

This positive view of professional commitment resulted in some cases in a degree of unearned trust, and an accountability system largely focused on inputs (quality of teaching expertise and sufficient resources), whilst external visits to schools were often more advisory than inspectoral, with only a limited number of regional and local bodies developing more interventionist initiatives. A final reason lay in the perceived professional expertise in curriculum and pedagogy which in some countries was then seen as the teachers' 'secret garden' (Eccles, in Lawton 1980, p. 22), and where inspections did take place, their quality and detail – and hence impact – were often determined by the personality, expertise and dynamism of significant individuals at the local level.

This rather fragmented form of accountability – a kind of neglected multi-based accountability with professionals often voluntary altruists – would be fundamentally challenged by the new economic and political realities of the 1970s. Nevertheless, this welfare state model contained a number of significant qualities which are necessary to any accountability model consciously adopting a more 'wicked' perspective. For example, relationships of (earned) trust are essential to the resolution to wicked problems as they require a variety of inputs into the definition of a problem, and of its best resolution. In addition, this model created the potential for micro-, meso- and macro-levels of interdependent accountability and inspection, and in so doing suggests the possibility of a considerable degree of responsibility by different levels in framing relevant accountability questions. This coheres well with the principle of subsidiarity, originally one of the key principles of Catholic social thought (Bosnich, 2010), but now seen as having much wider application, arguing as it does that nothing which can be done at lower levels of an organization should be performed at levels higher up. This is then also a political principle, as it prevents over-centralized power and control, and encourages individual and small group responsibilities in governance. Moreover, it also has the potential for a strong practical base, for if something can be done effectively at lower levels, those working at such levels will most likely understand the local context very well, and so be more aware of potential pitfalls and opportunities, which those more distanced from the situation may not appreciate. It is then important to keep in mind the potential of this model for the development of a multilayered shared accountability, as it fits a 'wicked' accountability approach extremely well. However, the political changes that came from the 1970s onwards brought forth accountability models which led in a very different direction.

From voluntary to mandated accountability

Welfare state forms of accountability were then either transformed or strongly influenced by political regimes into forms of accountability much closer to the 'mandated' end of a voluntary/mandated spectrum. Pollitt (1993) has described this movement as at least in part being one where professionals moved from being 'on top' in terms of determining local policy, to being 'on tap' to the demands of centralized control, these now normally being national, state or regional governments, with other lower-level accountability agencies (e.g. local authorities, inspectors and governing bodies) increasingly co-opted into steering professionals in conforming to central policy directives. Professional power by omission was then replaced by the much stronger central control, which issued much more focused and committed demands. Such demands were heavily influenced by the theoretical work of writers like Hayek (1944) who had argued that professional practice in welfare states was actually contributing to the creation of the kind of authoritarian state which the Allies had fought to prevent in the Second World War. This moral and political view was added to by works focusing on the benefits of the competitive private sector (e.g. Friedman, 1962), not only in enabling greater personal choice but also in providing better information to consumers. These views would then inform and create a radically different political, economic and moral position: instead of focusing upon the duty of the nation-state to provide for the welfare of all, it focused upon the right of the individual to greater personal freedom and responsibility, and for the use of these in markets which, it was believed, best distributed resources.

When combined with an increasingly critical literature on professional practice, the trust and autonomy formerly given to professionals were now viewed as incompatible with a market situation where consumers should be given the information to choose between the 'products' they wanted to 'purchase'. Unsurprisingly, accountability emphases moved from semi-voluntary notions to ones in which accounts by professionals to their political masters were mandated, and where inspection systems were often created to punitively enforce such obligatory emphases.

This change in the accountability model from one of neglectful trust to one of central power and direction then created a relationship between policymakers and professionals where the former increasingly possessed the power to demand compliant accounts of practice from the latter. Such movement in values and accountability was then highly challenging, even traumatic, for some 'producers', and strong resistance by some professionals still working from a foundation of personal responsibility and trust was perhaps unsurprising. It was also to be expected that accountability would move from a focus on inputs to that of outputs, and, as Maroy and Voisin (2017, p. 4) describe, this much heavier degree of mandated accountability was one where

> various dimensions and mechanisms . . . measure the outcomes of education systems and . . . hold individual or institutional actors accountable for reaching targets and goals fixed at the central level.

This new form of 'outcome' accountability thereby replaced earlier forms of input regulation. Moreover, and in expectation of professional resistance, more vertically downward one-source forms of accountability were also introduced. So, given the neoliberal economic and political claims of many new governments, and of international influences on governments which did not fully adopt this description, it was perhaps unsurprising that private sector models of accountability and inspection were often introduced, ones which used test result comparisons as the principal judgements of performance, along with an increasingly dominant objective of equipping students with the skills that would be needed in an environment of globalized market-competition. This holding to account by central governance of actors and institutions in achieving specified targets and goals was then seen in the policies of many governments. It was particularly strongly practised in 'Liberal' regimes – as reflected in US national legislation over the last twenty years, as well as in US states like Texas (Ozga and Grek, 2012), in English legislation following the 1988 Education Reform Act, and the creation of the inspectoral body Ofsted in 1992, and in the New Zealand

and Australian systems. Within such regimes, the public sector was viewed in increasingly private sector terms, educators were viewed as providers or producers of services in a market composed of other competing schools, and the 'clients' or 'consumers' of this service –government and parents – then required evidence to determine whether providers were performing acceptably, or whether individual consumer parents should choose a different 'product' for their child.

In this move from welfare state to a neoliberal accountability model, the answers to two highly important questions were changed. A first was the change of the answer to the question: 'Who is accountable?' The answer was that it would depend upon the political and economic assumptions underpinning the nature of the accountability. Under a welfare state model, it might only be teaching professionals who were accountable, but it could also include those working at other levels of the system. Curiously, under a very different fully developed *market* form of accountability, there should have been no real inspection procedures, for the market – in terms of the choices of its consumers – should have decided on the quality of those who were 'producing' the goods. Yet, as noted earlier, this market form of accountability lived uneasily next to political impulses of strong central governance, which were often used to enforce market behaviours through strong downwards accountability.

A second question follows from the first: 'To whom should the account be rendered?' In a welfare state model, it would need to reflect the fact that local, regional and national bodies might all need accounts rendered to them (and also by them as well). By contrast, a fully marketized model would require that only consumers of educational services in this market would need accounts rendering, but if the system was never fully privatised and marketized, then the state as well as more local consumers would also demand accounts rendering, and both in many cases then became major policy steers. Notions of accountability and inspection have then differed greatly, depending upon the political, economic and social assumptions of a society and its governance. In the process, accountability relationships would then also be heavily affected.

Accountability relationships

In the previous section, the distinctive nature of three different accountability systems has been described. In Table 11.2, the same accountability models are used to explore the kinds of relationships likely to exist between actors in such systems, principally because it is argued that those developed in the first two models are likely to be inadequate for developing the forms of relationship necessary for a wicked accountability system.

Table 11.2 then shows how different kinds of relationship emerge from different models of accountability. Maroy and Voisin (2017) suggest that such relationships are situated on a spectrum. At one end are those located within 'hard accountability' systems, which normally feature a focus on outcomes, high-stakes testing, strong control and punitive consequences for non-compliance to the standards demanded. At the other 'soft accountability' end are relationships situated within more loosely coupled systems which generate significant individual and institutional autonomy, and with fewer punitive consequences for those held accountable. The relationships in many current systems are generally more representative of hard accountability systems, deriving from a neoliberal preference for vertically downwards accountability, with educational systems being viewed by those demanding the account as one of a number of macro-instruments needed to drive particular educational policies to better compete with other nation-states in a global marketplace. This is a view which has transcended the supposedly distinct policies of different political parties. The pronouncement made in 1998 by David Blanket, the UK Secretary of State for Education and Employment in a New Labour government, could just as likely have been written by the Opposition spokesperson:

> Learning is the key to prosperity – for each of us as individuals, as well as for the nation as a whole. Investment in human capital will be the foundation of success in the knowledge-based global economy of the twenty-first century. This is why the Government has put learning at the heart of its ambition.

The quality and purpose of student learning was then firmly located within a picture of national economic growth, and a number of managerial instruments, particularly that of New Public Management (Hood, 1991), were then used to control and steer educational institutions and practitioners towards greater political and economic compliance. In this process, the use of testing and inspection systems to measure outputs, and the public dissemination of such results, have often been highly stressful to those working within schools (Ball, 2003; Berliner, 2011; Young and Szachowicz, 2014; Bottery et al., 2018), as they have been subject to high-stakes testing, and nuanced information has been simplified to match the supposed limited information needed by non-specialist consumers. Part of such simplification occurs through an emphasis on quantitative results, with little appreciation or tolerance for what was seen by some as little more than contextualized qualitative ambiguity. Once again, David Blunkett (2000),

Table 11.2 The Varying Nature of Accountability under Three Different Systems

Types of accountability/ Aspects of accountability	Welfare state accountability	Neoliberal vertical accountability	Wicked accountability
Nature of accountability relationship	Some vertical accountability, but much horizontal peer based	Heavily vertically downward	Multi-focused, with both horizontal and vertical accountability, strong organizational subsidiarity
Input/output focused	Highly input focused	Highly output focused	Mixtures of input and output
Nature of trust between parties	Strong assumed trust, but some acquired practice trust	Predominantly low calculative trust	Practice- and interaction-based: potential multiparty interdependence
Producer experience of inspection	Often infrequent and low-stakes, lacking stress but also potentially lacking an improvement stimulus	As outcome and high-stakes in nature, defined, likely to be compliant and stressful	Multiparty agreement needed, likely to be demanding but potentially rewarding
Nature of control	Large measure of professional independence by neglect	Highly directive largely from central government or its proxies	Control by employers, but potentially much multiparty interdependence
Degree of conformity	Limited enforcement by others, some degree of professional conformism	Normally highly conformist and performative	Potential for considerable empowerment but also demanding and possibly stressful
Degree of performativity	High degree of producer independence	Highly performative	Need for independent thought and high degree of **interdependence**
Quantitative/qualitative evidence	Producer-led small-scale quantitative and qualitative	Government-defined material normally in large-scale quantitative form	Multiparty mixture of nuanced quantitative and qualitative
Nature of materials and issues inspected and practised	Potential for tame micro-/meso-framing, balanced by some wicked expertise	Potential for macro- government-defined tame material followed by micro-meso conformist practice	Multiparty discussions at micro-meso-macro levels over wicked problems and best ways forward

in talking about the nature of useful research, was not alone amongst politicians in arguing that 'We are not interested in worthless correlations based on small samples from which it is impossible to draw generalisable conclusions.'

If much of the qualitative and contextualized insight of practitioners is to be so summarily dismissed, this will not bode well for the development of more trusting and collaborative accountability and inspection relationships, and the principle of subsidiarity will then be largely dismissed, with the real danger, as Ball (2003, p. 217) argues, of then translating 'complex social processes and events into simple figures or categories of judgements'. Such steers would also be framed by the kind of tame thinking and understanding discussed earlier, which would be highly unsuitable for developing educational systems with more subtle understandings of wicked problem. The tools used for such accountability and inspection will then be insufficiently nuanced for deeper, more contextualized and qualitative accounts to be rendered and discussed; and if the wrong measuring tools are used, one cannot expect to properly evaluate a complex process, and people may then be blamed for problems which, given the tools provided, are impossible to fully understand and describe.

The consequence of much current high-stakes testing then leaves little room for collaborative discussion, for in vertically downwards accountability systems, a monopoly of insight is claimed by those holding power in determining such issues. Yet when only one group of stakeholders – or their proxies – determine essential aims, skills and abilities, then this group is highly unlikely to be interested in worthwhile discussions with others on what the aims should be, how the problems should be defined and what skills and attitudes will be needed to deal with future challenges. Unless the need for more wicked forms of thinking is recognized, and for a greater variety of stakeholders to participate in the definition and best resolutions of educational problems, then the prospects for creating forms of education which understand and build notions of the wicked and the tame into their epistemology and pedagogy will be severely limited.

A further important consequence of this kind of accountability relationship is then the highly corrosive effect it can have upon trust relationships between educators and governments, which then threaten not only mental well-being but individual sustainability as well (Bottery, 2004; Bottery et al., 2018). In addition, if the kinds of cooperative relationships essential for a more nuanced and educative accountability are not valued, then this may also hinder the kinds of collaboration and interdependence needed for dealing with wicked problems. In so doing, attempts at more creative teaching and management strategies will be inhibited, as creativity, almost by definition, involves a degree of experimentation in which some attempts will – necessarily – prove unsuccessful, and which practitioners may fear to try if interpreted by governments only as evidence of poor practice. The danger of this kind of pressure, as Lauder et al. (1998) pointed out, is that people may then become so conditioned to control and direction by others that they develop a 'trained incapacity to think openly and critically' (p. 51). It is perhaps unsurprising then that Bottery et al. (2008) similarly found that many English headteachers they interviewed felt that the punitive nature of the English inspectoral body was never far from their thoughts. Penny, for instance, said that 'whatever we are discussing, it's always got the Ofsted element, it's always there' – and worried that her less experienced teachers were becoming increasingly reluctant to try more creative approaches in their teaching, because for them Ofsted was 'very scary stuff'. Alison, another English headteacher, admitted that current testing procedures were very strong inducements 'to stick to tried and tested formulas' and that this applied particularly strongly to those classes designated for external testing, where the temptation was then to only explore more creative avenues with children 'who [were] not going to be publicly examined just yet'.

Practitioners are then not only steered away from creative discussions but are also driven towards an increased performativity of practice (Ball, 2003). In so doing the flexibility needed for responding to new challenges is diminished. By reserving such power and steerage to themselves, governments using such punitive downwards accountability are then highly likely to exclude other voices and other opinions from influencing the aims and purposes of an education system, and therefore from having input into its accountability and inspection operations. The ultimate result is then very likely to be that the kind of collaborative stakeholder involvement essential for more subtle and nuanced definitions of wicked problems and resolutions will be prevented from forming.

Educational leadership and the existential threat of accountability and inspection

Much of the aforementioned is reflected in how educational leaders have responded to such changes in accountability and inspection. Many have felt the need to existentially negotiate a new role which provides them with a degree of personal fulfilment whilst also satisfying official requirements, somewhere on each of the following dimensions:

- From nurturing a concept of future citizenship to promoting one of consumerism;

- From championing the priority of an equity of need to advocating the priority of individual choice;
- From embracing forms of collective action for a greater public good to developing the value and practice of competition for personal and institutional gain;
- From exercising an appropriate subsidiarity role to being the base of hierarchically based policies and their implementation.
- From being service providers and public educators to being promoters and implementers of competitive policy, and coordinators of internal high-stakes testing;
- From being major contributors to communal goals to being leaders of institutional competitive advantage;
- From viewing the public as partners in achieving communal goals to viewing them as consumers in an educational marketplace in which they are one of many providers;
- From information being seen as open and public for furthering community action to seeing information as a weapon of non-disclosure in providing competitive institutional advantage.

Such personal existential negotiation probably takes place with any movement from one form of accountability to another when long-held personal values and personal sustainability are threatened. The existential threat – or promise – of movement to new forms of accountability and inspection is a very personal one, for personal sustainability does depend not only upon personal values but also upon personal resilience. Some individuals can absorb enormous amounts of pressure and yet still keep on fighting for what they believe, whilst others with similar values may submit to pressures much more quickly. The extra work involved in changing school practice due to new legislative directions, as well as many other pressures, may result in many 'exhausted leaders' feeling the need to quit. Yet some do cope better than others: as noted earlier (Bottery et al., 2018) one Hong Kong principal said he was working for fourteen hours on most days, and loving it, largely because of his strong motivation to prevent his school from closure. Not only then does one need to be acutely aware of individual differences, but of how circumstances and reasons can change individual capacity.

Existential leadership pressures may then arise whenever a move from one form of accountability and inspection to another occurs. However, personal sustainability doesn't always align with newly introduced personally preferred forms of change. Fullan (1991) has shown how even when individuals personally approve new approaches, they may still find it difficult to incorporate them into their practice because of other pressures faced, and the cost in terms of overwork and stress caused in changing practice may so reduce their energy that the adoption of such positive reforms may be much more limited than actually desired. Existential pressures are then likely to be present not only in the move from more-preferred to less-preferred accountability regimes, but even when the move is towards a more-preferred option. This is important because implementational stress will probably also occur for many educators wanting to adopt more wicked forms of practice and ensuing forms of accountability and inspection. It is then important to examine the differences between current accountability regimes and ones built upon more wicked notions, in order to examine how educators might be sustained during such change. One then needs to be clear not only about the ultimate purposes of wicked forms of accountability and inspection but also about the process of movement towards them.

Developing wicked forms of accountability and inspection

'Wicked accountability' is, unsurprisingly, underpinned by ways of thinking which begin with an understanding of the differences in nature between tame or wicked problems. A particularly distinctive aspect of wicked accountability lies in that it provides a much better understanding of an extended stewardship role, by demanding the application of wicked thinking to present and future problems. Its accountability instrument, the inspectoral body, would then also have demands placed upon it, for its members also need to appreciate the implications of this approach, not only in terms of how an inspectoral body should be composed but also in terms of its practice.

In line with its underpinning logic of the likelihood of imperfect, 'messy' and shared solutions to many problems, wicked accountability should not be seen as the agenda of one group of stakeholders, however powerful they may be, but as an account emerging from an inspection process conducted by a diversity of interested parties. Because activities focusing on education are not confined to those teaching at its various levels, but are also the focus of macro- and meso-governance bodies, the same process of multiparty wicked inspection should extend beyond those educational institutions to the inspection of its micro-, meso- and macro-governance as well. In sum, wicked accountability and inspection need to employ multiparty inspection teams to examine not just the levels of education practice but the levels of accountability practice as well. Inspections should then not be seen as single-focused exercises, but as collaborative *inter*dependent undertakings, in which discussions of the problems emerging at different levels of education and its inspections are shared and collective attempts are made to resolve them.

The varied nature of inspection teams members, and the focus of the activities they should undertake, are crucial, and for a number of reasons. First, if the best ways forward on wicked issues are generated by drawing on a variety of viewpoints, then an inspection process needs conducting in the same manner. Second, if the causes and effects of many problems are likely to be dispersed between different levels, it then follows that examining the interactions between educational activities at these different levels will be highly important if a more complete understanding of problems and resolutions are to be achieved. Such teams will then need macro-, meso-, and micro-level representation, which will likely mean governmental, regional and local representation (parents, local businesses, academics and representatives from the institutions being inspected). The leadership of such inspection bodies will be critical here, and its role will be one of facilitating the framing of questions and of developing a consensus on best ways forward for the problems considered.

Such inspectoral bodies will, like their counterparts being inspected, initially need considerable education and coaching, not training, in wicked and tame processes, because wicked inspection has to be the intelligent application of critical thought to contextualized instances of practice, and not the application of generalized rules and procedures which take little account of such contexts. Indeed, the principle of diverse representation is so important that it may require a degree of statutory insulation from practical concern, as concerns about the size, time, cost and education of both institutional educators and inspection team members should not compromise the central purpose of ensuring that wicked forms of inspection actually do take place.

This is not to dismiss the more traditional aims of inspection systems: continued assessment will be needed on issues of teaching quality, test results, student behaviour and institutional and financial management, but these issues will be increasingly assessed in terms of whether they are framed in a sufficiently wicked manner, and whether problems and their responses are couched within wicked forms of reasoning. Again, and crucially, educative feedback will need to be provided by an inspection team to the institutions being inspected, through discussions on how thinking and practice can be made more wicked, before thoughts of disciplinary action are considered. There then would need to be a sustained initial period for the education of both inspectoral bodies and those being inspected, and only when agreement is reached by a team that sufficient understanding has been gained (and not that an allotted time has been used up) should decisions be considered as to whether institutions and individuals within them need further educative, coaching and supportive help, or whether moves towards more remedial and disciplinary action are required.

Now it has already been noted how neoliberal forms of accountability and inspection have taken many educational institutions down paradoxical roads of demanding greater competitiveness in a market situation, whilst at the same time requiring a greater conformity to central government mandates. Wicked forms of accountability and inspection, however, need to develop expanded mindsets for those inspected, in which threats currently facing society are better understood and ways for them to be raised educationally are proposed. Central to such understanding will be an appreciation of the spectrum of differences between tame and wicked thinking, differences which require new ways of thinking not only for those being inspected but also, as argued, for those in inspectoral bodies assessing how well institutions are performing on such requirements. So as well as a central role of inspection being one of judging how well standards are being met, the creation of wicked accountability and inspection bodies – perhaps named OFCORE (the Office for Complex Organisational Responses) – would also need to focus on the nature of wicked processes, in the expectation that, as generations of students move to adulthood, such understandings are transferred and practised in the wider society. So, *inspection* would then not be the only key word describing OFCORE's function. As importantly would be those of *education* and *coaching*, as much disciplinary action following poor performance would need delaying until the better understanding and practice of wicked mindsets was established. Inspection bodies would then also need to be tasked with providing long-term external help and support for educational institutions, and a highly important coaching role in the development and application of such wicked thinking.

Beginning to apply wicked and tame distinctions to accountability and education

How does one begin to educate towards a nuanced understanding of the differences between tame and wicked thinking, and their application to the accountability of personal and institutional practice? Perhaps a simple, but not simplistic, introduction would be the reflection and discussion upon a number of educative questions, allied to appropriate coaching advice. These questions could provide a strong basis for understanding how differently problems and resolutions need to be viewed, and then need be used by stakeholders, inspection teams and practitioners in not only developing a better understanding of wicked and tame problems, but also in examining how such concepts relate to everyday practice, and crucially, whether they are currently being applied to wicked problems emerging at different levels.

A first opening question could then be: *'What do you see as the difference between tame and wicked problems?'* This is a basic question but is essential if one is to gain a good insight into where individuals and groups currently are in understanding such terms. A second opening question could then be: *'What are the best ways forward in resolving such problems?'* Both of these are key questions for they ask for an understanding of the distinction in detail and subtlety, for if more wicked than tame thinking is to be used, a very clear understanding of the nature of the two terms is required. This should then lead to a third question: *'Are "tame" and "wicked" problems different in nature, or different in degree on a spectrum of meaning?'*

A fourth question would then ask, *'Which problems and resolutions have been framed in a tame manner in your institution, or in your functioning?'* This question facilitates the application of such understanding to practice. An initial grasp of the terms 'tame' and 'wicked' will be needed once more, before such a reflective examination can be made, and the explanation of such application will provide others with a clear idea of the level of conceptual understanding used by the respondents.

A fifth question would ask: *'Which recent requests/demands/questions coming from other bodies do you believe have been framed in a tame rather than a wicked manner, and why?'* Some stakeholders, probably ones located at higher levels, may initially not relish this challenge to their thinking, which others are invited to critique. But this model of accountability requires a move from a mindset of top-down vertical accountability to one of a multilateral wicked accountability in the search for the best definitions of problems and of ways forward in their resolution, and this reflective critique of previous practice is then an essential element and consequence of such accountability.

A sixth question is a logical development from the previous ones. It asks, *'How can these previous requests/demands be re-fashioned to develop a better understanding of a wicked reality and its problems?'* This once more requires the application of an understanding of tame and wicked differences, and whilst this may be highly challenging to some, it will also be highly educative in developing a better understanding of the nature of past thinking at different levels, and of what now needs discussion and possible adjustment.

A seventh question asks specific questions about the formulation of institutional problems: '*How far have you gone in defining the nature of wicked problems encountered in your institution or in your functioning?*' Under a wicked accountability model, blame cultures will likely diminish with the greater acceptance of human limitations. Critical discussions of what still needs to be done, or what has been attempted but so far has only been partially successful, will be much less likely to be viewed as part of such a blame culture. Instead, they are more likely to be viewed as discussions for possible improvement rather than as confessions of inadequate thinking and practice, or even of personal and institutional failure. When mistakes are seen as events from which lessons can be learnt, rather than as examples of malfunction, an ethos of trust is likely to be reinvigorated, greater creativity is more likely to be attempted and individual and institutional sustainability will then be strengthened.

An eighth question asks: '*Which problems and best ways forward do you believe are now framed in your institution or in your functioning in a wicked manner?*' This question once more asks for personal understandings of what wicked problems and best ways forward are, and whether they have been correctly identified in practice. However, this question can also help develop another element of wicked practice, that of the contribution of a variety of interested parties, and so a follow-up ninth question would then be: '*Which different views within and beyond your institution's functioning have needed incorporating into such a discussion?*'

As with the formulation of problems, so with best ways forward: a tenth question is one of returning to and properly identifying tamer problems, for it asks, '*Which problems in your institution or in your functioning do you believe still remain amenable to "silver bullet" resolutions?*' This question does not rule out the high probability that some problems can be solved in this manner. Indeed, it may help identify the 'converts' to notions of wicked problems which see the world as composed *only* of such complex issues. An eleventh and accompanying question on best ways forward would then be, '*Which problems in your institution or your functioning are only amenable to "silver buckshot" or "messy" best ways forward?*'

Such educational and coaching questions on the differences between tame and wicked thinking then are essential for initial inspection discussions if the foundations for personal and institutional questioning are to be laid, and for a deeper understanding of the nature and effect of other, wider threats. Moreover, as understanding deepens, so will be the subtle and contextualized nature of such questions, and of a movement towards application. This will then develop the accountability relationship to one where three extra questions are asked, which move onto issues of action. A twelfth question would then ask, '*What strategies and actions have you taken with institutional problems which you have categorized as "wicked"?*' A follow-up thirteenth question would then be, '*What have you learnt both negatively and positively about this experience?*' A final question would ask, '*Would you tackle the problem differently next time, and how would this approach differ from the previously used approach?*'

Such initial education and coaching could then provide the conceptual foundations for a deeper understanding of threats not only at the micro- and meso-levels of practice but also beyond these to threats emerging from the macro-level which may challenge personal and institutional functioning, and which thereby provides much of the epistemological and practical underpinning for an extended stewardship education code.

Conclusions

Whilst this chapter has focused on accountability and inspection questions in institutions concerned with education, its ultimate intention has been to stimulate thought on finding ways of making wicked thinking not just a major change in teaching, leadership and governance, but, more importantly in making it a principal frame by which the wider society examines present and future threats, with accountability and inspection being transformed into mechanisms which provide a first link between how education and other systems function, and how society thinks about its own and the wider environment's sustainability. A foregrounding of wicked accountability and inspection systems could have profound educational implications as educators, institutional leaders and students better understand coming challenges, and in so doing educate them into how to respond more intelligently when adults and citizens. The purpose and practice of educational systems – and of other systems using the same approach – then begins to change, and in addition new questions are asked about the functions of accountability and inspection, and particularly about how they are more useful, and more educational, when their adversarial nature is reduced, so that they are re-fashioned to help create a more trusting and rational dialogue between different groups of stakeholders. By better understanding that we live in a complex 'wicked' world, and that the inadequate framing of problems and solutions can be highly damaging, more educative links can then be formed between such institutions and the wider society, as such practice also improves the sustainability of both.

The choice of a wicked accountability and inspection system then suggests new answers to old questions, and not just for educational systems, for this model of accountability suggests the need to reject models based on the vanity, certainty and power of one group of stakeholders, and instead argues for the adoption of a model of accountability which has at its core an ethic of personal humility, which advocates the need for many to contribute to problem solutions. With a tame model, Schein (2013) argues, students may be schooled into telling others what is their truth, largely because they have been schooled into believing that the older, the wealthier and the powerful in their society know what is true and what is false. If they choose this path, they will be confident in supporting a culture which finds it easy to assign blame to others – both at home and abroad – for instances of failure, because they have been schooled to believe that silver bullets can be found to solve even the most difficult problem, and therefore that most instances of failure come from others' personal or cultural limitations. In choosing a very different path, one underpinned by greater personal humility, they are *not* being taught that their views are 'of lower or of lesser account than others' (Grenberg, 2005, p. 2), but rather that the understanding of all human beings is limited by our individual natures, and that other voices need to be listened to if more nuanced, subtle and shared understandings are to be attained. In seeing such an accountability system as a support rather than as a way of steering others to conform to a dominant group's policies, students are then educated into the virtues of listening to others and their opinions, as they come to understand that others may have insights to complement their own. They will also be much more wary of the easy blame of others, as they grow to recognize that they know that there is so much that they and others don't know. By then they may have also come to understand that the embrace and application of 'wicked' thinking may be one of the most ethical things they can do and that it is one of the greatest gifts that educational systems can give to them.

Such a model for accountability and inspection would then have major implications for the kinds of educational leadership responses used in tackling covert and overt threats, as such leadership needs transforming into a collaborative leadership, where *most* are seen as being capable of being leaders within an institutional team, as they understand the nature of threats faced, the frames needed to combat such threats and develop relationships with others in a team which improves its practice by creating greater trust and knowledge between its members. Accountability teams should then be based on an underlying logic of creation where this model of collaborative leadership is also utilized. Such inspection and institutional teams may then have many leaders, with different kinds of expertise, fulfilling different roles, but still having room for the kind of facilitative leader who coordinates different personalities and attributes into a coherent institutional team, which then provides coherent responses to the threats faced. It is then to the development of this changing nature of educational leadership for an uncertain age that we finally turn.

12

Educational Leadership for a World of Covert Threats

Introduction

Societies and their schools face a number of emerging threats. Some of these have not been generally recognized because their full effects have yet to be experienced and others have not been fully appreciated because they have not been fully understood. This makes them covert, rather than overt, threats, and all the more hazardous because of this. This chapter returns to the nature of these threats and suggests that they can be usefully grouped into four distinct areas – those of temporal myopia, of epistemological concerns, of process issues and of leadership focused threats. These groupings help provide a framework by which educational leaders can better identify and deal with them. Further, it has also been argued that there are a number of 'frames' – ways of viewing their role – which educational leaders need to adopt in order to better understand and combat such threats. This chapter also provides a final summation of these frames which underpin the enlarged steward element of the leadership role.

By describing the threats and then considering the ways in which an educational leadership role needs changing, we argue for a greater stewardship orientation. The ethical underpinning of this has been extensively described, in Chapter 10, but a description of the best way in which this stewardship role should be enacted still remains. In this book, a number of leadership models have been considered, the conclusion being reached that the most suitable model is almost certainly a form of collaborative leadership, where all those within a leadership team understand not only the types of threat faced but also the approaches or 'frames' that need to be used in combatting such threats. This kind of leadership, it has been argued, requires the development of higher levels of relationship within a team than is found in most other models, in order to create greater trust and shared knowledge. So a final task lies in describing the nature and dynamics of such a leadership model, which might well be used not just by educational teams but also by other occupations and professions. This chapter then begins with a review of the threats posed.

Four sets of covert threats

The earlier descriptions of individual threats have allowed one to dig deeper into their particular characteristics; however, being able to assign them to larger groups of similar threats provides a wider view of their potential connections and therefore of a wider set of alternatives by which to combat them. So a first set of threats can be described as being caused by *human temporal myopia*. Such threats are then driven by a lack of awareness of how past events can impact present decisions and how it is similarly dangerous if attention is so fixated on present problems that future events are ignored. This book has examined how the spread of many previous pandemic diseases over the last 10,000 years has been a consequence of groups of human beings moving from the greater mobility of hunter-gathering lifestyles into adopting the more static and crowded behaviours of agriculturalists and city dwellers, behaviours which are now exacerbated by the vast increase in globalized travel over the last fifty years, which transports new diseases to static populations with no natural protection. Further, it has been assumed that many future environmental changes would only become problematic some distance into this future, yet there are increasingly present-day experiences which have taken many by surprise as they have occurred well before they were expected. So a first set of threats are those where we fail to learn lessons from the past and underestimate those which are occurring now or are probably only a little way from emerging into an unpredictable future.

A second set is that of **epistemological** threats – ones which threaten us because of the way in which we think about issues. Three different kinds have been discussed in this book. The first are those where human beings underestimate issues of complexity and uncertainty. In so doing, they run the danger of adopting 'tame' rather than 'wicked' views of the way the world works and of assuming that most causation is simple, linear and predictable, when many problem are much more complex, systemic and unpredictable. A second kind of epistemological threat occurs when societies prioritize particular economic ideologies over more socially and environmentally conscious approaches. By assigning priority to assumptions of resource exploitation, efficiency and consumption, humanity is then depicted as essentially composed of selfish and competitive individualistic consumers, rather than beings who are at least as caring, cooperative and socially responsible. Such assumptions have had major impacts upon many present social practices, on our treatment of other human beings and on the way we have viewed the natural environment upon which we depend. A final epistemological threat, visible within many political environments currently, is that of the rise of populist movements and their leaders, which adopt non-rational stances towards evidence, argument and logic, and try to seduce individuals into points of view which claim the truth, but which are largely the creation of a social media lacking robust critique, and often based on unproven conspiracies and rumour.

A third set of covert threats are **process threats** – physical processes which are unrecognized, or insufficiently recognized and understood, the impact of which can lead to high levels of instability in both the human and natural environment, and which significantly contribute to a time of great uncertainty. One area is that of connectivity – digital, social and environmental – where there can exist both an under-connectivity, as, for example, when human beings lack full appreciation of their links with the environment; but there is also a hyper-connectivity, as social links through greater digital connectivity may be enhanced, but they can also lead to much personal stress and intrusions into privacy. Another process threat is the lack of appreciation of the impact of exponential as opposed to arithmetic growth, for instance, when people believe that processes like Covid-19 expand slowly and arithmetically, rather than rapidly and exponentially. Exponential increase then often leads to genuine surprise at the speed of expansion and only then is it realized that it may be impossible to radically slow the speed of this process. Exponential growth is also seen in the manner in which human populations increase, and in the consequent exponential consumption in a world of finite resources. It is this combination that can lead to people fearing the approach of another kind of process threat – that of tipping points, where systems become so disrupted by the speed and size of change that a new 'normal' may be created which poses grave threats to both human and environmental sustainability. The final process threat – that of positive feedback – is also a major contributor to tipping points – as, unlike its counterpoint negative feedback, this process doesn't bring a system back to previous levels of functioning, but exacerbates situations so that the more that processes like ice-melt increase, the more that they are likely to increase, and may then cause huge damage to human and environmental sustainability.

A final set of covert threats – **leadership focus threats** – concentrates on the underlying assumptions of educational leadership models, as some of these steer leaders into focusing on aspects of reality, or on interpretations of that reality, which do little to develop a greater awareness of the kind of threats described earlier. One area here is the traditional educational leadership focus on micro- and meso-events, consisting of either person-to-person or small group interactions, or the functioning of larger groups or institutions. Such foci are both understandable and necessary, yet, as seen, many challenges occurring at micro- and meso-levels originate at the macro-level, and to respond appropriately to such challenges requires a greater understanding of such origins.

A second area of *problematic* leadership assumptions lies in the continued championing of educational leadership roles which are based upon visions of a reality where linearity, hierarchy and control dominate. Yet in an age when wicked problems and highly systemic complexities increasingly result in unpredictable and unexpected events, assumptions of linear thinking need to be replaced by ones which much better appreciate the complex nature of many systemic interactions. As Western (2018) has suggested, we now need to see organizations as 'ecosystems within ecosystems', and leaders as not only having to manage their own institutional ecosystem but understanding the processes of those impinging upon it. In such situations, assumptions of the effectiveness of a hierarchical leadership by individuals then need replacing by the development of more collaborative relationships, not only with other members of educational institutions but also with those in positions of larger systemic authority and with stakeholders who can broaden and enrich problem understanding. The concept of control then needs reducing in order to encourage the development of more creative ways of looking at present challenges, which then invoke the need for not only a greater *intellectual* humility that comes from better understanding the nature of wicked problems but also a *socio-emotional* humility which helps develop the contributions of others in finding the best ways forward. Finally, one needs to add to this list the existential threat that high-stakes testing creates, as such testing not only diminishes the possibility of better developing much-needed collaborative approaches but also threatens the sustainability of many of those working within the role.

The frames for steward leadership

Now if these are the major sets of current emerging threats, new ways of thinking – new frames – will be needed to inform the role. Such frames have been referred to and developed throughout the book, and will now be pulled together to provide their final restatement.

A much greater emphasis upon stewardship within the role

So a principal – perhaps *the* principal educational leadership frame – is that which embraces an enlarged stewardship role. Stewardship, as already noted, is a concept implicit within the role, for such leadership is at least in part a calling to help individuals live more fulfilling and sustainable lives. However, the role needs to transcend the concerns of these levels by recognizing that a much larger conception of human sustainability needs embracing, which is facilitated not only by societal values and practices but at least as importantly by the preservation and protection of the natural environment, for it is this which underpins the sustainability not only of human functioning but also of all life on this planet. This then is not only a stewardship for human beings but a stewardship for the global environment as well. Educational leaders then need to embrace this new and crucial part of their role, whilst communicating its need to their students, their colleagues and their communities. In so doing, they raise others' awareness of present and future responsibilities in this area, and how such recognition should be used to critique personal plans and ambitions, not only currently but also into the long future

The need for a more prominent macro-frame in educational leadership thinking

A second frame then extends the first: for if many incidents occurring at the micro- and meso-levels are generated at larger macro-level contexts, then focusing leadership work at lower levels will very often amount to little more than treating the symptoms rather than the causes of such incidents. This is particularly true for the sustainability of the leadership role, as the role's sustainability would be substantially improved by a better understanding of what at the macro-level has generated lower-level impacts.

It would, however, be wrong to assume that the cultivation of such a macro-frame – or indeed any of the frames discussed – should only be foci for individual leaders. If such changes are to have significant effects upon the leadership role, as well as the institutions they work within, and the wider society, strong macro-political endorsement and appropriate resource investment will be needed. As already noted, a significant steer would come from the creation of new educational and coaching purposes for accountability approaches and their inspection vehicles. Understanding the need for such changes at the macro-level will then be essential to a changed leadership role.

The need for the role to be more informed by the incidence of previous macro-threats

Despite the fact that some may doubt that necessary connections exist between previous macro-threats and the development of a new role for educational leaders, there are important lessons to be learnt from them. One is that the causes of previous mass extinctions strongly suggest that humanity is living on a planet where such mass extinctions will probably occur again, and there is good evidence to suggest that we are entering a sixth planetary species extinction, for which humanity is primarily responsible. A second and under-recognized lesson from the deep past is the movement from mobile hunter-gatherer to more static agricultural and then urban lifestyles, which have facilitated the emergence of many zoonotic diseases. Covid-19 is the latest but only one example, and it is probable that more will follow.

A third macro-lesson from the deep past is the early overuse by expanding populations of the finite resources around them which, when combined with unpredictable regional climate change, could lead to that civilization's collapse. The lesson from these to the present day is that we may be creating the same conditions again, as many societies continue to assume the possibility of infinite economic growth and consumption on a planet with limited finite resources, at a time when the world climate is changing for the worse.

The need for the role to be more informed about longer-term future projections

Whilst educational leaders need to look back in time for present-day lessons, they also need to look forward to possible threats in the future. However, care is needed here: a key theme throughout this book is that we live in a world with degrees of complexity and uncertainty which may make it impossible to fully comprehend, and therefore predict and control the future. Strathern (2007) suggests that it is largely the false – and tame – belief that we *can* understand the unfolding of emerging events in this future which has led to so many highly inaccurate future projections. Yet we have to predict from necessarily limited sets of information with necessarily limited sensory organs and brain capacity. So whilst there may well be similarities with past events, complex interactions in new contexts mean that future events will almost certainly never precisely replicate those of the past, and we may choose the wrong trends as the major steers of a human and global future. The further into the future we go, the less certain we should be about what to expect, and this is why Kay and King (2020) suggest that we necessarily move towards and must learn to deal with such 'radical uncertainty'.

However, this does not mean that nothing can be sensibly said about the future. Rather, we need to be aware of the siren calls of those claiming a false certainty, and be very careful and measured in what we claim. This is why the IPCC claims never talk in absolutes but only in terms like 90 per cent or 95 per cent certainty (e.g. IPCC, 2014, 2018, 2019/20): the evidence for instance of global warming is now overwhelming, but there always remains the possibility of new data, new evidence altering this picture.

However, it is also the reason why there needs to be a balance to counter such provisionality and is why at the first IPCC conference in 1992, Principle 15 became better known as the Precautionary Principle, as it stated that

> Where there are threats of serious or irreversible damage, lack of full scientific certainty shall not be used as a reason for postponing cost-effective measures to prevent environmental degradation.

The caution is then balanced by the concern: you may never be absolutely sure (and you will need to keep looking for more confirmatory and dis-confirmatory evidence), but when it is evident that taking no action will cause much greater damage than acting on the basis of the present evidence, then you must be proactive. This then is the lure not of false certainty but of measured action based on the evidence. This is the kind of deliberation needed to investigate the future. Forward projections, and discussion on how they need addressing, and what contributions education can make to such understanding and awareness are then essential frames for an educational stewardship role.

The need for leaders to better understand the causal linkages between the macro-, the meso- and the micro-levels, and how these affect their role

Having a more prominent macro-frame for the leadership role helps to raise awareness of the impact these macro-processes and events have upon meso- and micro-levels. The reasons for particular forms of micro- and meso-level management may then on many occasions be better understood as emanating, at least in part, from levels and systems well beyond where they impact. For a profession and leadership oftentimes focusing upon the personal and institutional, a clearer understanding of such linkages would help better understanding of the real origins of micro- and meso- events. As noted earlier, micro- and meso-events may only be downstream symptoms of larger upstream threats, and threats are seldom understood or resolved by focusing on symptoms rather than their causes.

So this book has emphasized the need to better understand the movement from macro- to meso- and micro-, because present leadership models often pay insufficient attention to the effects that the macro- can have. It is very important to also understand that meso- and micro-practices can have major effects upon the macro-level. For example, it was not very long ago that the primary criticism of the affluent West's excessive consumption of meat was because of the long-term effects upon a person's health. However, the principal threat from eating meat is increasingly being relocated to the macro-level, as it is recognized how damaging the raising of huge numbers of domestic animals (and their consumption of vast amounts of grain) can be to large areas of previously pristine wilderness and how such actions are significant contributors to greenhouse gas emissions. Linkages between levels and systems then are not one-way: whilst some top-down causations have major effects upon micro- and meso-areas of sustainability, bottom-up effects in the form of consumption practices – particularly when human populations are now close to eight billion – can have significant effects upon macro-level sustainability.

A greater appreciation of a deeply complex world

Such interactions between different levels then add to a much greater complexity than is often realized. As noted earlier, such complexity has at least four different faces. A first form – 'systemic' complexity – refers to a world of larger and smaller systems, actors, elements and parts interacting so intricately that it may be virtually impossible to predict the outcomes of such interactions, and many events will then be unpredictable 'emergent consequences' (Levy, 1992). A second form – 'epistemic complexity' – is concerned with what we can know about the external world, with some issues claimed to be 'known knowns', others admitted to be 'unknown knowns', more that are 'known unknowns' and probably many more that are 'unknown unknowns ' (Rumsfeld, 2002). If there is much more that we know we don't know, and where we are not even aware of what we don't know that we don't know, then working within a model of reality assuming the epistemologically safe and the comfortable will be a highly dangerous assumption to make.

If epistemic complexity is concerned with what we can know about the external world, the third form – 'relational complexity' – is concerned with what we can know about our internal world, about the gaps in our understanding of ourselves and of others in any form of relationship. Stern's (2021) 'Jumee window' suggests that relationships with others are complicated because there are things that we know and don't know about ourselves, and there are also things that others know and don't know about us. This raises the probability of misunderstandings between people and so of creating even greater complexity and unpredictability. Together, epistemic and relational complexities suggest that if the information we receive through our limited cognitive and sensory abilities is also mediated by selves that only partly know themselves, then any processing of the external world is going to be even more selective and partial, and will add to the difficulty in making sense of an external reality – and of our relationships within it.

Finally, 'wicked' complexity derives from the notion of 'wicked' problems, which, because they are context-bound and unique, means that they have to be dealt with on a highly individual basis, in which failure is always possible, because their resolutions lack the safety net of standardization that 'tame' problems very often possess. It is why leaders are highly unlikely to be able to raise morale or creativity in their schools in any kind of standardized way. Even more problematic is that different individuals may well understand and describe a wicked problem differently, and some may even deny that there is a problem to be concerned about. The problems surrounding Covid-19 have very often been wicked because there are sizeable minorities who do not believe that the disease constitutes as large a problem as experts or politicians claim – or indeed that it actually exists. There are others who believe that the use of vaccines to combat it is in actual fact the **real** problem. Whilst at first blush such issues may not seem to be *educational* problems, they are actually highly important ones, for they ask leaders to consider three critical questions:

1. How can people understand and communicate when they have different beliefs?
2. What is the basis for declaring something to be true or false?
3. How should such considerations affect a leader's approach to their educational leadership role?

Enacting steward leadership: Building relationships in an age of uncertainty

There is real need then to foreground such issues as well as understanding the danger of assuming any complete certainty. Yet we live at a time when a great deal of news, media, government policies and societal beliefs lead citizens down hubristic rather than humble paths. This is a problem that transcends education and its leaders, but education is probably an excellent place to address such issues, for a central part of its role, I suggest, is to open up such debate about understanding and uncertainty, and then to find ways of reaching acceptable forms of consensus. One of the first acts in doing so would then be to build the kinds of teams which not only understood these issues of complexity and uncertainty but which could communicate them to others and facilitate their discussion. A critical role of educational leaders then is to build enriched forms of relationships within such teams, and it is to this that we now turn.

How is such an enriched form to be developed? Assume two individuals: one is a homeowner wanting to alter the kitchen, much of which will be through removing dated cupboards, getting rid of old wallpaper and probably the plaster behind them. The other is the builder looking at the job for the first time: the cupboards can be easily taken out, but then the wall behind them may need taking back to the brickwork if other problems appear. The homeowner asks for a price for the work, and the builder shows some hesitancy: if the plaster and brickwork are fine, then the cost of parts and labour can be calculated, but until further investigation, he explains, this can only be an estimate. He needs to see what the full situation is (i.e. he needs to reduce the uncertainties in the work) before he can provide a more accurate price.

If the two have never met before, then there may be some tension, as the homeowner doesn't know whether to trust the builder on this provisional estimate, as the builder may be using this as a means of increasing the price later. The builder understands the homeowner's caution but still doesn't want to commit to a price until he is more certain of what he is dealing with. Now if the builder has satisfactorily executed previous work for the homeowner, then a level of relationship trust will likely have already been established, and the homeowner will probably agree to the initial estimate and accept that until further work is done, this is an area of uncertainty that needs living with. Trust is then the critical facilitator here, most often established by previous contact and practice.

In situations of uncertainty, then, developing relationships normally need ways of increasing the level of trust. Where a higher level of relationships has already been established, necessary resolutions can then be more quickly worked towards. If both are satisfied with the end result of this work, then the experience increases the level of this trust relationship, and when they next meet to discuss further work, and other instances of uncertainty are met, the relationship will probably be sufficiently robust to permit initial actions (problem-solving followed by provisional agreed resolution) to also move forward quickly.

This is a small example of how many relationships need to be developed when a problem is confronted in situations of uncertainty. If a shared relationship of trust is not built, then neither of the parties are likely to be comfortable in working closely together. Moreover, as situations of uncertainty develop into periods of wickedly uncertain problems, the level of relationship required needs to be at least maintained, and more likely improved. Schein and Schein (2018, p. 108), in arguing that we live in times of 'volatility, uncertainty, complexity, and ambiguity', suggest that dealing with such situations will not be possible where others are given instructions to work within narrowly defined functional silos, and where often there is little personal engagement between the individuals allocating such functions and those carrying them out. Schein and Schein therefore argue that it is essential in present and future organizations to begin cultivating higher-level personal relationships between all those working in the organization. They suggest that one needs to begin by changing the nature of the organization, and that a critical part of that is by moving from coercion, control and transactional relationships towards higher-level relationships, where knowing the other person is more than a pragmatic attempt to improve efficiency but one which is intended to create long-term interactions, where genuine interest is shown in finding out about the other as a person, their likes and dislikes, their personal skills and issues.

Now the levels of relationships Schein and Schein propose closely match suggestions by the current author (Bottery, 2004) on building richer forms of trust (see Table. 12.1).

Comparing and combining these two models together strongly suggest that a critical element in the building of higher-level relationships comes from developing more sophisticated forms of trust between individuals, and these are not best created by focusing on task-oriented bonds between members of a team, but rather by first developing relationship-oriented bonds, which increasingly include, as identified in the 'practice' and 'identificatory' trust of Table 12.1, genuine interest in and care for the other. In Chapter 3 it was suggested that the most appropriate type of leader for complex and turbulent times were probably those who were inclusive and facilitative; who understood the importance of context; who enabled discussions with others in defining the nature of problems and their solutions; who possessed the personal humility to accept the provisional nature of most findings; and, finally, who were comfortable in living with uncertainty.

All of these characteristics remain essential, but in the light of the kind of collaborative leadership which this book suggests now needs developing, they

Table 12.1 Building Relationships, Building Trust

Relationship types	Levels of leadership relationship (Schein and Schein, 2018, Chapter 2)	Levels of trust (Bottery, 2004, Chapter 6)
Level minus 1 and Calculative trust	Level minus 1: Very basic relationship of impersonal coercion and control	Very basic 'calculative trust': a trust goes no further than calculating how much a person can be trusted
Level 1 and Role trust	Level 1: Transactional role and rule-based supervision, service and most forms of 'professional' relationships	'Role trust' – A form of trust which depends upon how much a person 'representing' a profession can be trusted simply because they are a member of that profession
Level 2 and Practice trust	Level 2: Relationships based upon knowing the person, cooperating with them and developing more trusting relationships	'Practice trust': where through continued interaction individuals get to know and care for one another, their hopes and challenges, and who they are
Level 3 and Identificatory trust	Level 3: Emotionally intimate total mutual commitments	'Identificatory trust': very intimate level of trust creating strong emotional caring bonds – which can also produce much rancour if such trust is broken

need to be viewed as more than just the qualities which a single individual leader must possess, but rather as the qualities which *all* within a leadership team dealing with wicked problems in turbulent times must possess.

Individual leaders, it has already been argued, are seldom able to resolve wicked problems on their own, even if they are blessed with high levels of the qualities described earlier. Before such problems can be effectively tackled, *teams* of individuals with such qualities are needed, and in order to create such teams, a trusting and caring approach is required in order to forge such bonds before the intellectual tasks generated by wicked problems can be fully shared, and the kinds of frames which they need to adopt can be fully developed. Blake and Mouton's (1985) suggestion of a 'managerial grid' is then essentially correct in describing two main leadership orientations – task- and relationship-oriented. However, because individual leadership capabilities will be insufficient for dealing with many of the wicked problems increasingly presenting themselves, a collaborative team approach will be essential. If this is the case, then the development of such collaboration will initially not be so much an intellectual task as a socio-emotional cultivation of relationships. Critically, then, these need building *before* a team can effectively frame the intellectual tasks for dealing with wicked problems. In short, if you haven't got the right level of relationships in a team, you almost certainly haven't got the right level of collaboration to best manage the wicked problems faced. This is also likely to be significantly different from forms of 'distributed' forms of leadership, where the concern is with the passing on of tasks to others lower in a formal hierarchy, rather than on socio-emotional ways of building relationships which facilitate teams of leaders working together.

The focus on developing relationships was well illustrated for the present writer by the case study of 'trouble-shooter' English headteachers discussed earlier in this book (and in Bottery et al., 2018, Chapter 7). These headteachers were employed at a regional level to go into severely disrupted schools at a moment's notice in order to bring structure and calm back to the institution. They could be there for three months or three years, depending on the presenting problems and the time it took for attempted remediations to work. The relevant issue for this chapter is that the strategies adopted by these headteachers were remarkably similar to the attempts at forging stronger relationships described earlier. Their initial core strategy was quite different from what many might think necessary, but which has also been reported by Thornton (2021) with respect to Covid-19 and the prioritization of well-being over learning in the first phase of the crisis in secondary schools in New Zealand. In the case of the 'trouble-shooter' headteachers, it was what they called 'healing the school': trying to repair the fractured and acrimonious relationships therein. There was no employment of the kind of transformational and charismatic leadership behaviours which some might expect from such impressive individuals, nor was there any initial focus on boosting the school's results. Instead, they saw their role as one of helping all within the institution – *and* the community surrounding it – to come together to re-form relationships of trust, support and care, before any move was made to focus on improving results. Significantly, this prioritization of relationships over tasks by such 'trouble-shooter' headteachers increasingly became a source of friction between them and those at more senior levels requiring evidence of improving results, and was one of the reasons why several of the team left as they felt that such an early focus was a damaging and backward step in the rebuilding of these relationships.

Developing collaborative steward leadership

So an initial and essential part in the development of a more collaborative leadership is one of narrowing the status gap between 'followers' and 'leaders', ones in which Schein (2016) suggests leaders primarily do the 'telling' and followers will do either the 'implementing' or 'asking' if clarification is needed in the orders. So individual leaders convinced of the need to form less hierarchical and more collaborative groupings will need to admit two things. First, that there is a great deal that they don't know that they need to know; and second, that there is a great deal that others in their organization and beyond may know which would be extremely useful in defining and resolving problems.

Schein (2016) argues that changing the nature of such relationships requires that leaders 'ask' more, whilst those lower in a hierarchy 'tell' more. There are also other terms which could aid such transition – words like 'advise', 'contribute' and 'participate' – as they better express the belief that the thoughts of others lower in formal status in an organization are worthy of consideration and incorporation. Similarly, 'ask' is a good word for suggesting that those senior in a hierarchy should respect the views of others, as words like 'enquire' and 'listen' might add to frame the kinds of behaviours needed by those with senior formal status in closing the gap in a hierarchy of relationships. In so doing, views of how relationships 'up' and 'down' a hierarchy can be transformed into more collaborative ones may be better developed. In so doing, argues Western (2018, p. 301), one then reshapes the organization by changing the style of leadership, and in so doing one is able to 'harness and unleash dormant talent, skills, knowledge and energy'.

In then moving from hierarchical to more collaborative leadership cultures, relationships need to be changed, and changing such relationships entails a change in the language and attitudes of those who have influence upon its policies and practices not only within but also beyond the organization. Primary external influencers on educational institutions will likely be governments and their inspection teams. Internally there will also need to be further development in relationships with students, as they need educating into the virtues of listening to the opinions of others, and so coming to better appreciate that others may have 'truths' which enrich and complement their own values and insights. In so doing, they can be educated into the intellectual humility that comes from knowing that there is so much that they don't know. So whilst the problems faced by those within institutions now exist within contexts of volatility, uncertainty, complexity and ambiguity, the foundation of coping with such changes lies in building teams which can best deal with such conditions. These teams also need to be grounded in an intellectual humility in order to deal intelligently with wicked problems; but they also need to be grounded in a socio-emotional humility, so that they come to respect and bring to bear the different talents spread across the organization.

Developing ethical dialecticians in a world of covert threats

A couple of decades ago, the current author (Bottery, 2004) proposed that educational leaders needed to be 'ethical dialecticians' if they were to meet the challenges brought about by an age of increasing globalization, fragmentation, commodification and control, all of which were impacting issues of trust, meaning and personal identity. How would such a leader match up to the threats faced by educational leaders today? I then argued that educational leaders should not be cut from the cloth of a standardized 'designer' leadership (Gronn, 2003), where governmental intentions seemed to be to turn out individuals, like early Hollywood starlets, who were equipped with sets of standardized skills, values and, one suspects, personalities. Instead, it was suggested that in such an interconnected age of global, national and local pressures on education, educational leaders needed to be aware that such interconnections were not simple, linear and uniform but complex, ambiguous and non-standard. They, therefore, needed to begin to orient their role towards future challenges, and to more greatly embrace the values of a global public good and cooperation, in contrast to the much-vaunted national and individual self-interest and competition. An awareness of their own personal and epistemological limitations meant that they needed to listen to others and to adopt a provisional attitude to any conclusions they might reach. At the same time, they needed to balance such caution at a necessary impermanence with an independence of personality underpinned by an internal moral compass. This meant that they needed the moral courage to formulate problems and solutions in contexts which provided more nuanced understandings than any officially sanctioned tame and linear ones.

Twenty years on, in the changed circumstances of today, much of this argument still seems relevant, and in some ways has been strengthened by the analyses of current covert threats, by the arguments for the adoption of new leadership frames and by the description of the ethical values underpinning an urgently required stewardship role. This large emphasis upon a macro-stewardship role is then one major development from the previous analysis. However, a second development is in recognition of the sheer scale of the complexity with which leaders now need to deal. Having to think now of organizations as 'ecosystems within ecosystems', and of having to manage their own ecosystem as larger ones impact upon it seems a major step change in how the role needs to be viewed. A further development has been the realization of the need for greater emphasis on a longer vision for such leaders, not just into the future, but into the deep past as well. Some of this future is emerging much more quickly than many had expected, and there is much from the past which can help inform our thought and reactions to this future.

A final development has been the need for 'leaders' rather than 'a leader'. The concept of an ethical dialectician might suggest a prescription for one formally appointed individual principal or headteacher, and whilst the tendency in some distributed leadership literature is to discount the importance of the person inhabiting this formal role, it has become increasingly clear that problems are most often best resolved by teams in which strong personal relationships exist, but which do not engage in a 'groupthink' (Janis, 1972) which excludes the opinions of those who do not hold the majority opinion. Rather, such disagreement needs to be seen as a fundamental part of a process which involves valuable input through argument to counter-argument and then to synthesis, where a particular expertise may be located in surprising places in an organization, but which must be nurtured so that that person can become a leader in a team of leaders.

Just as such teams of leaders must recognize the covert threats, so each individual within them must recognize the frames that they will need in order to counter them, and they must embrace the ethical foundations from which to work. They all need to recognize that others have important perspectives and points of view, and that the cultivation of higher-level relationships is essential in a world where individuals cannot resolve many problems on their own. These are all essential steward leadership qualifications, but each individual is likely to exercise a different form. Some will be leaders in particular areas of expertise; some will have particular strategic gifts; whilst others will have the qualities and skills of a bricoleur (Grint, 2008) making the best of what is available, rather than trying to impose a particular plan or solution from the beginning. Others will be more skilled at 'creating transformational environments . . . [rather] than in creating the innovation itself' (Marion and Uhl-Bien, 2001, p. 394). There will also be some who must be encouraged to show leadership, just as there will be those, possibly officially appointed to senior leadership positions, who will be most skilled at facilitating the collaboration of this team of leaders. How this will work, and what kinds of leaders will be necessary, will be decided by the nature of the educational mission, by the nature of the threats encountered, by the context in which it is encountered and by the natures and the interactions of the people who lead. In a world of covert threats, educational organizations need the collaborative leadership of ethical dialecticians. In a world of covert threats, then, a set of leadership frames need to be shared amongst a group of leaders who have developed a sufficiently high level of relationships with each other to enable trust to fuel what will be difficult, but ultimately rewarding, discussions and resolutions.

Afterword

This book began with the story of Sitting Bull, the Sioux Chief, saying that inside of him there were two dogs. One was mean and evil, the other was brave and good, and they fought each other all of the time, and when someone asked which one would win, Sitting Bull answered, 'The one I feed the most.' This is the choice that humanity now faces. We can feed our desires for infinite economic growth and endless consumption, or we can realize that we are one part of an interconnected but finite natural world and that there are much more important things to achieve than to focus on consuming this natural world. Indeed, if we abuse it, we abuse ourselves and threaten our own existence. If we continue to feed the first dog, we now have no excuse for not recognizing the consequences of our choice. If we instead choose the second dog, to live within planetary boundaries and to educate our children, and our children's children, into doing the same, we open up many different and better pathways of developing our well-being and sustaining the welfare of all who occupy this planet.

Appendix 1

Surviving and Prospering as an Educational Leader in an Age of Uncertainty

Ontological assumptions

- Work with the reality of uncertainty, not with the false promise of populist certainty.
- Recognize and accept the reality of a world of complex and wicked problems; don't be seduced by promises of being able to live in an essentially tame and simple world.

Epistemological assumptions

- Cultivate an intellectual humility – understand and accept that on your own, you may know very little about many situations. So look for contributory insights from others, but even then, accept that these may be only partially correct.
- Cultivate *a socio-emotional* humility, accepting that the best solutions to complex problems do not often come from individual solutions but rather from blending a variety of insights, and to do this you need to value and develop others' contributions.

Ethical assumptions

- Act within the parameters of the values of an ethical stewardship.
- Do not transgress the ethical boundaries of resource consumption, individual and group well-being and global stewardship.

Understanding threats

- Be aware of four groups of covert threats: the process, the temporal, the epistemological and those affecting the leadership focus, and frame your understanding of individual threats within these.
- Triage threats by working out the degree of potential harm they are likely to cause.

Scanning the past and the future

- Be aware of the causes and dynamics of past problems, and consider how you would best deal with them if they return.
- Discuss and prioritise with others the nature of possible and emerging future problems.
- Examine past successes and consider how they can be applied to similar challenges in the present and the future.

Team structures and dynamics

- Act upon the assumption that implementing large-scale changes which others will embrace is not only more likely to endure but more likely to be created through cooperative, caring and trusting relationships than through competitive and self-serving ones.
- Wicked solutions are best produced by multi-level collaborative teams, with inputs by different talents at different levels, but will seldom be created by hierarchies dominated by individual leaders or a caucus of powerful individuals.

Action plans

- Use the right tools for presenting problems: wicked problems need wicked solutions, not tame ones.
- Consider and list leverage points at micro-, meso- and macro-levels which could apply to possible and emerging future problems.

- Don't focus solely on problems: recognize and facilitate benign processes to counter more malign ones.

Action through calmness

- Learn to not jump into action; find the time to think through a problem in discussion with others.
- When there is no time, and no time for consultation, reflect on your stewardship values and act in accordance with these. *Then* recognize you need to find time *before* an emerging problem occurs, and discuss this with others and reach preliminary conclusions on actions before they happen.

References

Ackoff R. (1979) 'The future of operational research is past' *Journal of the Operational Research Society* vol. 30 no. 2 pp. 93–104.
Almond G. and Verba S. (1965) *The Civic Culture*. Boston: Little, Brown and co.
Amyes S. (2013) *Bacteria*. Oxford: Oxford University Press.
April K. (2013) *Steward Leadership*. Cape Town, South Africa: University of Cape Town Press.
Aristotle (1976) *The Ethics of Aristotle: The Nicomachean Ethics*. London: Penguin.
Attenborough D. (2020) *A Life on Our Planet*. London: Witness Books.
Ball S. (2003) 'The teacher's soul and the terrors of performativity' *Journal of Education Policy* vol. 18 no. 2 pp. 215–28.
Ball S. (2007) *Education plc*. London: Routledge.
Ball S. (2012) *Global Education Inc*. New York: Routledge.
Bambra C. (2006) 'Health Status and the Worlds of Welfare' *Social Policy and Society'* vol. 5 no. 1 pp. 53–62.
Bandura A. (1977) *Social Learning Theory*. Engelwood Cliffs, HJ: Prentice-Hall.
Bangs J., MacBeath J. and Galton M. (2011) *Reinventing Schools, Reforming Teaching*. London: Routledge.
Barabasi A-L. (2002) *Linked: The New Science of Networks*. Cambridge, MA: Perseus Publishing.
Barber B. (1984) *Strong Democracy*. Berkeley: University of California Press.
Barnard A. (2018) 'Defining hunter-gatherers: Enlightenment, romantic and social evolutionary perspectives' in Cummings V., Jordan P. and Zvelebil M. (eds), *The Oxford Handbook of the Archaeology and Anthropology of Hunter-Gatherers*. pp. 43–54 Oxford: Oxford University Press.
Barnovsky A. and Hadley E. (2015) *Tipping Point for Planet Earth*. New York: St. Martin's Press.
Bassey M. (1999) *Case Study Research in Educational Settings*. Buckingham: Open University Press.
Beauchamp G., Hulme M., Clarke L., Hamilton L. and Harvey J. (2021) "People miss people': A study of school leadership and management in the four nations of the United Kingdom in the early stages of the Covid-19 Pandemic' *Educational Management Administration and Leadership* vol. 49 no. 3 pp. 375–92.
Bell D. and Wang P. (2020) 'The case for hierarchy' *Palladium*, March.
Bellah R., Madsen R., Sullivan M., Swidler A. and Tipton S. (2008) *Habits of the Heart: Individualism and Commitment in American Life*. Berkeley: University of California Press.

Benedick R. (1998) *Ozone Diplomacy*. Cambridge, MA: Harvard University Press.
Berliner W. (2011) 'Teachers want to be treated as professionals' *The Guardian*, 3 October.
Benton M. (2003) *When Life Nearly Died*. London: Thames and Hudson.
Blake, Robert and Mouton (1985) *The New Managerial Grid*. Houston: Gulf.
Bloomberg (2017) 'Farming the world: China's epic race to avoid a food crisis' *Bloomberg News*, 22 May.
Blundell R., Costa Dias M., Joyce R., and Xu X.(2020) 'Covid-19 and Inequalities' *Fiscal Studies* vol. 41 no. 2 pp. 291–319.
Blunkett D. (2000) 'Influence or irrelevance: How can social science improve government?' *Research Intelligence* no. 71 pp. 12–21.
Bongaarts J. (2009) 'Human population growth and the demographic transition' in Mace G. (ed.), *The Impact of Population Growth on Tomorrow's World*. pp. 2985–90. London: Philosophical Transactions of the Royal Society.
Bore A. and Wright N. (2009) 'The wicked and complex in education: Developing a trans-disciplinary perspective for policy formation, implementation and professional practice' *Journal of Education for Teaching* vol. 35 no. 3 pp. 241–56.
Bosnich D.(2010) 'The "principle of subsidiarity"' *Religion and Liberty* Vo. 6 no. 4 pp. 1–4.
Bottery M. (1990) *The Morality of the School*. London: Cassell.
Bottery M. (1992) *The Ethics of Educational Management*. London: Cassell.
Bottery M. (1998) *Professionals and Policy*. London: Cassell.
Bottery M. (2000) *Education, Policy and Ethics*. London: Cassell.
Bottery M. (2003a) 'The management and mismanagement of trust' *Educational Management and Administration* vol. 31, no. 2 pp. 245–61.
Bottery M. (2003b) 'The end of citizenship? The Nation State, threats to its legitimacy and citizenship education in the twenty-first century' *Cambridge Journal of Education* vol. 33 no. 1 pp. 101–122.
Bottery M. (2004) *The Challenges of Educational Leadership*. London: Paul Chapman.
Bottery M. (2006) 'Education and globalisation: Redefining the role of the educational professional' *Educational Review* vol. 58 no. 1 pp. 95–113.
Bottery M. (2016) *Educational Leadership for a More Sustainable World*. London: Bloomsbury.
Bottery M. (2019) 'An ethics of educational leadership for turbulent and complex times' in Bush T., Bell L. and Middlewood D. (eds), *Principles of Educational Leadership and Management*. pp. 39–57. London: Sage.
Bottery M., Ping-Man W. and Ngai G. (2018) *Sustainable School Leadership: Portraits of Individuality*. London: Bloomsbury.
Bottery M., Ngai G., Wong P. M. and Wong P. H. (2008) 'Leaders and contexts: Comparing English and Hong Kong perceptions of educational challenges' *International Studies in Educational Administration* vol. 36 no.1 pp. 56–71.
Boulding (1968/1989) 'The economics of the coming spaceship earth' in M. Allenby (eds), *Thinking Green: An anthology of Essential Ecological Writing*. pp. 133–8. London: Barrie and Jenkins.

Braidwood R. (1957) *Prehistoric Men* (3rd ed.). Chicago Natural History Museum Popular Series, Anthropology, no. 37.

Brannen P. (2018) *The Ends of the World*. London: One World books.

Breakspear S. (2020) *Leading Through Disruption*. Queensland Education Leadership Institute webinar. https://qeli.qld.edu.au

Brody H. (2002) *The Other Side of Eden: Hunter-Gatherers, Farmers and the Shaping of the World*. London: Faber and Faber.

Brook B., Ellis E. and Buettel J. (2018) 'What is the evidence for planetary tipping points?' in Kareiva P., Marvier M., and Silliman B. (eds), *Effective Conservation Science*. pp. 51–57 Oxford: Oxford University Press.

Brown M., McNamara G., O'Hara J. and O'Brien S. (2016) 'Exploring the changing face of school inspections' *Eurasian Journal of Educational Research* no. 66 pp. 1–26.

Brundtland Report (1987) *Our Common Future. World Commission on Environment and Development*. Oxford: Oxford University Press.

Bryman (1992) *Quantity and Quality in Social Research*. London: Routledge.

Bryman, A. (2016) *Social Research Methods*. Oxford: Oxford University Press.

Bulkeley H. (2000) 'Common knowledge? Public understanding of climate change in Newcastle' *Australian Understanding of Science* vol. 9 no. 3 pp. 313–33.

Bush T. (2019) 'Models of educational leadership' in Bush T., Bell L. and Middlewood D. (eds), *Principles of Educational Leadership and Management* (3rd ed). pp. 3–17. London: Sage.

Butzer K. and Endfield G. (2012) 'Critical perspectives on historical collapse' *Proceedings of the National Academy of Sciences of the United States of America* 109 pp. 3628–31.

Cain S. (2013) *Quiet: The Power of Introverts in a World That Can't Stop Talking*. London: Penguin.

Cain S. (2020) *Quiet: The Power of Introverts in a World That Can't Stop Talking* London: Penguin.

Cameron D.(2006) 'Make people happier, says Cameron' *BCC News*, 22 May. http://news.bbc.co.uk/1/hi/uk_politics/5003314.stm

Chalmers R.F. (1999) *What Is This Thing Called Science?* (3rd ed.). Milton Keynes: Open University Press.

Cheok A. (2017) *Hyperconnectivity*. New York: Springer.

Clark C.(2012) *The Sleepwalkers; How Europe Went to War in 1914*. London: Penguin.

Clarke S. (2015) 'School leadership in turbulent times and the value of negative capability' *Professional Development in Education* vol. 42 no. 1 pp.1–14.

Clarke S. and Dempster N. (2020) 'Leadership learning: The pessimism of complexity and the optimism of personal agency' *Professional Development in Education*. https://dpo.lrg/10.1080/19415257.2020.1787196

Cline E. (2014) *1177: The Year Civilisation Collapsed*. Princeton: Princeton University Press.

Collins R. (1990) 'Market closure and the conflict theory of the professions' in Burrage M. and Torstendahl R. (eds), *Professionals in Theory and Practice*. pp. 24–43. London: Sage.

Conklin J. (2006) *Dialogue Mapping: Building Shared Understanding of Wicked Problems*. Chichester: John Wiley and Sons.

Corum J., Sheilk K. and Zimmer C.(2020) 'Different approaches to a Coronavirus Vaccine' *New York Times*, May 20.

Crawford M. (2019) 'Solo and shared leadership' pp. 57–72 in Bush T., Bell L. and Middlewood D. (eds), *Principles of Educational Leadership and Management* (3rd ed.). pp. 3–17. London: Sage.

Creasy R. (2017) *The Taming of Education*. London: Palgrave.

Crutzen P. 'Geology of mankind' *Nature*, no. 415 no. 23.

Cummings V. (2018) 'Hunter-gatherers in the post-glacial world' in Cummings et al. (eds), *The Oxford Handbook The Archaeology and Anthropology of Hunter-Gatherers*. pp. 438–455 Oxford: Oxford University Press.

Cummings V., Jordan P. and Zvelebil M. (eds) (2018) *The Oxford Handbook of the Archaeology and Anthropology of Hunter-Gatherers*. Oxford: Oxford University Press.

Cunliffe B. (2012) *Britain Begins*. Oxford: Oxford University Press.

Darvill T. (2010) *Prehistoric Britain* (2nd ed.). London: Routledge.

Dasgupta Review (2021) *The Economics of Biodiversity*. Crown Copyright.

Davidow W. (2011) *Over-Connected; the Promise and Threat of the Internet*. London: Headline Publishing Group.

Davidson J. and Rees-Mogg W. (1999) *The Sovereign Individual*. New York: Touchstone.

Davies B. (2007) 'Sustainable leadership' in Davies B. (ed.) *Developing Sustainable Leadership*. pp. 11–25. London: Paul Chapman.

Davis A. and White J. (2001) 'Accountability and school inspection: In defence of audited self-review' *Journal of Philosophy of Education* vol. 35 no. 4 pp. 668–681.

Davis J. (2016) *The Birth of the Anthropocene*. Oakland, CA: California University Press.

De-Shallit A. (1995) *Why Posterity Matters*. London: Routledge.

Demeny P. (2003) 'Population policy dilemmas in Europe at the dawn of the twenty-first century' *Population and Development Review* vol. 29 no. 1 pp. 1–28.

Diamantis P. and Kottler S. (2012) *Abundance: The Future Is Better Than You Think*. New York: Free Press.

Diamond J.(1987) 'The worst mistake in the history of the human race' *Discover*.

Diamond J. (1998) *Guns, Germs and Steel*. London: Vintage.

Diamond J. (2006) *Collapse*. London: Penguin.

Diamond J. (2012) *The World until Yesterday*. London: Allen Lane.

Donaldson G. (2013) 'The SICI Bratislava memorandum on inspection and innovation' Quoted in Brown et al. 2016.

Dorling D. (2013) *Population Ten Billion*. London: Constable and Robinson.

Downey S., Haas W. Sr. and Shannon S. (2016) 'European Neolithic societies showed early warning signals of population collapse' *Proceedings of the National Academy of Sciences USA* vol. 113 no. 35 pp. 9751–6.

Doyle and Locke (2014) *US Lacking Leaders; The Challenge of Principal Recruitment, Selection and Placement*. Ohio: Thomas Fordham Institute.

Dunbar R. (2010) 'Dunbar's number' in *How Many Friends Does One Person Need?* London: Faber and Faber, pp. 21–34.

Dunbar R. (2012) 'Can the internet buy you more friends' *TED talk*. youtube.com/watch?v=071pED729k8

Dunt I. (2021) 'Our origins offer hope for the future' p. 19 The 'I' 5th August.

Eatwell R. and Goodwin M. (2018) *National Populism*. London: Penguin/Random House.

Ehrlich P. (1971) *The Population Bomb*. London: Ballantine.

Engster D. (2007) *The heart of justice: Care ethics and political theory*. Oxford Scholarship online.

Esping-Anderson G.(1990) *The Three Worlds of Welfare Capitalism* London: Polity Press.

Etzioni A. (1993) *The Spirit of Community*. London: Fontana.

Etzioni A. (1997) *The New Golden Rule*. London: Profile Books.

Fagan B. (2005) *The Long Summer*. London: Granta.

Fagan B. (2009) *The Great Warming*. London: Bloomsbury.

Fergusson R. (1994) 'Managerialism in education' in Clarke J., Cochrane A. and McLaughlin E. (eds.) *Managing Social Policy*. pp. 93–114. London: Sage.

Figlio D. and Loeb S. (2011) 'School accountability' in Hanushek E., Machin S. and Woessmann L (eds), *Handbook in Economics*. pp. 383–421. The Netherlands: North Holland Publishers.

Finlay N. (2018) 'Personhood and social relations' in Cummings V., Jordan P., Zvelebil M. (eds), *The Oxford Handbook of the Archaeology and Anthropology of Hunter-Gatherers*. pp. 1191–203. Oxford: Oxford University Press.

Flannery T. (2005) *The Weather Makers*. New York: Grove Press.

Flannery T. (2015) *Atmosphere of Hope*. London: Penguin.

Francis M. (2020) 'Just how infectious is Covid-19 popular science' *Popular Science*, popsci.com

Fredette John, Marom Revital, Stelnert Kurt and Witters Louis (2012) 'The promise and perils of hyperconnectivity for organizations and societies' in Dutta Soumitra and Bilbao-Osorio Benat (eds), *The Global Information Technology Report 2012 – Living in a Hyperconnected World. INSEAD*. pp 113–120.

Freud S. (1930) *Civilisation and Its Discontents*. London: Hogarth Press.

Friedman M. (1962) *Capitalism and Freedom*. Chicago: University of Chicago Press.

Friedman T. (2006) *The World Is Flat*. London: Penguin.

Fukuyama F. (1991) *The End of History and the Last Man*. London: Penguin.

Fukuyama F. (1996) *Trust: The Social Virtues and the Creation of Prosperity*. London: Penguin.

Fullan M.(1988) *What's Worth Fighting for in the Principalship?* New York: Teachers College Press.
Fullan M. (1991) *The New Meaning of Educational Change.* London: Cassell.
Fuller E. (2012) 'Examining Principal Turnover' *National Education Policy Centre.* Available at http://nepc.colorado.edu/blog/examining-principal-turnover
Gardner D. (2009) *Risk: The Science and Politics of Fear.* London: Virgin Books.
Gecas V. and Burke P. (1995) 'Self and identity' in Cook K., Fine G. and House J. (eds), *Sociological Perspectives on Social Psychology.* pp. 41–67 Boston: Allyn and Bacon.
Gilligan C. (1989) 'Moral orientation and moral development' in Held V.(ed), *Justice and Care.* pp. 31–46. Oxford: Westview Press.
Gladwell M. (2000) *The Tipping Point.* London: Little, Brown and Co.
Goldin I and Mariathasan M. (2014) *The Butterfly Defect.* Princeton: Princeton University Press.
Grace G. (1994) 'Education as a public good: On the need to resist the domination of economic science' in Bridges T. and McClaughlin T. (eds), *Education and the Marketplace.* pp. 126–38. London: Falmer.
Green A. (1997) *Education, Globalisation and the Nation State.* London: Macmillan.
Green A., Preston J. and Janmaat G. (2006) *Education, Inequality and Social Cohesion* London: Palgrave.
Greenleaf R. K.(1977) *Servant Leadership.* New York: Paulist Press.
Grenberg J. (2005) *Kant and the Ethics of Humility.* Cambridge: Cambridge University Press.
Grint K. (2008) 'Wicked problems and clumsy solutions' *Clinical Leaders* vol. 1 no. 22 pp. 11–25.
Grodzins M. (1957) 'Metropolitan segregation' *Scientific American* vol. 197 pp. 33–47.
Gronn P. (2003) *The New Work of Educational Leaders.* London: Paul Chapman.
Guardian (2020a) 'Official report [2016] that said UK was not prepared for pandemic is published' 22 October.
Guardian (2020b) 'Arctic finds a "new page" in climate emergency' 28 October.
Gunderson L. and Holling C. (eds) (2002) *Panarchy: Understanding Transformations in Human and Natural Systems.* Washington, DC: Island Press.
Gunter H. (2016) *An Intellectual History of School Leadership Practice and Research.* London: Bloomsbury.
Gutman A. and Thompson D. (1996) *Democracy and Disagreement.* Cambridge, MA: Belknapp Press.
Hamilton C.(2004) *Growth Fetish.* London: Pluto Press.
Hardin G. (1977) 'Who cares for posterity' in Pojman L. andPojman P. (eds), *Environmental Ethics.* pp. 350–7. Belmont, CA: Wadsworth.
Hardin G.(2006) 'Lifeboat ethics' in Pojman L. and Pojman P. (eds), *Environmental Ethics.* pp. 443–52. Belmont, CA: Wadsworth.

Hargreaves A. and Fink D. (2007) 'Energising leadership for sustainability' in B. Davies (ed.) *Developing Sustainable Leadership.* pp. 46–64. London: Paul Chapman Publishing.

Harvey F. (2020) 'World population in 2100 could be 2 billion below UN forecasts, study suggests' *BBC News,* 15 July.

Hayek F. (1944) *The Road to Serfdom.* London: Routledge and Kegan Paul.

Head B. (2008) 'Wicked problems in public policy' *Public Policy* vol. 3 no. 3 pp. 101–18.

Head B. and Alford J. (2015) 'Wicked problems: Implications for public management and policy' *Administration and Society* vol. 47 no. 6 pp. 711–39.

Heater D. (2004) *A History of Education for Citizenship.* London: Routledge-Falmer.

Heilbronner R. (1975) 'What has posterity ever done for me?' in Pojman L. and Pojman P. (eds), *Environmental Ethics.* pp. 347–50. Belmont, CA: Wadsworth.

Henson R. (2011) *The Rough Guide to Climate Change.* London: Penguin.

Hernandez J. (2008) *Journal of Business Ethics* vol. 80 no. 1 pp. 121–8.

Higginson J. (ed.) *Selections from Michael Sadler.* Liverpool: Dejsli and Meyorre.

Higham T. (2021) *The World before Us.* London: Viking/Penguin.

Hirsch F. (1977) *The Social Limits to Growth.* London: RKP.

Hodgen E. and Wylie C. (2005) 'Stress and wellbeing among New Zealand principals' http://www.nzcer.org.nz/research/publications/stress-and-well-being-among-new-zealand-principals-report-new-zealand-principa?cPath=130_131&products_id=1555

Homer-Dixon T. (2006) *The Upside of Down.* London: Souvenir Press.

Hood C. (1991) 'A public management for all seasons?' *Public Administration* vol. 69 pp. 3–19.

Hourani A. (2005) *A History of the Arab Peoples* London: Faber and Faber.

Hovden E. and Lindseth G. (2002) 'Norwegian climate policy 1989–2002' in Lafferty W., Nordskog M., Askre H.(eds), *Realizing Rio in Norway.* pp. 143–68. Oslo, Norway: University of Oslo.

Howard P. (2013) 'Human resilience in the face of biodiversity tipping points' in O'Riordan T. and Lenton T. (eds), *Addressing Tipping Points for a Precarious Future.* pp. 104–26. Oxford: Oxford University Press.

Hughes T., Carpenter S., Rockstrom J., Schefflier M. and Walker B. (2013) 'Multiscale regime shifts and planetary boundaries' *Trends in Ecology and Evaluation* vol. 28 pp. 389–95.

Hulme M. (2009) *Why We Disagree about Climate Change.* Cambridge: Cambridge University Press.

Huntingdon S. (2004) *Who Are We? America's Great Debate.* New York: Free Press.

Intergovernmental Panel on Climate Change (IPCC) (2014) *Climate Change 5th Synthesis Report.* Switzerland: IPCC.

Intergovernmental Panel on Climate Change (IPCC) (2018) *Global Warming of 1.5 Summary for Policymakers.* Switzerland: IPCC.

Intergovernmental Panel on Climate Change (IPCC) (2019/2020) *Climate Change and Land Summary for Policymakers*. Switzerland: IPCC.
Isakjee A. (2017) 'Welfare state regimes: A literature review' University of Birmingham: IRIS Working Paper no. 18. www.birmingham.ac.uk/iris
Jackson T. (2021) *Post-Growth: Life after Capitalism*. London: Polity Press.
Jacoby S. (2018) *The Age of American Unreason in a Culture of Lies*. New York: Vintage Books.
Janis I. (1972) *Victims of Groupthink*. Boston: Houghton Miflin.
Johnson N. (2007) *Simply Complexity*. Oxford: One World publishers.
Johnson S. (2001) *Emergence*. Harmondsworth: Penguin.
Johnstone C. (2019) *Seven Ways to Build Resilience*. London: Robinson.
Kant I. (1997) 'Of duties to Animals and Spirits' in Heath P. and Schneewind J. (eds), *Lectures on Ethics*, pp. 212–13. London: Methuen.
Kaufmann S. and Stutzle I. (2017) *Thomas Piketty's 'Capital in the Twenty-First Century'*. London: Verso.
Kay J. and King M.(2020) *Radical Uncertainty* London: Bridge Street Press.
Kellstedt P., Zahran S., Vedlitz A., (2008) 'Personal efficacy, the information environment and attitudes towards climate change and global warming' *Risk Analysis* vol. 28 no. 1 pp. 113–26.
Kennedy R. (1968) Speech at Kansas State University March 18, 1968.
Kent J. (2009) 'Individualised responsibility and climate change' *Cosmopolitan Civil Societies Journal* vol. 3 no. 1 pp. 132–49.
Keynes J.M. (1963) 'Economic possibilities for our grandchildren' in Johnson E. (ed.), *Essays in Persuasion*. pp. 358–373. New York: W. W. Norton & Co.
Klare M. (2004) *Resource Wars*. New York: Owl Books.
Klare M. (2012) *The Race for What's Left*. New York: Picador.
Klein M. (2014) *This Changes Everything*. London: Allen Lane.
Kolbert E. (2014) *The Sixth Extinction: An Unnatural History*. London: Bloomsbury.
Koser (2007) *International Migration*. Oxford: Oxford University Press.
Krosnick J., Holbrook A., Lowe L. and Visser P. (2006) 'The origins and consequences of democratic citizen's policy agendas' *Climatic Change* vol. 77 pp. 7–43.
Kruuk H. (1972) 'Surplus killing by carnivores' *Journal of Zoology* vol. 166 pp. 233–44.
Kuhn T. (1970) *The Structure of Scientific Revolutions*. Chicago: Chicago University Press.
Kunzig R. and Broeckner W. (2008) *Fixing Climate*. London: Green Profile.
Lanchester J. (2010) *Whoops! Why Everyone Owes Everyone and No One Can Pay*. London: Penguin.
Land T. and Ingram J. (2013) 'Food security: Twists and turns' in O'Riordan T. and Lenton T. (eds), *Addressing Tipping Points for a Precarious Future*. pp. 81–103 Oxford: Oxford University Press.
Lauder H., Jamieson I., Wilkeley F. (1998) 'Models of effective schools: Limits and capabilities' in Slee R., Weiner G. and Tomlinson S. (eds), *School Effectiveness for Whom?* pp. 51–69. London: Falmer.

Lawton D. (1980) *The Politics of the School Curriculum*. London: Routledge and Kegan Paul.

Leick G. (2001) *Mesopotamia: The Invention of the City*. London: Penguin.

Lenton T. (2013) 'Tipping points from a global perspective' in O'Riordan T. and Lenton T. (eds), *Addressing Tipping Points for a Precarious Future*. pp. 23–46 Oxford: Oxford University Press.

Lenton T., Howell S. and Williams T. (2013) 'On the origins of planetary-scale tipping points' *Trends in Ecology and Evolution* vol. 28, no. 7 pp. 380–2.

Lenton T., Held H., Kriegler E., Hall J., Lucht W., Rahmstorf S. and Schellnuhuber (2008) 'Tipping elements in the earth's climate system' *Proceedings of the National Academy of Sciences* vol. 105 no. 6 pp. 1786–1793. www.pnas.org/content/105/6/1786.full (accessed on 21 April 2011).

Levin K., Cashore B., Bernstein S. and Auld G. (2012) 'Overcoming the tragedy of super wicked problems: Constraining our future selves to ameliorate global climate change' *Policy Sciences* vol. 45 pp. 123–52.

Levy S.(1992) *Artificial Life*. New York: Random House.

Leydet D., Carlson A., Breckenridge A., Barth A., Ullman D., Sinclair G.; Milne G., Cuzzone J., Caffee M. (2018) 'Opening of glacial Lake Agassiz's eastern outlets by the start of the Younger Dryas cold period' *Geology* vol. 46 no. 2 pp. 155–8.

Lifton J. (1993) *The Protean Self: Human Resilience in an Age of Fragmentation*. New York: Basic Books.

Lincoln Y. and Guba E. (1994) 'Paradigmatic controversies, contradictions, and emerging confluences' in Denzin N. and Lincoln Y. (eds), *Handbook of Qualitative Research*. pp. 163–88. London: Sage.

Lindberg S. (2013) 'Mapping accountability: Core concepts and sub-types' *International Review of Administrative Sciences* vo. 79, no. 2 pp. 202–26.

Linden E. (2006) *The Winds of Change*. New York: Simon and Schuster.

Lingard T. (2013) 'It tips both ways' in O'Riordan T. and Lenton T. (eds), *Addressing Tipping Points for a Precarious Future*. pp. 233–6. Oxford: Oxford University Press.

Lipsky M. (1980) *Street-Level Bureaucracy*. New York: Russell Sage Foundation.

Lovelock J. (2006) *The Revenge of Gaia*. London: Penguin.

Luft J. (1963) *Group Processes: An Introduction to Group Dynamics*. Palo Alto, CA: National Press Books.

Lynas M. (2020) *Our Final Warning: Six Degrees of Climate Emergency*. London: Fourth Estate.

MacPhee R. (2019) *End of the Megafauna*. New York: W.W. Norton and Co.

MacPhee R. and Marx P. (1997) 'The 40,000-year plague: Humans, hyper-disease, and first-contact extinctions' in Goodman S. and Patterson B. (eds), *Natural Change and Human Contact in Madagascar*. pp. 169–217 Washington: Smithsonian Institution Press.

Management in Education (2016) vol. 30 no. 3: Special issue on Sustainable development goals.

Marion R. and Uhl-Bien M.(2001) 'Leadership in complex organizations' *Leadership Quarterly* vol. 12 no. 4 pp. 389–418.

Maroy C. and Voisan A. (2017) 'Think piece on accountability UNESCO' Background paper prepared for the 2017/8 Global Education Monitoring. pp. 1–26.

Marshall G. (2015) *Don't Even Think About It: Why Our Brains Are Wired to Ignore Climate Change*. London: Bloomsbury.

Martin P. (1973) 'The Discovery of America' *Science* vol. 179 pp. 969–974.

Martin P. (1984) 'Prehistoric overkill: The global model' in Martin P. and Klein R. (eds), *Pleistocene Extinctions: The Search for a Cause*. pp. 354–403. New Haven: Yale University Press.

Martin P. (2015) *A Short History of Disease*. Harpenden: Pocket Essentials.

Marx K. (1971) *Grundrisse*, McClelland D. (ed.). London: Macmillan.

Mason M. and Macarthy S. (1996) *When Elephants Weep: The Emotional Lives of Animals*. London: Vintage.

McEwan I. (2010) *Solar*. London: Jonathan Cape.

Meadows D. (1999) 'Leverage points: Places to intervene in a system' in *The Sustainability Institute*. pp. 1–20. VT, USA: Hartland.

Meadows D. (2008) *Thinking in Systems*. Vermont: Chelsea Green Publishing.

Meadows D., Randers J. and Meadows D. (2004) *Limits to Growth Vermont*. Chelsea Green Publishing Co.

Merton R., Gray A., Hockey B., and Selvin H. (eds) (1952) *Reader in Bureaucracy*. Glencoe: The Free Press.

Middleton G. (2017) *Understanding Collapse*. Cambridge: Cambridge University Press.

Midgely M. (1983) *Animals and Why They Matter*. Harmondsworth: Penguin.

Mitchell M. (2009) *Complexity: A Guided Tour*. Oxford: Oxford University Press.

Monbiot G. (2009) 'The population myth' *The Guardian*, 29 September.

Morgan G. (2004) *Images of Organisation*. London: Sage.

Mudde C. and Kaltwasser C. (2017) *Populism: A Very Short Introduction*. Oxford: Oxford University Press.

Munz R. and Reiterer A.(2009) *Overcrowded World*. London: Haus Publishing.

Noddings N. (1995) 'Caring' in Held V. (ed), *Justice and Care*. pp. 7–30. Oxford: Westview Press.

Norgaard K.M. (2011) *Living in Denial*. Cambridge, MA: MIT.

Northouse P. (2016) *Leadership* (7th ed.). London: Sage.

Nye J. (2002) *The Paradox of American Power*. Oxford: Oxford University Press.

Oreskes N and Conway E. (2011) *Merchants of Doubt*. London: Bloomsbury

O'Riordan T., Lenton T. and Christie I. (2013) 'Metaphors and systemic change' in O'Riordan T. and Lenton T. (eds), *Addressing Tipping Points for a Precarious Future*. pp. 3–20. Oxford: Oxford University Press.

Ohmae K. (2006) *The End of the Nation State*. New York: McKinsey and Co.

Oliver N. (2012) *A History of Ancient Britain*. London: BBC books.

Ord T. (2020) *The Precipice: Existential Risk and the Future of Humanity*. London: Bloomsbury.
Oreskes N. and Conway E. (2012) *Merchants of Doubt*. London: Bloomsbury.
Orwell G. (1949/2021) *1984*. London: Collins Classics.
Osborne D. and Gaebler T. (1992) *Reinventing Government*. New York: Plume.
Ozga J. and Grek S. (2012) 'Governing through learning: School self-evaluation as a knowledge based regulatory tool' *Researches sociologiques et anthropologiques* vol. 43 no. 2 pp. 83–100.
Parkin S. (2013) 'Leadership for sustainability' in O'Riordan T. and Lenton T. (eds), *Addressing Tipping Points for a Precarious Future*. pp. 194–212 Oxford: Oxford University Press.
Partridge E. (2003) 'Future generations' in Jamieson D. (ed), *A Companion to Environmental Philosophy*. pp. 377–90 Oxford: Blackwell.
Perryman J. (2006) 'Panoptic performativity and school inspection regimes: Disciplinary mechanisms and life under special measures' *Journal of Education Policy* vol. 21 no. 2 pp. 147–161.
Piaget J. and Inhelder B. (1956) *The Child's Conception of Space*. London: RKP.
Picketty T. (2017) *Capital in the Twenty-First Century*. Cambridge, MA: Harvard University Press.
Pielke R. Jr. (2007) *The Honest Broker*. Cambridge: Cambridge University Press.
Piff P., Kraus M. and Keltner D. (2018) 'Unpacking the inequality paradox' in Olson J. (ed), *Advances in Experimental Social Psychology*, vol. 57. pp. 53–124. Burlington: Academic Press.
Plsek P. (2001) 'Why doesn't the NHS do as it's told?' Plenary address to NHS conference July 2001.
Pollitt C. (1993) *Managerialism and the Public Services* (2nd ed.). Oxford: Basil Blackwell.
Ponting C. (2007) *A New Green History of the World*. London: Vintage.
Popper K. (1945) *The Open Society and Its Enemies*. London: Routledge and Kegan Paul.
Popper K. (1982) *The Logic of Scientific Discovery*. London: Hutchinson.
Powell M. and Barrientos A. (2004) 'Welfare regimes and welfare mix' *European Journal of Political Research* vol. 43 pp. 83–105.
Princen T. (2005) *The Logic of Sufficiency*. Cambridge: MIT Press.
Rawls J. (1970) *A Theory of Justice*. Harvard: Harvard University Press.
Raworth K.(2017) *Doughnut Economics*. London: RH Business Books.
Rayner S. (2006) *Wicked Problems: Clumsy Solutions* – diagnoses and prescriptions for environmental ills. Jack Beale Memorial Lecture Sydney, Australia, July.
Read D., Bistrom A., Granger Morgan M., Fischoff B. and Smuts T. (2004) 'What do people know about global climate change?' *Risk Analysis* vol. 14 pp. 971–82.
Rees M. 2005 *Our Final Century*. London: Penguin.
Reynolds T., Bostrom A., Read D., Morgan M. (2010) 'Global climate change? survey studies of educated laypeople' *Risk Analysis* vol. 30 no. 10 pp. 1520–38.

Rhodes R. (1994) 'The hollowing out of the state: The changing nature of the public service in Britain' *Political Quarterly* vol. 65 no. 2 pp. 138–51.

Rifkin J. (2000) *The Age of Access*. London: Penguin.

Rittell H. and Webber M. (1973) 'Dilemmas in a general theory of planning' *Policy Sciences* vol. 4 pp. 155–169.

Ritzer G. (2004) *The Globalisation of Nothing*. Thousand Oaks, CA: Fine Forge Press.

Rizvi F. and Lingard R. (2009) *Globalizing Education Policy*. London: Routledge.

Rockstrom J. and Klum M. (2015) *Big World, Small Planet*. New Haven: New Have Yale UP.

Rockstrom et al. (28 other authors) (2009) 'A Safe Operating Space for Humanity' *Nature* vol. 461 pp 472–5.

Rogers P., Jalal K. and Boyd J. (2008) *An Introduction to Sustainable Development*. London: Earthscan.

Rorty R. (1989) *Contingency, Irony, Solidarity*. Cambridge: Cambridge University Press.

Rousseau J. (1999) 'Discourse on the origins of inequality' in Coleman P. (ed.), *The Social Contract and Discourses* Oxford: Oxford World Classics.

Rumsfeld D. (2002) U.S. Department of Defense news briefing in February 2002.

Ruppel C. and Kessler J. (2017) 'The interaction of climate change and methane hydrates' *Review of Geophysics* vol. 55 no. 1 pp. 126–68.

Sadler M. (1979) 'How far can we learn anything of practical value from the study of foreign systems of education?' Address given at the Guilford Educational Conference on Saturday, 20th October, 1990' in Higgenson J. (ed), *Selections from Michael Sadler: Studies in World Citizenship*. Liverpool: Dejall and Meyorre.

Safi M. (2021) 'WHO chief warns of "catastrophic moral failure" over jabs distribution' *Guardian*, 19 January 2021.

Sahlins M. (2011) 'The original affluent society' in *Stone Age Economics*, 2nd ed., pp. 1–40. London: Aldine transaction.

Sandel M. (2020) *The Tyranny of Merit*. London: Penguin.

Sandvik H. (2008) 'Public concern over global warming' *Climatic Change* vol. 90 no. 3 pp. 333–341.

Scheffler M. (2016) 'Anticipating societal collapse: Hints from the Stone Age' *PNAS* vol. 113 no. 39 pp. 1073–5.

Schein E. (2013) *Humble Enquiry*. San Francisco: Berrett-Koehler Publishers.

Schein E. (2016) *Humble Consulting*. San Francisco: Berrett-Koehler Publishers.

Schein E. and Schein P. (2018) *Humble Leadership*. Oakland, CA: Berrett-Kohler Publishers.

Sheninger E. (2014) *Digital Leadership*. Thousand Oaks, CA: Corwin Press.

Schumpeter J. (1942) *Capitalism, Socialism, and Democracy*. London: Allen and Unwin.

Schweitzer A. (1949) *Civilisation and Ethics*. London: Allen and Unwin.

Scott J. (2018) *Against the Grain: A Deep History of the Earliest States*. New Haven: Yale University Press.

Senge P. (2006) *The Fifth Discipline*. London: Random House.

Sennet (1998) *The Corrosion of Character*. New York: W.W. Norton.
Sergiovanni T. (1996) *Leadership for the Schoolhouse*. San Francisco: Jossey Bass.
Sheninger E. (2014) *Digital Leadership*. Thousand Oaks, CA: Corwin Press.
Simon H. (1956) 'Rational choice and the structure of the environment' *Psychological Review* vol. 63 no. 2 pp. 129–38.
Sinclair-Wilson J. (2013) 'Endgame' in O'Riordan T. and Lenton T. (eds), *Addressing Tipping Points for a Precarious Future*. pp. 285–8. Oxford: Oxford University Press.
Singer P. (1981) *The Expanding Circle*. Princeton: Princeton University Press.
Skinner B.F. (1972) *Beyond Freedom and Dignity*. London: Jonathan Cape.
Slovic P. (2000) *The Perception of Risk*. London: Earthscan.
Smith J. (2013) 'Media coverage of tipping points' in O'Riordan T. and Lenton T. (eds), *Addressing Tipping Points for a Precarious Future*. pp. 243–57. Oxford: Oxford University Press.
Smith L. (2012) *The New North: The World in 2050*. London: Profile Books.
Snyder T. (2017) *On Tyranny: Twenty Lessons from the Twentieth Century*. London: The Bodley Head.
Spielman K. (2018) 'The emergence of forager-farmer interactions in North America' in Cummings V., Jordan P., Zvelebil M. (eds), *The Oxford Handbook of the Archaeology and Anthropology of Hunter-Gatherers*. pp. 881–902. Oxford: Oxford University Press.
Spinney L. (2017) *Pale Rider*. London: Vintage.
Spring J. (2014) *Globalization of Education*. London: Routledge.
Stanley J. (2020) *How Fascism Works: The Politics of Us and Them*. New York: Random House.
Starr K. (2015) *Education Game Changers: Leadership and the Consequence of Policy Paradox*. Lanham, MD: Rowman & Littlefield.
Steffen W., Grinevald J., Cruzen P. and McNeill J. (2011) 'The Anthropocene: Conceptual and historical perspectives' *Philosophical Transactions of the Royal Society* vol. 369 pp. 842–867.
Stern J. (2020) 'Do you follow: Understanding followership before leadership' *Management in Education* vol. 35 no. 1 pp. 58–61, July 2020.
Stern J. (2021) 'Uncertainty and mortality: Two stubborn particulars of religious education' in Franck O. and Thalen P. (eds), *Religious Education in a Post-Secular Age*. pp. 123–38. London: Palgrave.
Strathern O. (2007) *A Brief History of the Future*. New York: Carroll and Graf.
Strogartz S. (2003) *Sync: The Emerging Science of Spontaneous Order*. Harmondsworth: Penguin.
Subbaro K. (2020) 'Covid-19 vaccines: Time to talk about uncertainties' *Nature* vol. 586 p. 475 (20th October).
Sunker H. and Otto H.(1997) *Education and Fascism*. London: Falmer Press.
Tawney R. (1921) *The Acquisitive Society*. New York: Harcourt Brace.
Taylor F.W. (1911) *Principles of Scientific Management*. London: Harper and Row.

Temulkuran E. (2019) *How to Lose a Country*. London: 4th Estate.
The I (2021) 'Oslo urged to halt deep-sea mining plans' 13 April 2021.
Thomas C. (2017) *Inheritors of the Earth: How Nature Is Thriving in Age of Extinction*. London: Penguin.
Thornton K. (2021) 'Leading through Covid-19: New Zealand secondary principals describe their reality' *Educational Management Administration and Leadership* Vol. 49 no. 3 pp. 393–409.
Toffler A. (1970) *Future Shock*. London: Bodley Head.
Tufekci Z. (2020) 'The overlooked variable in the key to the pandemic' *The Atlantic*, 3 October.
Uhl-Bien M. and Marion R. (2008) *Complexity Leadership Part1: Conceptual Foundations*. Charlotte Carolina: Information Age Publishing Inc.
Uslaner E. (2002) *The Moral Foundations of Trust*. Cambridge: Cambridge.
Varoufakis Y. (2020) 'The crisis of the 2020s – and how to solve it' *Guardian*, 5 September.
Verweij M. and Thompson M. (2011) *Clumsy Solutions for a Complex World*, Verweij M. and Thomson M. (eds). pp. 1–31 London: Palgrave Macmillan.
Vollset et al. (2018) 'Population and fertility by age and sex for 195 countries from 1950–2017: A systematic analysis for the Global E . . . study' *2017 The Lancet*. https: dot.org/10.1016/SO14
Waal F. de (2017) *Are We Smart Enough to Know How Smart Animals Are?* London: Granta.
Walker A., Quian H., Zhang S. (2011) 'Secondary school principals in curriculum reform' *Frontiers of Education in China* vol. 6 no. 3 pp. 388–403.
Wallace-Wells D. (2019) *The Uninhabitable Earth*. London: Penguin.
Ward P. (2008) *Under a Green Sky*. New York: Harper-Collins.
Ward P (2010) *The Flooded Earth*. New York: Basic Books.
Washington H. and Cook J. (2011) *Climate Change Denial*. London: Earthscan.
Wayne M. and Bolker B. (2015) *Infectious Disease*. Oxford: Oxford University Press.
Weart S. (2005) *The Discovery of Global Warming*. Cambridge, MA: Harvard University Press.
Webster-Wright A. (2009) 'Reframing professional development through understanding authentic professional learning' *Review of Educational Research* vol. 79, no. 20 pp. 702–739.
Weisman (2013) *Countdown*. New York: Little, Brown and co.
West A. and Nikolai R. (2014) *Welfare Regimes and Education Regimes*. London: LSE Research Online.
Western S. (2019) *Leadership: A Critical Text* (3rd ed.). London: Sage.
Wilkinson R. (1996) *Unhealthy Societies: The affliction of inequality*. London: Routledge.
Wilkinson R. and Pickett K. (2009) *The Spirit Level*. London: Penguin.
Wilkinson R. and Pickett K. (2019) *The Inner Level*. London: Penguin.
Wilson E. O. (2003) *The Future of Life*. London: Abacus.

Woods P. and Roberts A. (2016) 'Distributed leadership and social justice' *International Journal of Leadership in Education* vol. 19 no. 2 pp. 138–156.

World Meteorological Organisation (2021) '2020 was one of the three warmest years on record' 15 January. https://public.wmo.int/en/media/press-release/2020-was-one-of-three-warmest-years-record

Wragg Sykes R. (2021) *Kindred: Neanderthal Life, Love, Death and Art*. London: Bloomsbury.

Wright N. (2011) 'Between "Bastard" and "Wicked" leadership? School leadership and the emerging policies of the UK Coalition government' *Journal of Educational Administration and History* vol. 43 no. 4 pp. 345–362.

WWF(2008) *Living Planet Report*. Available at http://www.panda.org/about_our_earth/all_publications/living_planet_report

Young D. and Szachowicz P. (2014) 'Responding to principals' rising responsibilities' *Education Week*, 4 February.

Young M. (1956) *The Rise of the Meritocracy*. Harmondsworth: Penguin.

Zahran S, Brody H., Grover H. and Vedlitz A.(2006) 'Climate change vulnerability and policy support' *Society and Natural Resources* vol. 19 pp. 21–27.

Zalaziewicz J. and Williams M. (2012) *The Goldilocks Planet*. Oxford: Oxford University Press.

Zilhao J. (2014) 'The Neanderthals: Evolution, palaeoecology, and extinction' in Cummings V., Jordan P. and Zvelebil M. (eds), (2019) *The Oxford Handbook of the Archaeology and Anthropology of Hunter-Gatherers*. pp. 177–190. Oxford: Oxford University Press.

Zolli A. and Healy A-M (2012) *Resilience*. London: Headline.

Index

accountability
   and inspection   198–219
   models of   199–205
   relationships   206–9
   threats   210–12
Ackoff, R. (and 'messes')   130
ageing populations   69–70
ancient community collapse   96–9
ant behaviour   44–5
anthropocene   96
'anticipatory obedience' (Snyder)   116
Arrhenius, S.   27
Assassination of Archduke Ferdinand   42–3
Attenborough, D.   186, 188–9, 193
'authentic reflexivity' (Webster-Wright)   20

bacteria doubling   67
Bandura, A.   45
Barnovsky, A.   96, 126–7
Beauchamp, G.   4
benign covert processes   77–81
Benton, M.   18, 95
Biden, J. (U.S. President)   24, 36, 121, 138
Bottery, M.   4, 7, 13, 50, 65, 70, 103, 111–12, 136, 146–7, 209–10, 230–4
Braidwood, R.   88
brain functioning   29, 32
Brannen, P.   18
bravery   164, 166–7
bricoleur (Grint)   235
Brody, H.   29
Brown, M.   9
Brundtland   18
Bryman, A.   46
bubonic plague   119, 166
building relationships   228–32
Bulkeley, H.   35
Bush, T.   22

Calendar, D.   27
Cameron, D.   119
Captain Tom Moore   177
care   164, 166–7, 180
changing environmental conditions   5
chess board bet   66–7
child-centred code   8, 10
China   ix, 26, 40, 69, 104, 148, 150
civil society   164, 167–8, 180–1
Clark, C.   43
Clarke, S.   20, 40
climate change   ix, 12
   causes of inaction   24–41
   disinformation   28
   facts   26–8
   stability   28
climate stability   85–7
Cline, E.   18
Clinton, H.   37
collaboration   198, 199, 209
collaborative leadership   218–19, 232–3
common good   163, 177
complexity   x, 15–17
   climate   28
   epistemic   16, 48–50, 58
   relational   16–17, 51–2, 58
   systemic   16, 44–8, 58
   wicked   17, 51–9
conditioning, classical and operant   47
connectivity   14, 70–5
   and Covid   74–5
   digital   14, 74–5
   environmental   15, 71–2
   hyper   14
   social   14, 72–4
consequentialist ethics   183, 184, 193
conservation, ethic of   185–6
context, importance of   16, 20–1, 35–6, 38–40, 46, 56, 72–3, 78–80, 99–100, 125–7, 143–8, 159–61, 174, 184, 207, 228

control 164
Conway, E. 28
Cook, J. 28
cooperation between human species 94–6
COP 26 ix, 24
Covid 19 ix, 3–5, 12, 14, 17–20, 24
  Covid concerns 171–6
  as an educational aid 162–81
  effects on national politics 83–4
  and tipping points 148–50
'cowboy world' 71–2
Crawford, M. 22
'critical' educational literature 9
cultural transmission code 7–8, 10
Cummings, V. 29, 73, 89

dandelions 28
Dasgupta, R. 7
Davidson, J. 12, 104
Davies, H. 6, 33
Demeny, P. 69
demographic transition 70
Dempster, N. 40
Denisovans 94–5, 100
deontological ethics 183–5
De-Shallit, A. 19
'designer' leadership (Gronn) 234
Diamond, J. 18, 90
distributed leadership 4, 22, 79, 91, 135, 232, 236
'Doughnut Economics' (Raworth) 189
Doyle, P. 6
Dunbar, R. 73

Early Civilisation Collapse 18
ecological sustainability 6–7
economic code 8
educational codes 7, 10–11
educational leaders and macro-level change 39–40
educational leader's role x, 5–7, 19–22
education as a democratic space 103, 120–2, 168, 199
'The End of the Nation-state' (Ohmae) 104
epistemological assumptions 237
epistemological concerns 220–2
ethical dialecticians 234

ethic of care 184, 188, 193
ethic of imperative sufficiency (Princen) 84
Etzioni and communal values 119
expanding circle of ethical concerns (Singer) 6
exponential growth 14, 66–70, 77, 86, 128, 129, 131, 138, 148–52, 157–8, 164, 168–9, 187, 222
  and Covid-19 68
  and population growth 68–70

Fascism 103, 116, 118
Fergusson, R. 13
Fink, D. 6, 33
followers 33–4
fossil fuels ix
frogs in water 148, 150, 170
Fullan, M. 199, 212
future time frames 18–19
'fuzzy generalisations' (Bassey) 78, 156

Gaebler, D. 83
Gardner, D. 29
GDP 111, 118
Gecas, V. 34
global extinction events 18, 84, 95–6
globalisation
  cultural 12
  on educational leadership 4
  of leisure 4
  of trade 4
global-level institutions 104–5
global threats 25
global warming, causes of 26–7
Goebbels, J. 115
'goldilocks planet' 85
Goldin, I. 14, 75
'greedy organisations'(Gronn) 77
Green, A. 12
Greenleaf, R. 6
groupthink (Janis) 235
Guardian 3
Guba, E. 45
Gunter, H. 9

Hadley, E. 96, 126–7
Hardin, G. 19
Hargreaves, A. 6, 33

'healing' a school 146, 232
Healy, A-M. 18
heater 12
Heilbronner, R. 19
Hernandez, J. 6
Homo Sapiens
    and megafaunal extinctions 91–4
    relationships with other
        hominids 94–5, 100–1
    species responsibility 185
    under-connectedness 71
Hourani, A. 43
Hovden, E. 36
humility
    epistemology and ethics 20, 46, 57, 72, 79–80, 194–6, 218, 223, 233, 237
    intellectual and socio-emotional 223
hunter-gatherers
    sustainable lifestyle 88–9
    thought patterns 26, 29
    transition to agriculture 88–91
hysterisis 126

individualism, effects on climate policies 38–9
individual well-being 180–1
Inhelder, B. 45
inter- and intra-generational 9, 18–19
intergenerational education 70
intergenerational equity 193–4
interglacial periods 85–6
IPCC 32, 76, 134–8, 163, 176, 226

Jacoby, S. 28
Johari Window (Luft) 52
Johnstone, C. 18
Jumee Window (Stern) 52, 228

Kant, I. 187–8
Kay, J. 18
Keeling, D. 27
Kellstedt, P. 32
Kennedy, R. 118–19
Kessler, J. 15
King, M. 18
Klare, M. 18, 40, 98, 121, 192, 194
'known knowns' 16, 48–52, 237
Kohlbert, E. 18
Krosnick, J. 32

leadership qualities for wicked problems 55–6
leadership sustainability 6–7, 12, 33, 152–4
leadership threats 220–3
leverage points 39, 69, 143, 154–60, 180, 182, 238
Levin, K. 25, 35
Levy, S. 43–4
Lincoln, Y. 45
Lindseth, G. 36
Lingard, T. 9
linkages between micro, meso and macro 12–13
Locke, S. 6

machine metaphor 164–5
macro-frame 9
macro-power groupings 103–5
mandated accountability 202, 204–6
Mariathasan, M. 14, 75
Maroy, C. 9
Marshall, G. 29, 30, 33
Masai warrior 73
Meadows, D. 39, 63, 68, 145, 154, 156, 182
megafaunal mass extinctions 91–4
Mencken, H. L. 54
Middleton, G. 18
multi-level
    collaboration 238
    problems 53–5
    sustainability 11–15
    understanding 36–40
multinational corporations 103, 105
multispecies sustainability 187–9
Munz, R. 69

'naming and shaming' 65
Nation State
    competition 40–1
    cooperation 40–1
    as a resurgent power grouping 102–22
Nazism 115–16
Neanderthals 94, 100–1
negative capability 20, 148
neoliberal accountability 200, 202, 206–8

neoliberalism   9, 34, 94, 102, 106–9,
    111–15, 191
'nesting' of citizenship loyalties
    (Heater)   103
New Public Management   207
New Zealand   4, 92, 119, 205
Norgaard, K.   26, 33–8
Norway   34, 36–9, 202

OFCORE
    assumptions   237
    questions   215–17
    teams   214
Oreskes, N.   28
Osborne, D.   83
'overkill' hypothesis (Martin)   92

Partridge, E.   19
past macro-threats   17–18
performativity   210
Piaget, J.   45
Picketty, T.   107, 113, 120
planetary boundaries (Rockstrom)   186
poking with a sharp stick (Broeckner)   87
population growth   3, 14, 18, 68–70,
    83–4, 97–9, 131, 150, 159,
    168–9, 187, 225
populism   113–14, 117, 121
populist
    concerns   114
    irrationalism   115–18
    leaders   102, 106, 111, 113, 115–19,
        153, 222, 237
    state   113–18
positive and negative feedback   14, 15,
    64–6, 86, 123, 128–31, 135,
    151–3, 157–8, 222
prehistoric events
    constructions   86, 89
    natural disasters   86–7
Princen, T.   71–2
process threats   220, 222
public good   83, 109, 118, 120, 122, 163,
    168, 181, 211, 234

quiet introverts (Cain)   21–2

rationality as an ethical choice   194–5
Raworth, K.   9, 186–90

Read, J.   26
Rees-Mogg, W.   12, 104
Reiterer, A.   69
relational leadership   51, 59, 228–31
Reynolds, T.   27
Rittel, H.   17, 28, 53–4
Rizvi, F.   9, 12
roadmap limitations   196–7
Roberts, A.   22
'R' rate or number   14, 168
Rumsfeld, D.   16, 48, 50–2, 227
Ruppel, C.   15
Russia   ix, 26, 40, 104, 115

Sadler, M.   78
Sandal, M.   120
Sandvick, H.   34
SARS   130, 146
'satisfice' (Simon)   20
Schein, D.   229–30
Schein, P.   229–30
Schweitzer, A.   188–9
Scott, J.   88–90, 97
scramble for resources   97–9
Sennett, R.   12
Sergiovanni, T.   6
Sheninger, E.   74–5
Sitting Bull   5, 236
Skinner, B. F.   45
Sky News and climate change   152
Smith, I.   40
'Snowball Earth'   64, 95, 125
social communitarianism   118–20
social reconstruction code   8, 10
solutions
    clumsy or messy   54–6
    silver bullet *vs.* silver buckshot   53–5,
        58, 79, 109–10, 130, 156, 196,
        216–18
'spaceship earth' (Boulding)   71
Spanish Flu   3, 168–9
speed of change
    with animals   76
    with humans   76
Spinney, A.   3
Starr, K.   12
steering and rowing   83
stewardship   x, 6–7
stewardship code   8–11, 22

stewardship frames   223–7
stewardship leadership   5, 10, 59, 84, 182–97, 220–35
stewardship role   8–9, 11, 84
'street-level bureaucrats' (Lipsky)   76
subsidiarity   203–4
sufficiency, types of   191–3
'super-wicked' problems   25, 35
Szachowicz, P.   12

tame and wicked differences   53–4, 214–17
'tame' problems   53–7, 79–80, 110, 117, 127, 135, 148, 184, 195–7, 213–16
'tame' processes   28
tame world views   195, 197
temporal myopia   220, 221
'thick' and 'thin' trust (Uslaner)   115
Thornton, K.   4
threat assessment   29–31
threat groupings   220
three-phase model   4–5
throwing stones and birds (Plsek)   80
tipping points   15, 99, 123–40, 143–61
    benign tipping points   48–50, 124
    and covert processes   128
    and Covid-19   129
    early warning signals   145–7
    educational   131–3
    environmental   129–30
    meanings   124–5
    reversibility/irreversibility   126–7
    and rising temperatures   110, 150–2
transactional leadership   20–1, 47, 58, 74, 91, 136, 230, 231
transformational leadership   21, 58, 79, 91, 135, 232, 236
'trouble-shooter' principals   146, 232
Trump, D.   38, 115, 116, 121

trust relationships   2–3, 4, 12, 22, 58–9, 73, 106, 110–16, 133, 200–1, 208–9, 216–18, 229–32
Tyndall   27

UK   4, 13, 37, 89, 104, 146, 149, 177, 207
uncertainty   x, 17, 20, 163–6, 172, 180
under-recognised processes   13–15
United States   21, 26–7, 34, 37–40, 74, 104, 112, 115, 178, 199, 202

vaccines   3, 152, 228
veil of ignorance (Rawls)   193–4
Voisin, A.   9
voluntary accountability   2–2, 204–5

Wallace-Wells, D.   5
Ward, P.   14
Washington, H.   28
Weber, M.   17, 28, 53–4
Webster-Wright, A.   20
Weismann, A.   67
welfare state agendas   82–3
Western, S.   22, 57
'wicked accountability'   204–5, 212
'wicked' complexity   17, 52–9, 110, 123, 136, 186, 200, 221, 228, 230, 233
'wicked' inspectoral bodies   212–14
'wicked' problems   17, 25, 35, 52–9, 75–80, 109–11, 127–30, 136, 147, 155–7, 184–7, 194–203, 208–23, 228–34, 237–8
Woods, P.   22

Young, M.   12

Zahran, S.   34
Zolli, A.   18
zoonotic diseases   5, 90, 93

www.ingramcontent.com/pod-product-compliance
Lightning Source LLC
Chambersburg PA
CBHW062127300426
44115CB00012BA/1835